Reproducing Jews

Body, Commodity, Text

Studies of Objectifying Practice

A series edited by

Arjun Appadurai, Jean Comaroff,

and Judith Farquhar

Reproducing Jews

A Cultural Account of Assisted Conception in Israel

Susan Martha Kahn

Duke University Press Durham and London 2000

© 2000 Duke University Press

All rights reserved

Printed in the United States of America on acid-free paper ∞

Designed by C. H. Westmoreland

Typeset in Sabon with Frutiger display type by Keystone Typesetting, Inc.

Library of Congress Cataloging-in-Publication Data appear

on the last printed page of this book.

Contents

Acknowledgments

This book could not have been written without the intellectual and emotional support of many people both in the United States and in Israel. Susan Gilson Miller was an important source of advice and support during every stage of this project. At Harvard University, Michael Herzfeld, Begona Aretxaga, Mary Steedly, and Arthur Kleinman provided crucial comments, criticisms, and suggestions. I am very grateful to Daniel Boyarin, Faye Ginsburg, Sarah Franklin, Marcia Inhorn, Carmel Shalev, David Golinkin, Helen Epstein, and Madeline Kochen for reading sections of the manuscript and offering invaluable insights. Any sins of commission or omission in the following pages are obviously my own. My new colleagues at Brandeis University have been very supportive. I particularly thank Shulamit Reinharz, Sylvia Barack Fishman, Helene Greenberg, Sylvia Fuks Fried, Marc Brettler, and Jonathan Sarna. The help, interest, and collegiality of Don Seeman, Adam Weisberg, Samantha King, and Dana Isaacoff were important to me throughout this project. Although Janet Adelman and Ruth Wisse teach literature, not anthropology, their intellectual examples have been very inspiring to me. I thank Florence DeVecchi for making the study of anthropology so interesting to me in the first place.

In Jerusalem, I am very grateful to my friends, particularly Judy Paikin, Gladys Groner, Dani Groner, Tessa Manoim, Dorit Ortal, Susie Schneider, Tali Birkhan, Susan Moser, Renee Goutmann, Batya Kallus, Menachem Kallus, Tslila Zagagi, Yael Shaul, Shosh, Katya, Tamar, and Golda, for their friendship, warmth, and hospitality. They kept me sane, invited me over for delicious meals, and challenged me to think carefully about the many ideas this project generated. Getting to know Dr. Carmel Shalev was one of the great perks of this project, and her extremely generous intellectual input into my early thinking about these ideas was invaluable.

The staff at various hospitals and clinics in Israel were generally very helpful, and this work could not have been completed without their consent and participation. Many of them were also great fun to be with. The women in the "maybebaby" group in Jerusalem cheerfully tolerated my "spying," as they called it, and it was a pleasure to be part of their ongoing exploration of the dilemmas of childbearing and to share the joy of two pregnant members. The unmarried women I interviewed shared the intimate details of their reproductive lives with me, and I hope I have done credit to their stories. I also thank the many rabbis, librarians, taxi drivers, bus drivers, and others who helped me navigate my way around Israel, both literally and figuratively.

This research was assisted by a grant from the Joint Committee on the Near and Middle East of the Social Science Research Council and the American Council of Learned Societies with funds provided by the U.S. Information Agency. I am also grateful for support from the Center for Jewish Studies at Harvard University, the Memorial Foundation for Jewish Culture, and the Charlotte Newcombe Doctoral Dissertation Fellowship. Finally, I want to thank the National Foundation for Jewish Culture for awarding this project their 1998 Sidney and Hadassah Musher Publication Prize.

I am very grateful to Ken Wissoker, Rebecca Johns-Danes, and Paula Dragosh at Duke University Press. I also thank Nancy Zibman for preparing the index.

I dedicate this work to my mother with deep gratitude for her unwavering support.

Reproducing Jews

Introduction

A Jewish baby is born to a woman on the outskirts of Jerusalem. The baby is healthy, the mother is happy, guests bring gifts, and the child is welcomed to the world. The birth is remarkable because the woman conceived the child without having sexual intercourse and the baby has no identifiable father.

This reproductive moment is not the virgin birth of Christian Scripture; it is an ongoing, contemporary phenomenon in the state of Israel. Indeed, such births occur quite regularly in Israel as part of a small but growing trend among unmarried Jewish women who give birth to children they have conceived with anonymous Jewish donor sperm.

An unusual confluence of social, legal, and rabbinic forces have enabled the birth of these children. First, many Israelis have enthusiastically embraced new reproductive technologies as reasonable solutions to childlessness and, in the case of a growing number of unmarried women, as legitimate alternatives to sexual intercourse as pathways to pregnancy. Second, the Israeli medical community has recognized the potential for procreative innovation inherent in these technologies and has positioned itself at the cutting edge of their research and development. Third, Israeli legislators have drafted regulations to provide broad-based, and in many cases unprecedented, access to these technologies. Finally, contemporary orthodox rabbis have spared no effort to determine appropriate uses of these technologies that are commensurate with traditional rabbinic understandings of relatedness.

These dynamics present numerous analytical foci. In this study, I have chosen to (1) illustrate how rabbinic beliefs about kinship are made literal through the social uses of new reproductive technology in Israel, with a particular focus on the construction of maternity and paternity in rabbinic kinship cosmology; (2) illuminate the curious conceptual and practical overlaps between secular and religious uses of, and beliefs about, these technologies; (3) analyze how rabbinic beliefs about kinship create the potential for unmarried Israeli women to reproduce via reproductive technology; (4) show how the bodies of unmarried Jewish women are imagined as reproductive resources in legal discourse regarding the new reproductive technologies in Israel.

First, some descriptive comments about my research site and the "nexus of power" that shapes the use of the new reproductive technologies in Israel (Ginsburg and Rapp 1995: 5). At the time of my research in the mid-1990s, there were more fertility clinics per capita in Israel than in any other country in the world (twenty-four units for a population of 5.5 million, four times the number per capita in the United States). Moreover, Israeli fertility specialists have emerged as global leaders in the research and development of these technologies, making Israel a regional hub for infertility treatment that attracts patients from all over the Middle East and Europe. In addition, all the new reproductive technologies, including artificial insemination, ovum donation, and in-vitro fertilization, are subsidized by Israeli national health insurance. Thus every Israeli, regardless of religion or marital status, is eligible for unlimited rounds of in-vitro fertilization treatment free of charge, up to the birth of two live children. This commitment theoretically obligates the state to subsidize hundreds of thousands of dollars of infertility treatment (one cycle of in-vitro fertilization treatment in the United States can cost anywhere between $5,000 and $20,000) as a standard part of the basic basket of health services.[1] Finally, Israeli lawyers have actively fought for legislation guaranteeing broad-based access to reproductive technology, whether by challenging existing regulations that limit access to these technologies or by drafting innovative legislation regarding their use. Indeed, in 1996 Israeli legislators passed the Embryo-Carrying Agreements Law, making Israel the first country in the world to legalize surrogate mother agreements, provided that they are publicly regulated by a government-appointed commission. Since that time, a number of surrogacy contracts have been negotiated and carried out.

Contrast this extraordinary state support for reproductive technology with the striking degree to which treatments that limit family size remain unsubsidized in Israel. Family planning services do not receive state support and are funded only on a charitable basis. Contraceptives are not generally part of the basic basket of medical services covered by Israeli health insurance, and abortion, though legal, is subsidized only in certain cases.[2]

A word about Israeli pronatalism is crucial here, for the overwhelming desire to create Jewish babies deeply informs the Israeli embrace of reproductive technology.

The barren woman is an archetype of suffering in the Israeli/Jewish imagination. From the childlessness of the matriarchs in the Book of Genesis, about which every Israeli schoolchild learns from the age of six, to the later biblical image of Hannah weeping over her inability to have children, Israelis learn that barrenness is a tragic fate for a woman. The childless woman is to be pitied and prayed for; her suffering is the quintessential form of female suffering and her joy at childbirth the quintessential form of female joy. Childlessness is no less tragic for a Jewish man who is commanded to procreate according to Jewish law; failure to do so prevents him from fulfilling an obligation of central importance in Judaism. The biblical commandment to "be fruitful and multiply" thus resonates deeply for Jews in Israel, particularly for religiously observant Jews for whom reproduction is understood as an imperative religious duty that is foundational to their entire way of life.[3]

For Israeli Jews the imperative to reproduce has deep political and historical roots as well. Some feel they must have children to counterbalance what they believe to be a demographic threat represented by Palestinian and Arab birthrates. Others believe they must produce soldiers to defend the fledgling state.[4] Some feel pressure to have children in order to "replace" the six million Jews killed in the Holocaust. Many Jews simply have traditional notions of family life that are very child centered. Finally, there are a range of cultural sensitivities to practices designed to limit Jewish births, given that such policies were often employed in various diaspora contexts as part of other anti-Semitic measures.

Historically, the imperative for Israeli Jewish women to reproduce has been reinforced by various state policies. In the 1950s David

Ben-Gurion, the first prime minister of Israel, gave 100 lira awards to "Heroine Mothers" who had ten or more children. In 1967 the Israeli demographic center was established "to act systematically to realize a demographic policy directed at creating an atmosphere and the conditions for encouraging a birth rate, which is so vital to the future of the Jewish people" (Yuval-Davis 1987). In 1968 the Fund for Encouraging Birth was established to offer subsidized housing loans and increased child allowances for Jewish families with three or more children. In 1983 the Law on Families Blessed with Children was passed, which provided subsidies for families with three or more children (Yuval-Davis 1987).[5]

Jewish citizens of the Jewish state come from only three places: from immigration, from conversion and from Jewish mothers. Since immigration is unpredictable and conversion hotly contested, Israeli Jewish women are left as the primary agents through which the nation can be reproduced as Jewish. In a country in which reproduction is of such primary importance, Jewish women are under extraordinary pressure to reproduce, whether they are married or unmarried.

It is important to note that the social uses of new reproductive technologies in Israel take place within a cultural context where there are complex social divisions between Israeli Jews. These divisions cross lines of Jewish ethnicity, religious affiliation, and class background. In fact, the social uses of these technologies often reify these distinctions in unexpected and curious ways. In addition, these technologies are being integrated within an economic and political context in which there is rapid economic growth, ongoing conflicts between Jews and Palestinians, and many other active and intense cultural dramas. This is the backdrop for the pursuit of assisted conception for all Israelis, religious and secular, Jewish and non-Jewish, married and unmarried, infertile and fertile.

Methodology

My methodological inspiration for this study evolves out of George Marcus's call for "multi-sited research . . . designed around chains, paths, threads, conjunctions, or juxtapositions of locations in which the ethnographer establishes some form of literal, physical presence with an explicit, posited logic of association or connection among sites that in fact drives the argument of the ethnography" (1995: 105).

I conducted the research for this study as an unmarried, secular, Jewish American woman without children. It is important to mention that unlike many American Jews, I received no religious education as a child, was not part of any sort of Zionist youth group, and have no close family in Israel. My background is that of an acculturated, assimilated American Jew; I was raised in a cosmopolitan city, in a neighborhood that included Mennonites, Bahais, Dharma Datus, and Protestants. I first went to Israel at the age of twenty-three, en route to farther reaches, and found the place compelling. It was only then that I began to learn Hebrew, study traditional Jewish texts, and become absorbed in the study of the Middle East more broadly.

The problem of the Jewish ethnographer who chooses to do ethnography of Jews has been addressed by Jonathan Boyarin in his essay "Jewish Ethnography and the Question of the Book" (1992). I accept Boyarin's proposition that my "critical stance" is inevitably informed by my identification with the collectivity that I have chosen to study and, more importantly, by their identification with me as "one of them." Yet I would like to contend that my dual status as insider and outsider has afforded me a unique opportunity as a fieldworker. Indeed Boyarin suggests that Jewish ethnography is well served by those "who are Jewish by origin and identification, but marginal to the 'putative' Jewish community in terms of their social position and critical stance" (1992: 68); a contention not without its own problems, and certainly not one that is meant to imply that secular Jewish ethnographers have any sort of monopoly on writing good Jewish ethnography. To be sure, compelling and convincing ethnography has to do with a lot more than the degree of identification between the ethnographer and her subject. The fact that I am a Jew who is writing about Jews simply means that the distance between subject and object is somewhat collapsed. For while I am Jewish, I am writing about Israelis as an American, I am writing about religious Judaism as a nonobservant woman, and I am writing about motherhood as a woman without children. The distance between subject and object thus expands and contracts, creating a dynamic tension that has hopefully served to illuminate the issues addressed in this ethnography.

My ethnographic research spanned two consecutive years from August 1994 to July 1996 and is concentrated in three spheres. In the first, I conducted thirty-five in-depth, open-ended interviews with unmarried Israeli women, either those who had had children via artificial insemination or those who were seeking to get pregnant via artificial insemination. I also participated in an ongoing "support group" of unmarried women in Jerusalem, which met monthly to discuss the various issues involved in having a child outside marriage. These two formal activities were supplemented by long hours of participant-observation with many more unmarried women and their alternatively conceived children.

In the second sphere I was a participant-observer in the fertility clinic at a small hospital in Jerusalem, where all the reproductive procedures are determined by Jewish legal (Halakhic) considerations. I include in this sphere of research the many interviews I conducted with various medical professionals, be they doctors, nurses, or social workers, at this hospital and other hospitals and clinics throughout Israel.

In the third sphere, I interviewed rabbis and other orthodox Jews involved in issues related to the uses of reproductive technology. This sphere of research was grounded in both traditional ethnography and text study, for during these interviews I would inevitably be referred to articles and other materials in which rabbinic deliberations on these issues were explained. I am not an Halakhic scholar, and therefore my research into Halakhic source material was often guided by these secondary source materials, which I read in both Hebrew and English; the citations for these materials are provided in detail in the succeeding chapters. Most interviews and conversations in each sphere were conducted in Hebrew and later translated by me from field notes.

It is important to point out that my ethnographic work focuses on

Israeli Jews, not on non-Jewish Israeli minorities or on Palestinians living in the Occupied Territories. Although Israeli Palestinians and other non-Jewish Israeli minorities have equal access to fertility treatment in Israeli hospitals, state policies regarding the appropriate uses of reproductive technology are constructed with attention to Halakhic concerns about relatedness; Islamic and Christian attitudes are manifest in individual use of these technologies, not in state policy.[6] Thus I would like to make it clear that when I refer to "Israelis" or "Israeli society," I am referring to Israeli Jews and Israeli Jewish society, unless noted otherwise.

In chapter 1, I examine how unmarried women use new technologies to have children and how these alternative pathways to pregnancy are being created and understood by the social actors themselves. In chapter 2 I analyze the uneasy relationship between secular and religious law in Israel regarding the legislation of reproductive technology and explore how this legislation challenges the traditional family as the exclusive locus of legitimate reproduction. As part of this analysis I suggest a theoretical framework for understanding the various cultural discourses that come to bear on the social uses of the new reproductive technologies in Israel. In chapters 3 and 4 I describe the dynamics through which rabbinic conceptions of kinship become explicit by examining rabbinic debates over the appropriate uses of the new reproductive technologies, and I contextualize these interpretive dramas in their present-day Israeli cultural milieus. In chapter 5 I examine the potential social consequences of the Israeli surrogacy law with specific attention to how this legislation depends on the bodies and reproductive capacities of unmarried women. In chapter 6 I present my main theoretical arguments. Here I problematize Marilyn Strathern's model for theorizing the new reproductive technologies and their consequences for thinking about kinship. Strathern suggests that as soon as reproduction gets technological, biogenetic relatedness inevitably gains conceptual power, but in Israel more diverse beliefs about relatedness somehow prevail.

1

"The time arrived but the father didn't":

A New Continuum of Israeli Conception

If you're not a mother, you don't exist in Israeli society.
—Social worker in a Jerusalem fertility clinic

It is a hot Jerusalem night in July, and I am sitting on a large, rooftop patio with six Israeli women. We are drinking Diet Coke and lemonade, eating pretzels and olives, and discussing reproductive decisions and dilemmas. These women have been meeting monthly for over a year as a support group for unmarried women who are considering artificial insemination. Everyone refers to it as the "maybebaby" group.

They know I am writing about them, in fact they call me the "spy," but I have assured them that I will not reveal their real identities (all names have been changed to protect the identities of participants) and so I have become a regular member. We have all gotten to know each other over the past months, and everyone is joking around. Tonight a new member has joined, so everyone gives more personal background information than usual. After a long, informal chat about work, politics, food, and relationships, the "formal" discussion begins with a go-around.

Hagit, a thirty-eight-year-old teacher who lives in Jerusalem, goes first:

> I see each stage of getting pregnant in and of itself, to look at the whole process from beginning to end is like looking at a huge mountain, it's too much. I try not to think about it, the more I think about it the less natural it seems. There is a limit to all the thinking you can do. Other people just get pregnant and are parents without thinking twice about it, why should I obsess about something that is so natural for most people? I was thinking a lot about it, how do it, with a man or not, the

sperm bank. I chose the sperm bank because to make an agreement with someone you don't love to have a child is very problematic. It seems unfair to divide the child in two before he is even born. Working out the problems in a relationship is difficult enough.

You have to get shots, then checkups, then go to work, then shots, checkups, ultrasound, work, fit in Pesach vacation, and on and on. If all goes well it should only take a month from first checkup to interviews to insemination. But with me it takes longer because I have trouble getting pregnant. I took a Chorigon (hormone) shot yesterday and I get the insemination tomorrow morning at 7:30 A.M. [Everyone wished her luck.]

Katya, a forty-year-old nurse, was next:
I'm taking a break. I got through all the stages until they told me I need a measles vaccination and must wait three months to continue. It's given me time to think. I'm going to Turkey to take a break, I'm not so sure now that I really want to raise a child alone. I started thinking about how hard it is to be a single parent. I'm not sure that's what I want. I know what it is to be tired, I know how much work it is to have a baby, I'm not so sure now.

Tamar, the new member, spoke next:
I grew up in Jerusalem but I live in London now. I was married for ten years to an Israeli guy, my high school sweetheart. After a few years, I found out he was infertile, it's a long story, but we ended up breaking up. I had five unsuccessful inseminations in London, and so I came back to Israel for a few months to check out the options here, and to see my family and friends. Maybe I will have better luck here, I thought.

An interesting thing happened a few weeks ago, I met an old friend from the army, a gay man, and we started talking. It turned out he really wants a child, too. So it seemed perfect, and we got very excited about it. But now I am starting to feel less sure about it, he wants too much from my life. I am leaning toward the sperm bank again. I think it's important what you say, Hagit, that you don't want to divide the child before he is born. I sort of assumed that people who chose the sperm bank option were people who had trouble forming relationships, but I'm not so sure that that's true, maybe it comes from a certain maturity about the relationship that you are in.

Everyone thanked Tamar and welcomed her to the group. Chana spoke next; she said she had made no "progress" and was still in the thinking stages. Then came Vardit. She said that she had recently told the women in her office that she was starting to inseminate, and they were all very supportive. "It was a big step," she said, "to talk about it at work. I was afraid of the reactions. But I was missing so much time because of all the doctor's appointments I had to say something. One woman in my office made it seem very simple, she just said to me: 'the time arrived, but the father didn't.' It makes it much easier now that everyone knows."

The discussion on that hot July night echoed many of the individual interviews I conducted with unmarried Jewish women, both heterosexual and lesbian, religious and secular, who were seeking to get pregnant via artificial insemination in Israel. In addition to confronting a wide range of emotions in their journeys to become mothers, they had to be extraordinarily determined and persistent to navigate the sea of logistical hurdles that make up the Israeli insemination bureaucracy. A complex kind of reproductive agency informs these pathways to pregnancy. It is a reproductive agency that assumes reproduction is something one can take into one's own hands and accomplish on one's own, that is bolstered by deep cultural beliefs that motherhood is the most primal and natural goal for women, and that is enabled by the traditional rabbinic belief that children born to unmarried women are considered legitimate, full-fledged Jews.

In this chapter I delineate eight stages that help conceptualize unmarried women's experiences of artificial insemination and autonomous motherhood in Israel. The stages serve as a heuristic device to make literal a new process through which Jews are reproduced in Israel. These stages are not always discreet, nor do they often flow smoothly one after the other. Rather, they are often interrupted by long gaps, as women cope with the frustrations of unsuccessful inseminations, lingering doubts, or other intervening life events. Nevertheless, when read as a sequence, these stages illuminate the lived experience of artificial insemination for unmarried Israeli women.

I animate these stages with select commentaries culled from interviews with a random assortment of thirty-five unmarried Israeli women I interviewed between 1994 and 1996, as well as those in the "maybebaby" group. The unmarried mothers among whom I gathered life stories and whose lives I shared during my fieldwork were randomly assembled; they do not constitute any sort of spatially bounded population, nor are they united by any particular ethnic characteristics, besides the fact that they are all Israeli Jews. They comprise a group only because they were the women who agreed to participate in my research during a particular two-year time period.

I conclude my explication of the eight stages that characterize assisted conception for unmarried women in Israel with additional perspectives on autonomous motherhood made manifest in the experiences of Israeli lesbians and unmarried religious women who conceive via artificial insemination. I then examine short narratives about artificial insemination as an individual strategy for negotiating loss in specific instances.

How Did You Get Pregnant?

When I arrived in Israel to begin my research with unmarried Israeli women, I was initially quite embarrassed to ask what seemed to be very intimate questions about personal reproductive choices, but I was quickly put at ease by my research subjects and their apparent willingness to divulge the intricate details of their reproductive lives. I think the fact that I was both single and Jewish made it easier for them to confide in me, for they could identify with me as being like them. And yet I think the fact that I was an American reified the distance between us and made it clear that they had to explain things carefully to me and could not take it for granted that I would understand anything. Most of my research subjects had been to college, so the concept of research was familiar to them and the form of discourse between interviewer and interviewee was not alien or off-putting. Moreover, most of the unmarried women I interviewed were economically advantaged. They held well-paying jobs, most of them owned their own cars, and most had traveled abroad; in other words, they were part of the Israeli middle class. Most were Ashkenazi (Jews of European origin), though a substantial minority was Sephardi or Mizrachi (Jews of Spanish, North African, or Asian origins). Ethnicity was not a central category for delineating my research subjects, however; not only did they come from various ethnic backgrounds, they seldom invoked ethnicity as a significant characteristic of their individual identities. In addition, it must be understood that the women I interviewed were overwhelmingly secular, for reasons that will become clear.

The community I studied, then, must be understood as an "imagined" one, and it was I, the anthropologist, who was imagining it. Unmarried Israeli mothers themselves do not self-identify as a distinctive group; their self-definitions range from descriptions of their political beliefs to their jobs to their cities of birth or residence.

I conducted almost all my interviews in the homes of the women I interviewed, often with babies sleeping in the next room or with children jumping around on the sofa beside me. I think being in their own homes helped the interviewees feel more comfortable, even if it sometimes made it difficult for me to concentrate. I became friends with some of the women I interviewed, and as I got to know them more personally they would invite me over for babies' birthdays, holiday celebrations, and so on. It was in these more informal meetings that I learned a lot about their lives and the contexts in which they made their reproductive choices. Some of the women I met also invited me to accompany them on their visits to the fertility clinic.

I told everyone I knew and everyone I met about my research. It would turn out that so-and-so's sister was getting artificially inseminated, or so-and-so's hairdresser had just had a child on her own, or the ex-wife of someone's brother was in fertility treatment. These kinds of leads led me to my interviewees. I would ask if I could call the person in question, and the liaison would either give me the phone number directly or call ahead first. Eventually, I was able to make these initial phone calls with a minimum of anxiety. But I could never quite get over how strange it felt to call up people, out of the blue, and ask them if I could interview them about how they got pregnant, or how they wanted to get pregnant.

Once a woman agreed to be interviewed, I usually went to her house and spoke with her there, though sometimes I initially met interviewees in cafes or in their workplace. The "house interviews" would last anywhere from one to four hours. Sometimes they would last significantly longer: I called one woman in Haifa who was the mother of a three-year-old son whom she had conceived through artificial insemination, and she invited me to stay with her for the weekend, sight unseen. After these initial meetings, I would arrange follow-ups depending on the circumstances. In addition, I posted signs in fertility clinics in Jerusalem, Tel Aviv, and Haifa that said I was a Ph.D. candidate at Harvard University and was interested in interviewing women who had been artificially inseminated or who were considering it. These public notices were significantly less effective for contacting interviewees than word of mouth.

After I had been in Israel for almost a year and a half, unmarried women began to find me. I had become known as someone who knew a lot about the reproductive resources in the country and as someone who knew what was involved in fertility treatment. One of my favorite "informants" turned up at my door one cold March afternoon after having met some friends of mine camping in the desert. She wanted to get artificially inseminated, and my friends told her that I had information about how to do it in Israel.

Almost all the women I interviewed I found "through the grapevine." Israel is a small country, people very helpful, and I slowly found my way from one person to another over the course of many months. Indeed, the research would have been impossible in a place where reproduction was considered to be a more private matter than it is in Israel. There was a level of openness and a readiness to reveal intimate facts that continually surprised me and proved crucial to the success of my research.

It is important to point out, however, that I encountered this openness among a very particular population in Israel: secular Jews who were using reproductive technologies not to solve infertility but to achieve autonomous conception. It would have been significantly more methodologically problematic to concentrate my research exclusively on infertile Jews, particularly those who are religiously observant. Not only do outsiders generally encounter resistance trying to enter more religious social worlds in Israel, infertility is often shrouded in secrecy and shame in these communities, making it even more difficult to conduct in-depth ethnographic research.

Before I describe the eight stages I have delineated, it is important to understand some additional features of the social context in which unmarried women in Israel choose to pursue pregnancy via artificial insemination. Unmarried Israeli women make this choice within a culture of high visibility and state support for unmarried mothers. In fact, though far from ubiquitous, unmarried mothers have long been a familiar part of the social landscape in Israel. Some are war widows whose husbands were killed while serving in the Israeli army. Others are divorcees, whose numbers are growing as Israeli divorce rates rise.[1] Still others are unmarried mothers by choice, who choose to have children outside marriage while living in stable, long-term relationships with their male partners (Israel has one of the highest cohabitation rates in the world).[2] Many are new immigrants from the former Soviet Union; since 1989 over one million of these immigrants have arrived in Israel, over half of whom are women, and many of whom are single parents. Finally, some are unmarried women who choose to conceive on their own, either via reproductive technology or through other means.[3]

Unmarried Israeli women who choose artificial insemination also benefit from a secular social climate in which the traditional stigma associated with out-of-wedlock births has ceased to retain its negative force. For most secular Israelis, sex outside marriage is relatively common, and the virtues of virginity enjoy little currency. The fact that a woman deliberately conceived a child out-of-wedlock is not a sign of promiscuity for these Israelis; it is a manifestation, perhaps desperate though certainly understandable, of the legitimate desire to have a child and become a mother.

In 1992 the Knesset explicitly recognized the economic hardships faced by single parents with the passage of the Single-Parent Families Law. The law subsidizes single parents in three main areas: housing, childcare, and tax exemptions. Single parents receive advantageous mortgage rates and rent supplements, reduced kindergarten fees and social security allowances (on top of the flat allowance that the government allocates to families with children), and tax exemptions for single-parent families and reductions in the municipal property tax on their apartments. In addition, since April 1994, single-parent families have received a discount in their payments to the National Health Funds. This support indicates that the state feels a responsibility toward the children being raised by single parents and exhibits an appreciation of the financial difficulties they face, be they single parents by choice or by circumstance. Moreover, state support for unmarried mothers could be understood to begin even before conception, for we have seen how access to reproductive technology is heavily subsidized by Israeli national health insurance funds, regardless of marital status. The funds cover all forms of technological treatment, from the relatively simple procedures related to artificial insemination — including blood tests, AIDS tests, ultrasounds, fertility monitoring, hormonal treatments, and doctors visits — to technologically advanced procedures such as IVF, micromanipulation, GIFT, ZIFT, and so forth.[4]

These state policies, which not only recognize and support single parents but also subsidize the pursuit of single parenthood, contribute to the growing social acceptance of unmarried mothers, particularly within more secular Jewish communities in Israel. Indeed, as one thirty-nine-year-old unmarried woman told me, it is considered much worse to be a childless woman than it is to be an unmarried mother. She said: "My friends are encouraging me to get pregnant on my own. They told me I would be a great mother. They said that a husband I could always get, but children! To have children the time runs out. I should get pregnant now, while I can, and the husband will come later." Another woman I interviewed, an unmarried mother in Jerusalem, articulated a cogent explanation for this social acceptance:

Once a child is born in Israel it will always be accepted. The way a woman got pregnant isn't held against her; for example, if she is raped the child is still considered legitimate. There is no word for an illegitimate child in Hebrew. Once the child is born, the society accepts him. Israel is very lenient to single women. The society accepts the child because of Jewish culture. The nuclear family is difficult to circumvent psychologically, but not Halakhically. A single mother threatens that, but not terribly. The idea that children should be born is very strong in Israel.

In sum, though having a child out-of-wedlock is still not socially encouraged in Israel, unmarried women who do so make that choice in a society where the pressure to be a mother is intense, where single mothers are not uncommon, where the stigma against out-of-wedlock births has ceased to retain its cultural force, where the special economic needs of single parents are understood by the government, and where state health insurance subsidizes all forms of reproductive technology regardless of marital status.

Make no mistake, most unmarried Israeli women see artificial insemination as a last resort and make every attempt to "normalize" these instances of reproduction by integrating their children into existing family networks. Indeed, unmarried women articulate their reproductive agency from within the context of traditional family relationships and with the desire to perpetuate those relationships. They tend to define their actions in conservative terms, despite the potentially radical and destabilizing consequences of their actions.

A New Conception Continuum

Stage 1

Unmarried heterosexual Israeli women who choose to get pregnant via artificial insemination select an option that exists along a continuum. They can marry a man to start a family, sleep with a man for the express purpose of having a child, contract with a man to have a child outside a romantic relationship while sharing parenting responsibilities,[5] adopt, choose artificial insemination with a known donor, or choose artificial insemination with an unknown donor. Undoubtedly, new options will be created by future convergences of social and technological forces. At the same time, unmarried women who choose artificial insemination are not necessarily choosing among options that they perceive to be equally available. Because a woman's chances of getting married are thought to diminish significantly after the age of thirty in Israel, the "choice" to get pregnant via artificial insemination is often not articulated as a choice between having a child within a marriage or outside one, but as a more basic choice between having a child or not having a child. Indeed, the regulatory limit that excludes unmarried Israeli women under the age of thirty from insurance coverage for artificial insemination reifies the assumption that a woman would not, or should not, choose the course of unmarried motherhood unless and until other avenues for maternity have failed to materialize. Thus those seeking state-sponsored access to this technology are all women in their thirties and forties who feel the "clock ticking" and who have not found a man to marry; or who have chosen not to marry, or who are divorced or widowed and have not, or are not, interested in getting remarried.

Artificial insemination was seldom articulated by the women I interviewed as the ideal pathway to pregnancy. Many of the heterosexual women I interviewed would have preferred to have a child within a marriage or partnership with a man. Some chose to get pregnant via artificial insemination because they felt they had limited options and no time to waste. Others felt that the opportunity to get artificially inseminated represented a wonderful new option that freed them from having to wait for a man to achieve motherhood. Still others emphasized that artificial insemination was more "natural" and "better" than other available options. In the narratives that follow, unmarried Israeli women articulate multiple motivations and rationalizations to explain their reproductive choices.

Nitza, a forty-one-year-old physical therapist who lives in Jerusalem, explained why she chose artificial insemination:

> I recently ended a relationship and don't have children. I've had a lot
> of different relationships, but it would take another year at least to

have kids, a long time. I've led a busy, happy single woman's life, hobbies, dancing, sports. When I turned forty, I had to sit down and say yes or no. I started to ask my doctor questions about artificial insemination, and he said that according to the law I had to see a psychiatric social worker. So I started to meet with a social worker who helped me think through the process. I spoke to other women who had done it and talked to family and friends, both female and male. I got lots of positive feedback, but lots of doubts will always accompany the decision, that's just the kind of person I am. I never asked my male friends directly about donating sperm. For them it is probably too difficult, too complicated. I know I'm going to be all alone in this. I'm very independent.

For Tali, a thirty-nine-year-old state employee in Tel Aviv, the decision to use artificial insemination was a painful one:

I cried all the way home from the first appointment at the fertility clinic. It was very sad, very lonely. It's not the best option, but it's the option I have right now. After my last relationship ended, it was the end of hope for a nuclear family. . . . Sometimes I look at what I'm doing and I can't believe it. I'm such a big supporter of family values and the nuclear family. I'm basically very conservative in my outlook, and it does seem strange, though it is starting to feel natural now. It's my right. It's dichotomous, I guess.

Etti, a forty-year-old university administrator in Beer Sheva, felt similarly:

You have to mourn a lot of things. You are not going to have a fairy-tale life. It's not like you love a man and out of this love comes a child. Instead, you make a child and then maybe you can build a relationship afterward. You have to ask yourself what kind of woman am I? There's a real mourning about being alone. The hardest thing is doing it alone without intimacy. I couldn't rely on luck to meet someone and had to take action. So I asked myself: how do I want to do this?

For Hagar, a thirty-seven-year-old photographer in Tel Aviv, the decision to get artificially inseminated was also difficult:

It took me a long time to make the decision. I was hoping to find a man and do it the regular way; I had objections to bringing the child up alone. Single motherhood is not my first choice, but I wanted to take the pressure off. I'm afraid to wait. . . . I'm hoping I'll find a husband.

Once they had let go of the idea that they were going to have a child within a marriage, many of the heterosexual unmarried women I interviewed considered other options. They ultimately chose artificial insemination because they believed it was easier and "better" than having sex with a man in order to get pregnant, it was less costly and less complicated than adoption, and it presented an opportunity to have "one's own" genetic children.

Nomi, a forty-year-old educator who lives in Haifa, decided that artificial insemination was preferable to adoption and sleeping with a man to get pregnant:

> I considered adoption, sleeping with a man, and artificial insemination. I had a man in mind but then I decided against it, it would create a complicated situation. He was married, and I was afraid that the child would leave and decide to go live with a normal family. Adoption costs a lot of money and is hard for a single woman. I couldn't just go sleep with a man I didn't know, that's not me.

Ruby, who lives on a kibbutz in central Israel, also considered adoption:

> Originally I really wanted to adopt. I went to Sherut Leumi Hayeled [Children's services] to adopt an older child, but the connection with them wasn't good. It was a bureaucratic nightmare. I had several candidates in mind to sleep with, but I was afraid of rabbinic law. I heard that according to rabbinic law, the father can claim a boy at age six, and I didn't want to risk it. So I went to the doctor.

Rita, a forty-one-year-old executive in Tel Aviv, considered adoption as well, but then decided she would rather gamble on her own genes:

> When it looked like I was really not going to get married, I thought about adoption, but I figured that if I'm going to have a kid I'd rather gamble on my own genes. I don't think you can discount genetic heritage, and I've got a good one. So I decided to try artificial insemination.

For some, artificial insemination offered a "clean," efficient, and safe alternative to sexual intercourse outside marriage. The donors are screened, the sperm is checked for HIV, and there is no "lying" involved; the donors have given their sperm freely, so it does not need to be "stolen" from them through sexual intercourse. For these women artificial insemination was articulated as more "honest" than sexual intercourse as a means of obtaining sperm. Indeed, many of these women mentioned that they had thought about "stealing sperm" (what one recent immigrant even labeled "the Israeli thing to do") as dishonest and unjust and a bad way to start human life; "stealing sperm" means sleeping with a man in order to get pregnant without telling him.

In a newspaper report on unmarried women and artificial insemination, one interviewee articulated the difficulties involved in "stealing sperm":

> Every man that I have sex with fears for his sperm as though they were a treasure and does not do anything without a condom. And rightly so, indeed he has something to be afraid of. I can give him every promise in writing that I will not seek his financial assistance and I will not ask him to recognize his paternity. . . . There are snares all along the way, from forty on, there are no more nice good single men, most are divorced or in the process, paying alimony to their ex, the really nice ones are married. With them I have a sexual relationship, but they are the most cautious. It is impossible today to have a child without your partner knowing it. Even if I tell them that I am protected because I am on the pill, they'll ask that we use a condom from fear of AIDS, if I ask to do it without a condom it will raise suspicions. If I am with a guy who engages in unprotected sex, he will practice withdrawal. And if I am with a guy who doesn't use a condom and is willing to complete the act inside, how can I make sure that he comes to me on my ovulation day?[6]

Chaya, a thirty-eight-year-old office worker I interviewed in Tel Aviv, had strong feelings about "stealing sperm":

> I didn't want to steal sperm. On my own I could do whatever I want, but as for my child, though it may sound romantic, I want him to start out clean and not from dirty things. To steal sperm is to begin not in a clean way.

Miriam, a thirty-seven-year-old therapist in Jerusalem, told me that she thought artificial insemination was an "honest" way to get pregnant:

> When I think about it emotionally, I think it is the most honest way, it is something that is very coherent with who I am, in relation to not lying, in relation to my lifestyle and my need for freedom. I still prefer a known donor, but I don't have time to wait for all the bureaucracy of importing sperm from California.[7]

Rachel, a forty-year-old therapist in Jerusalem, expressed a similar attitude:

> I thought about just sleeping with someone, but I thought it was ethically wrong to just sleep with someone; it's stealing, it's cheating, it's unethical to do it just to have kids. The ethical, moral, and health considerations led me to the sperm bank option. The health history of the donor was important to me, and you don't necessarily know that from someone you just sleep with.

Yael, a thirty-nine-year-old store owner in Jerusalem, concurred:

> I would sleep with a man. But I didn't want to do it and not let him know, unless there was a man who wanted to do it as a *mitzvah* [good deed]. Artificial insemination is the most honest way to do it because I can tell the child the truth: he does not have a father. That way there's no rejection from a father who doesn't live with him, because there is no father. This child is not going to have a father from the outside, it's clinical. I looked for the best way for me to do it wholeheartedly and honestly, and I feel like this is the most honest way for me to do it. No lying to the child, no lying to a man. It's a totally honest situation.

Yael articulates some interesting equations here: artificial insemination = honesty, sexual intercourse = dishonesty. These equations overlay those implicit in the statements of Chaya and Rachel above, that artificial insemination = cleanliness, sexual intercourse = uncleanliness. In other words, the dangers of physical contagion inherent in sexual intercourse overlap with the dangers of moral contagion inherent in dishonesty and stealing.[8] In configuring their decision to get pregnant via artificial insemination in these terms, these women borrow tropes familiar to anthropologists who identify conceptual oppositions as intrinsic to the construction of cultural meaning (Levi-Strauss 1969; Douglas 1966). As they choose unprecedented means to get pregnant, these women create ways of understanding their choice that make sense and are coherent with their cultural logic. Artificial insemination, constructed as clean, safe, efficient, and honest, is understood by differentiating it from what it is not: dirty, potentially dangerous, difficult to control, and dishonest.[9] By making this differentiation, these women are constructing beliefs that determine their reproductive choices and are conceptualizing a hierarchy that privileges artificial insemination over sexual intercourse as the superior way to reproduce autonomously.

Once an unmarried Israeli woman decides that artificial insemination is her preferred pathway to pregnancy, she must then negotiate the medical bureaucracy that organizes and controls access to reproductive technology in Israel. First, she must choose a clinic in which to pursue treatment. Then, after meeting a nurse or doctor at her chosen clinic for an informational and diagnostic interview, she must schedule evaluative interviews with both a psychiatrist and a social worker.[10] Once interviewed and approved, she must then return to the clinic to choose sperm with the assistance of the nurse or doctor in charge of sperm selection. After these hurdles have been successfully overcome, the insemination itself can begin.

Stage 2:
Fertility Clinics as Sites of Conception

Unmarried women who choose artificial insemination generally spend a lot of time in their chosen fertility clinic. Not only does it often take repeated inseminations to get pregnant, many women receive hormone injections and other forms of fertility treatment that must be regularly monitored. Clinic ambience, therefore, is often invoked as a significant factor in their experiences of insemination, as is the clinic staff, whose kindness or lack thereof makes lasting impressions on those seeking insemination.

Public Israeli sperm banks and fertility clinics are all governed by the same ministry of health regulations, so there are few significant operational differences between these clinics. Not all clinics are public, however. There are private fertility clinics in Israel that operate on a fee-for-service basis, and there have been reports that adherence to government regulations in these clinics has been somewhat irregular.[11]

Most of the women I interviewed sought inseminations in public, government-regulated clinics.[12] For these women, the choice of fertility clinic was relatively perfunctory, since each public clinic follows the same regulations, and they all offer essentially the same services. The choice of fertility clinic was informed mainly by geographical convenience to home or work, or by recommendations about a particular fertility specialist. Clinic choice was also informed by the fact that "religious" hospitals do not accept unmarried women patients, so unmarried women inevitably chose fertility clinics that did not function under rabbinic auspices. Those with proven fertility problems were more particular about the clinic in which they were inseminated, since their inseminations required more extensive hormonal and sometimes surgical preparations.

Tamar's choice was typical:

> I went to the clinic across the street from my parents' house. I'm there a lot, so it seemed convenient. It was very clean and had a very friendly atmosphere; all of the nurses were very helpful and the doctor was very nice, so I went ahead with it.

Rita did more research about fertility clinics before she chose Akiryah in Tel Aviv:

> I heard Akiryah and Hadassah were the best hospitals. My friend recommended Dr. Y because he's warmer than the other doctor; he has a better bedside manner. Since I thought I had no fertility problems I thought I didn't need a genius doctor, just someone who could give warmth and support. Dr. Y gave me an hour of his time. I went in prepared; I asked him everything, regarding legal complications, donor files, and so on. Where they are physically is a dump, yet you get good treatment. It's known as one of the best places. Teaching hospitals are better; there's more money for research and innovation. Why shouldn't I benefit from them trying to publish articles? You may get

nicer frills in private clinics, but the treatment isn't as good. It's the '90s, and the place is totally uncomputerized; it's all done on xeroxes and paper files. They work on card catalogs. They don't even have a computer. In the waiting room there are all these pictures of kids with notes that say, "Thanks Dr. Y!"

Most Israeli fertility clinics I visited were busy and unadorned, much like other public healthcare clinics in Israel. I was often struck by the friendly and informal, if often chaotic, atmospheres of these clinics, where waiting rooms were invariably full of a diverse range of patients, both young and old, religious and secular, Jewish and non-Jewish.

Yehudit, a thirty-eight-year-old accountant in Tel Aviv, narrated her experience at the fertility clinic thus:

In the waiting room, everyone waits together; the couples, the donors, the single women all sit together in the same room. Everyone hears what goes on, everyone sees the donor give the plastic container to the secretary. There's no ladies' room, only a men's room in the middle where the donors go to masturbate. I had to go to the bathroom and had to go to the men's room; it was a gross place. Half of the donors look like high school students. I heard them talk with the secretary about their weekend plans.

Yehudit's experience was not unusual. When sitting in the waiting rooms of these clinics, I was also struck by how little regard was given to patients' and donors' privacy, an aspect of medical care that I realized I was conditioned to experience and expect in healthcare settings. Doors were left ajar during examinations, diagnoses were yelled across waiting rooms, prescriptions were announced loudly. I would often overhear nurses and doctors giving advice and encouragement to patients as if they were speaking to their own cherished, yet somehow errant, children. From behind half-closed doors, nurses admonished: "Chaim-ke, tell your wife to come in for her Chorigon (hormonal) shot. . . . Yank-ele, we need another sperm specimen. . . . 'Hamouda' (dearie), don't think about the treatment this weekend, just have fun." Certainly, some clinics respected patient privacy more than others, and certainly the lack of privacy was more disturbing to some patients than to others.

Intimate and intense relationships often developed between unmarried women patients and the staff at their chosen fertility clinics. These relationships evolved in the context of ongoing and close contact between women and clinic staff as inseminations and various associated diagnostic procedures, like ultrasounds and blood tests, were repeated month after month. The fact that these women were pursing pregnancy without primary partners often made their relationships with clinic staff that much more intense, for the clinic staff were often the first ones to offer support after the disappointment of a failed insemination or to share in the joy of a positive pregnancy test. Many women described how they valued the clinic staff's advice and encouragement during their infertility treatments.

Among the women I interviewed, these relationships rarely extended beyond the fertility clinic, however; they were confined to the clinic and to the period of insemination. Some women who endured particularly lengthy and complicated fertility treatments invited the clinic doctor or the nursing staff to the *brit milah* following the birth of a boy baby, or to a more informal celebration following the birth of a baby girl. Some women sent photos of their babies to the clinics in which they were conceived, with notes of thanks. Indeed, every fertility clinic I visited had walls of photos with pictures of "their" babies.

For Etti in Beer Sheva, the metaphor of the clinic as family was explicit:

> The woman who did the ultrasound treated me like I was her sister, it was so unclinical. It feels like an extended family, it feels like they really want me to get pregnant, the nurse said she gets personally invested, the doctor has a big heart, he wants it to work, he really cares. It's too big to be just individuals, this feeling, it's the system, everyone really wants you to get pregnant, I find it very warm (*hamama*) like a greenhouse. The whole process is very personal, pleasant, and unclinical. Everyone says "Good Luck" every two minutes.

Tali in Tel Aviv also had positive and close relationships with the clinic staff:

The clinic itself is made up of a great bunch of people. . . . Their job is
that they love pregnant women. They feel every baby is a blessing and
that every woman deserves to be a mother. The nurses and secretaries
say, "We want to be part of your happiness, not just part of your
treatment, bring us the baby to see. We want to see what we made,"
and they DID help make it. They feel as if these are their babies, and
they ARE in some way. They want to see you pregnant. After every
treatment they all say *b'hatzlachah* [Good luck]. After the last time
when it didn't work, Dr. Y said to me: "You're not going to bring me
nachat [pleasure]? Bring me *nachat!*"

Dr. Levine, head of the IVF clinic at Hadassah Hospital in Jerusalem,
felt similarly. He explained the enthusiasm with which he and his
staff treats unmarried women:

I have no problem whatsoever with unmarried women having babies
on their own; I am very happy to help them. In fact, the nurses here
often give more support to the unmarried women.

The fertility clinic as a state organization can be understood to
function as a metaphor for the family in these instances, as unrelated
people are brought together to accomplish the work that is traditionally the family's purview, reproduction.

Stage 3:
Screening Unmarried Mothers to Be

At the time of this research, ministry of health regulations required
that after an initial meeting with the head doctor of the chosen fertility clinic, an unmarried woman seeking artificial insemination must
undergo two evaluations before she was "approved" for insemination. The evaluations were to be conducted by a psychiatrist and a
social worker, the rationale being that an unmarried woman who
chooses to be artificially inseminated must be professionally evaluated both for her mental health as well as for her economic and
social well-being.

Rachel Lavi, the senior social worker for the women's health clinic
in Tel Aviv, outlined the criteria that social workers use to determine

the eligibility of single women for insemination in the newspaper *Ma'ariv:*

— Age, not above 50 or below 30, exceptions to these limitations require special consideration, *the lower limit is intended to ensure that the woman has exhausted other alternatives,* and the higher limit is intended to ensure parental responsibility until the child turns 18 out of fear of orphaning the child.

— Financial basis: this includes a regular source of income, without dependence on others, that will allow for meeting the basic needs of a mother and child (food, dwelling, education, medical care) without the woman needing social security from the state.

— Stability and consistency in various areas of life: workplace, studies, the army.

— Emotional capability and stability in relationships, ability to give without receiving in return.

— Is the motivation for having a child primarily to ease her own loneliness or are the best interests of the child central?

— Emotional pathologies, did the candidate have, or has she ever had, mental illnesses or addictions?

— Her understanding of the responsibilities she is taking upon herself, grasp of reality, maturity, and ways of dealing with crises in the past.

— Her state of health.

— Her support systems, the quality of her family ties, availability and readiness to take from them assistance and support in the event of need.

— Motivation to become a mother, when did she begin to think about motherhood? What did she do in the past to attain this goal? What are her expectations from the child?

— Her self-image and her future vision of the family.

(emphasis mine)

Lavi explained:

We recommend that our opinion will be valid for two years only, on the condition that no significant changes have occurred in her life in the past two years. This is a government service. *The government is supplying the sperm* and we are given the mandate of deciding who is fit and who is not. We ask the same questions regarding adoption. The process the woman undergoes is not intended to make things difficult for her. To the contrary, it is attempting to ensure that she is able to raise the child in satisfactory conditions, that she is stable, mature, and economically self-sufficient. That she is aware of the difficulties, that she will be able to deal with a complicated pregnancy including bed rest, a multiple pregnancy, or a retarded child, if God forbid this should happen. We check to see if she will be able to get help from other sources, including friends and family, since after all there are not two parents here to share the responsibility. There are women for whom it would be a tragedy to have a child as a single parent and it is our job to tell them this. Afterwards, they feel grateful that we helped them to organize their thoughts (emphasis mine). Mayna Shenkar, "Just Me and My Sperm Donor," *Ma'ariv,* 19 December 1995

These regulations mirror those in the adoption model of chosen parenthood, in which prospective parents must be evaluated for their psychological and economic fitness to be parents. This despite the fact that unmarried women produce offspring who are biologically related to them, and biological relationships are traditionally seen as relationships beyond the purview of state intervention except in extenuating circumstances. What the adoption model offers is a way to vet prospective parents to ensure that they are capable of taking care of children before they are entrusted with them by the state. Yet, in this case, most women could, theoretically, obtain sperm through sexual intercourse and conceive children without state approval.

As soon as the state gets involved in controlling access to conception, it assumes a paternalistic role, both literally and figuratively. The role of "inseminator" moves laterally between the imagined father and the state. The vestigial assumption at work here is that the maintenance and welfare of the child is dependent on the entity that produces sperm for conception, whether that entity is the father or whether it is the state. As Lavi said: "The government is supplying the sperm."

The women I interviewed experienced these interviews in various ways. Some found them to be perfunctory, bureaucratic hurdles. Others were annoyed by the fact that they had to be approved to be mothers. A minority accepted these interviews as helpful, necessary measures designed to ensure the well-being of their child.

Yehudit in Tel Aviv said:

> I was annoyed, why do they have to ask all these questions? Like, why did I want to have a child through artificial insemination? What is my socioeconomic status? What is my family's reaction? If I was going out with men? The government is sponsoring it, my insurance is paying. The state wants to make sure, they want to make sure that this woman is okay so they don't have to give babies up for adoption. I can understand their need to do it, I had nothing to hide, let's just do it, I thought. There's a lot I am going through that I don't want to do, the shots, the ultrasounds, the diagnostics; the psychiatric evaluation was the least of it.

Rita in Tel Aviv felt similarly:

> If the interview is what they tell me to do, I do it. I went to see the psychiatrist, and it took all of ten minutes, he was chain-smoking the whole time, he just rubber stamped me. I think he just wanted to make sure I wasn't a drug addict who was going to have a baby in order to sell it. The social worker was more serious, it took an hour. She asked more involved questions, about economic status, education, whether I owned my own apartment, why I wasn't married. . . . She wanted to know how I would cope if I got sick, who would take care of the baby; I told her how our family works: when you're in trouble, you get support, very warm. I explained to her that the least of my worries were crisis situations; I know my sister would drop everything and come be with me. It's the daily logistics of being a single parent that I'm worried about. The long working days in order to pay the nanny [*metapelet*]. In crises my family will be with me; on the daily level it's hard.

Tsvia, a forty-two-year-old teacher in Haifa, commented:

> It made me angry that I would have to go through all sorts of interviews. Why should I have to be interviewed to be a mother when any

other woman can just go get fucked? It made me furious, that they have this public system that determines whether or not you can be a mother.

Chaya echoed Tsvia's experience:

The exam of whether I passed the criteria was long and annoying. I felt that they were really trying to get inside my head. What bothered the social worker was that I was too independent and what will I do if I need to ask someone for help. What does she want that I should say? That I'm dependent? I'm not! But I acted relatively nice, because I knew that my fate depended on this meeting.

Lana, a forty-year-old nurse in Jerusalem, in contrast, found the interviews quite pleasant:

The social worker was sweet to me, she just asked me questions like: did I own my own apartment, did I own my own car, what kind of job I had. The psychiatrist said to me: just promise me one thing: that you'll bring the baby to see me when he's born, and they don't say that to everyone. I just told them I wanted to get artificially inseminated because I didn't want to be pressured into getting married in order to have a baby.

Some women accepted the interviews because they felt that the state was looking out for the best interests of the child to be conceived. As Tali in Tel Aviv explained:

I believe this type of screening is an important thing. The bottom line is that we are not talking about the normal way of raising a child and if the public infrastructure is assisting and supporting it, it is important that it consider whether the woman is capable of raising the child alone. Concern for the welfare of the child is in my opinion legitimate. Just as the welfare services watch over children in regular families that have problems.

The fact that most unmarried women I interviewed encountered little formal resistance to their pursuit of autonomous motherhood could be interpreted to mean that the ministry of health's screening mechanisms were largely perfunctory. Or it could be interpreted to mean that I happened to interview women who were unlikely to be discriminated against for economic or psychological reasons by these regulations, since most were middle class and seemingly emotionally stable. In my discussions with social workers, however, I learned that my sample was not unusual; economic considerations were seldom, if ever, held against prospective mothers, and psychological disqualifications were extremely rare. My impressions were confirmed by Dr. Tzvi Zuckerman of Beilinson Hospital in Petach Tikva in an interview with the newspaper *Hadashot* (26 March 1993). Dr. Zuckerman explained that "despite the fact that the great majority of the applicants (for insemination) are college graduates, or graduates of other post–high school programs, the salary of those being treated by us varies between 2000–5000NIS net (in 1993, approximately $600–$1500 per month). . . . From more than 50 women who have applied to us, only three have been rejected for reasons of serious socioeconomic or mental problems."

Clearly, the state's interest in controlling access to insemination for unmarried women was loosely interpreted by those in charge of vetting prospective inseminees. Though obligated to evaluate the social and economic well-being of prospective unmarried mothers, it was clear that few social workers were eager to discriminate against unmarried women for all but the most serious psychological, as opposed to economic, reasons. As one social worker in Jerusalem explained: "It's my place to ask questions, not to give answers; very rarely do I say to the doctors that it is not a good idea to treat a woman. Who am I to decide whether a woman should get pregnant or not? I'm not God! As far as I'm concerned, women can get treatment as long as they are not pathological."

Stage 4:
"Choosing" Sperm

Once an unmarried woman has successfully passed the mandatory psychiatric and social worker interviews, she must meet with the nurse or doctor in charge of sperm selection at her clinic to choose sperm. She is not presented with a wide range of choices.

According to the ministry of health regulations regarding the operation of sperm banks (1987), women who receive artificial insemination in Israel may only receive sperm from anonymous donors, the majority of whom are Jewish.[13] Women may not choose between specific characteristics of the anonymous Jewish donors beyond the donor's "colors," be they dark or light, Ashkenazi or Sephardi, though, as we will see, these choices were relatively false ones.

Men who donate sperm must fill out extensive health histories, must be examined, interviewed and approved, and must obligate themselves to donate sperm on a regular basis over an extended period of time. In return they receive financial compensation for their efforts. The donors are all "students," according to those who worked in sperm banks. This information was explained to Rita in Tel Aviv thus: "The doctor told me that the donors are either medical students or MA students, no BA students. They are all tested for AIDS etc. and are given a full checkup. They are also given psychological testing. The whole checking process takes about eight months. Dr. Y says he interviews them to make sure they are nice people; he doesn't want them not to be nice."

"Being nice" and other unquantifiable personality characteristics often figured prominently in unmarried women's descriptions of their sperm donor. These personal qualities were often relayed to them by the person in charge of managing the clinic's sperm bank. One nurse, who chose sperm for several of the women I interviewed, seemed to understand her role as that of a matchmaker. She told many of these women that the sperm donor she selected was perfect for them, that if they met the man who donated, they would marry him, that they were very compatible types. This information seemed to make the women receiving inseminations feel good about the process.

Tamar explained:

> It was amazing. I'm so excited, there was a real connection between us (her and the nurse). We talked about all kinds of things so she could get a sense of me; we really connected. She said to me: "As soon as I saw you I knew the donor for you, it's too bad you can't meet him, you're very suited to each other."

It was by virtue of this connection, Tamar implied, that she got much more information about the donor than she thought she would:

> He is a psychology student, very creative, every time he brings his sperm in he writes a poem or a blessing on the container. The nurse said he makes her laugh all the time. That's just what I wanted: someone open and creative with a good sense of humor. It is very important that there be some connection with this person.

Miriam had a similar experience:

> I wanted to try and go for Iraqi sperm or something like that, something dark, but the nurse persuaded me not to. She said she knew the donor for me, he has blue eyes like me, she says he is very nice, very gentle. I told her I didn't want a genius, it was more important to me that the guy has social skills; we talked a lot about what kind of person I am, what kind of person the donor should be.

Yael in Jerusalem drew a parallel between choosing sperm and choosing a husband:

> It is very important for me to know the intellectual level of the donors; if I had gotten married I would have married a smart man. I'm not looking for a slow child. All I want is for the kid to be smart and healthy. She said she'd pick someone who will be extremely similar to me. She said since I would be a single mother it would be better if the child looked like me; I hadn't thought about that, but she had. "Ashkenazi heritage, brown eyes," that's what they wrote down. You can make the best of plans, but it's up to fate.

At other clinics, the sperm selection process was significantly less of a "feel-good" experience. Nitza explained:

> The nurse just sat there with a cigarette in her hand and said: "It will be okay, I just take a look at the girl and I know it will be okay. I'll bring you something good, don't worry." I didn't like it, there's a person who just sits there and decides, it seemed unethical, who does she think she is? God? They are only supposed to use the sperm so many times and who knows if they do or not? Who knows how many times they use the sperm? I said to her: "Aren't you going to ask me anything?" And the nurse said: "Do you mind if the hair is curly?" I couldn't believe it! I didn't want to tell her that I don't like blondes

because she was blonde and I didn't want to put her off, I'm in her hands, I don't want to make her mad. I didn't want her to get mad and give me bad sperm.

So I told her I preferred someone tall, then I asked if they screen the donors. She told me the donors were mostly medical students and law students, she said they test them for AIDS and ask them questions about their health. It's all frozen sperm by law, for health reasons. So I asked her: are they at least decent looking? And she said: "Kulam nireh kmo ben adam" [they all look like human beings]. I think they handled it badly. The decision as to whose sperm you get inseminated with should not be made at the last minute by the nurse who gets on the intercom and says to the lab: "Hey, send down this sample." . . . But this is what they have to offer here.

Leah, a thirty-six-year-old teacher in Tel Aviv, had a similar experience:

I had no choice about whose sperm was used. I just know it is medical students, and that they choose someone who looks like me with my background, Ashkenazi, but if a Yemenite woman went in there, they would find her Yemenite sperm. It has to be anonymous sperm because they don't want the mother going to the father and asking for financial support. I asked the doctors what they do with the sperm, after it is donated. It is frozen for a year so that all diseases, especially AIDS, are destroyed.

Yehudit took a pragmatic approach to sperm selection:

I asked what tests the donors were given, specifically I asked about mental diseases, I know there's a genetic component. Dr. P said he interviews the donors several times, most of them are students. I didn't involve myself at all in the technicalities. I didn't ask whether the sperm is frozen or not. Dr. P asked me what I wanted, and I said the donor should just be healthy. He asked if I wanted Ashkenazi, that was the only thing I could choose. I thought about it and I said yes, somewhere inside I guess I am prejudiced, because I prefer Ashkenazi to Sephardi. I fantasize about the donor, I call him "217," that's his number, all my friends know him as "217." I dream about it, too; I dreamt about six very Ashkenazi names and I knew the donor was one of these six.

Hagar makes the connection between the sperm with which she was inseminated and the young men that she saw in the waiting room. She identifies the sperm donors as the "fathers" and is relieved that "her sperm" was donated years earlier by someone she desperately hoped was unlike the undesirable characters she saw in the waiting room:

> I got frozen sperm that had been donated in 1990, it was written on the container. I knew that my sperm was old, but if I thought that those pimply faced teenagers were the father, those runny-nosed kids I saw in the waiting room, I would have been very unhappy. It didn't feel so nice, to see all those runny-nosed kids. It would not have been nice to think that they were the father. It didn't affect the decision to do it, it just wasn't nice. The whole process wasn't dignified. It's disrespectful for everybody, patients, donors, and doctors.

The matchmaking element surrounding sperm selection for unmarried women extends directly into matching the donor and recipient's Jewish ethnicity, which interestingly is assumed to be either Ashkenazi or Sephardi, either "light" or "dark," despite the fact that many Jews in Israel are of mixed ethnic origins. Sharon, a forty-one-year-old office administrator in Jerusalem, explains:

> The doctor asked what "color" I wanted. I said I didn't care, but then he said, for sure you don't want an Ethiopian or something, it will be too confusing for the child if he doesn't look like you. He told me that the eye color is the 'hint of the race,' and that I should go with someone who had blue eyes like me. So I agreed with him and got Ashkenazi sperm.

Tsvia in Haifa said:

> It's not important to me whose sperm was used, or whether it was Jewish or not Jewish, Sephardi or Ashkenazi. In fact, when you inter-breed it can be healthier. I just wanted a healthy baby. The doctor chose sperm that was like me, Ashkenazi.

Ruby on the kibbutz said:

> All I know is that the sperm comes from medical students. They asked for my preference regarding skin color and eye color. I'm not a racist

or anything, but I wanted to go with someone who looked pretty much like me, tall, Ashkenazi type.

We see in these accounts how women were encouraged to choose sperm that "looked like them," which in most cases meant "light" or of Ashkenazi origin. One woman I interviewed, a blonde, blue-eyed Jew of Polish origin, went to the clinic and specifically asked for sperm from a Yemenite Jew, reasoning that "the mix would make a beautiful child." She continued: "But when I went in, the nurse told me that the dark colors are dominant, and asked me whether I thought it was fair to make a child that looks like someone he will never know. I think she was right, so I chose to go with sperm from someone who is light like me." Thus, even though women ostensibly have the option of choosing the "colors" of their donor, all the women either preferred sperm that "looked like them" or were strongly encouraged to choose sperm that "looked like them."[14]

Phenotypic preference for matching the "color" of Jewish sperm to the "colors" of its recipient reflects one level of concern about what constitutes an appropriate "match" between donor and recipient. An appropriate match in this context maintains broader ethnic divisions in Israel between Jews of European origin and Jews of North African or Asian origin, despite the history of intermarriage between Jews from diverse ethnic and regional backgrounds. A range of cultural assumptions are clearly operating here. Certainly, there is no official policy that mandates the matching of Ashkenazi donor sperm with Ashkenazi unmarried women, but the informal practice of sperm selection seems to suggest that it is desirable to observe and maintain ethnic difference in this process. That the long simmering tensions between Jews of different ethnic origins in Israel should be played out in the realm of assisted conception is not surprising, for this is a realm in which such cultural dramas become most vivid.

Interestingly, despite the emerging scientific knowledge of the frequency of specific genetic mutations among Ashkenazi Jews — from Tay-Sachs to rarer recessive disorders such as Canavan's disease, Gaucher's disease, Niemann-Pick disease, Dystonia, etc. — I observed limited efforts in the public fertility clinics to restrict the social practice of matching unmarried Ashkenazi Jewish women with sperm donated by men of Ashkenazi origin. Donor sperm is screened for Tay-Sachs, but it was explained to me that the cost of more comprehensive genetic screening was simply prohibitive.[15] Since most unmarried women who seek anonymous donor inseminations are over the age of thirty-five, they routinely consent to amniocentesis tests once they are pregnant, with the assumption that if any genetic irregularities are found at that stage they will consider abortion. Beyond the test for Tay-Sachs, however, there were no efforts of which I was aware to limit the potential for the replication of genetic mutations among Ashkenazi Jews; for example, by deliberately matching Ashkenazi Jewish women with sperm donated by men of Sephardi or Mizrachi origin. It would seem that the statistical risks of replicating rare genetic mutations in conceptions between Ashkenazi Jews were either considered negligible or too expensive to guard against. Or perhaps risking the conception of a Jewish child with a rare genetic disease was considered preferable to deliberately conceiving a child whose mixed Jewish ethnicity would make him or her phenotypically unlike his or her mother. This clinical practice, motivated as it may be by economic or social considerations, certainly begs further investigation. Perhaps as knowledge about the variety of genetic disorders that seem to be prevalent among Ashkenazi Jews becomes more widespread, efforts will be made to ensure that Ashkenazi donor sperm is checked for the increasing range of identifiable genetic mutations.

Because the protocol surrounding sperm choice in Israel more closely resembles that of a traditional matchmaking agency than that of a regulated, consumer-oriented medical service, unmarried women's consent to it may emerge from a familiar set of associations with the process of consenting to the informed and personalized selection of a "mate" rather than the more unfamiliar process of evaluating and selecting a sperm donor based on particular individual characteristics. Moreover, unmarried women's consent suggests that they do not imagine themselves as "consumers" who are entitled to pick and choose goods in the reproductive marketplace, as has been observed in other contexts (Franklin 1997). Instead, their consent suggests that they understand their pursuit of conception as part of a more communal process of reproduction. The operative variables here are not the particular characteristics of an individual donor but the shared ethnic and religious identities of the donor and recipient. The fact that the donor and recipient are matched according to these characteristics guarantees that the child conceived in this union will assume an identity that is recognizable and acceptable in the communal idiom of the Jewish state.

Stage 5:
Insemination

Once the decision to artificially inseminate has been made, the interviews passed, the sperm selected, and the right time for conception calculated, it is finally time for the insemination itself. The average insemination is a remarkably low-key event; sperm is usually placed in a catheter, which is inserted into the woman's vagina, and then released in the location that will maximize the possibility of conception (either at the entrance of the uterus or inside the uterus). Once the sperm has been deposited, the woman must lie quietly for at least twenty minutes, and then she can be on her way. Here are five descriptions of inseminations:

> They put a diaphragm inside me that had sperm in it, then they put on classical music, turned the lights down low, and gave me a cup of tea.

> The doctor was very fatherly, he was gentle and lovely, and after he put the sperm inside me he wished me good luck.

> They are very considerate; they put the sperm inside me and covered me with a sheet. You're just lying there, with your feet in the stirrups, in this dead cockroach position. You're there for twenty-five minutes.

> They let me look at the sperm under the microscope before they put it in me. It hurt because my cervix wasn't open enough.

> The first time they did ICI (intracervical insemination), with "the dart." They don't tell you you're going to smell like a whorehouse for six hours afterward. The first time I was hysterical, I smelled so much of sperm, anyone who knows what sperm smells like would have recognized the smell. I had to go home; it was embarrassing.

Most women I interviewed had to undergo repeated inseminations until they achieved conception, others had to receive more extensive fertility treatments in order to get pregnant. These treatments included diagnostic surgical procedures, hormone pills and injections to hyperstimulate their ovaries, oocyte retrieval operations in which ova were extracted for in-vitro fertilization, etc. These medical regimens were often emotionally and physically debilitating and demanded extraordinary resolve and persistence.[16] In addition, once pregnant, some of the women I interviewed had difficulty keeping their pregnancies and had to cope with the emotional and physical trauma of miscarriage. For those who had difficulty conceiving and staying pregnant, family, friends, and clinic personnel were invariably supportive and encouraging. "Eventful" conceptions and pregnancies were not uncommon among the unmarried women I interviewed, because they were all older women for whom fertility problems are statistically more common.

Once conception was achieved, the subsequent biological processes of gestation and parturition are not, needless to say, different for unmarried and married women. The social experience of being an unmarried pregnant woman was often different, however, since pregnant women are generally assumed to be married. The unmarried women I interviewed innovated a range of strategies for negotiating these unwanted questions, from lying about being married, to wearing wedding rings, to simply replying they were not married.

Births were generally attended by the unmarried woman's close family or friends. Some women asked their mother or a close friend to act as their birth coach. Most were overwhelmed by visitors as they recuperated in the hospital after they had given birth, a customary occurrence following births in Israel.

Stage 6:
Postnatal Concerns (Circumcision)

Once unmarried women in Israel have given birth to their alternatively conceived children, a new set of decisions must be made. The most immediate concern for mothers of male babies is the arrangement of the brit milah circumcision ritual eight days after the boy's birth (many Israelis have innovated baby-naming ceremonies for female babies as well). The alternatively conceived sons of the unmarried women I interviewed all had circumcisions, as do the vast majority of Jewish baby boys in Israel, and these events were often huge catered affairs, as is customary among both religious and secular Jews in Israel.

Unmarried secular women who give birth to boys must often ask around to find a *mohel* (circumcisor) who is known to be more liberal and who will agree to perform a circumcision on a boy who has no father listed on his birth certificate; mohels who are more conservative may refuse to officiate at circumcisions for a boy born to an unmarried woman, out of concern that their participation would condone such conceptions. Nevertheless, that orthodox mohels, albeit more "liberal" ones, do inevitably officiate at these events implicitly legitimates these instances of reproduction. Ruby on the kibbutz described her son's circumcision thus:

> You should have seen the *brit!* What a laugh that was! Since there was no father listed on the birth certificate I decided not to go with the Ashkenazi rabbi who may have had trouble with the whole thing so instead I found a Yemenite rabbi who had no problem with it. We needed a *minyan* [prayer quorum of ten men], so I got together as many men from the kibbutz that I could, everyone made it very nice.

One brit I attended exemplified how social worlds sometimes collide when unmarried women have babies through artificial insemination in Israel. Ronit and Tsippi were lesbians who lived in a highrise apartment building in Ramat Aviv, a trendy, secular suburb of Tel Aviv. They were both in their mid-thirties, successful financially, and like their yuppie neighbors drove new cars, wore expensive clothes, and worked out at the neighborhood gym.

Tsippi was artificially inseminated at a fertility clinic in Tel Aviv and gave birth to a baby boy. Eight days after their son was born, they had a party in their apartment and invited a mohel to perform the circumcision.

For the brit, Ronit and Tsippi's apartment was filled with adults and children, both families and friends. Their nieces and nephews rolled around the living room on roller blades, their brothers and uncles sat on the sofas and yelled into their cellular phones, their mothers stood in the kitchen holding babies, wiping mouths of small children, and refilling the salad platters. When the ultraorthodox mohel appeared at the door, he was welcomed. He was either unperturbed or unaware of the fact that he was in a lesbian household. The mohel prepared for the circumcision, and all the activity in the apartment stopped for a moment while the mohel uttered the blessings. He skipped over the words in the liturgy where the baby is named as "son of" the father and just said the baby's name. The baby squealed as the circumcision was performed, and everyone resumed eating and talking, including the mohel.

After the party I asked Tsippi if she had ever considered not having her son circumcised. She was taken aback. "Of course not," she said, "it's too difficult to be different at school, in the army, everywhere." Then she cooed to her newly circumcised baby, "welcome to the Jewish people." For these secular lesbians in Tel Aviv, and for the ultraorthodox mohel who performed the circumcision, of their alternatively conceived child, maintaining cultural continuity, symbolized through religious ritual, was completely taken for granted regardless of how the child was conceived.

Stage 7:
Postnatal Concerns (Family Support)

The natal families of the unmarried women I interviewed, both heterosexual and lesbian, were universally forthcoming with emotional, financial, and practical support for their alternatively conceived relatives after they were born. Before conception and during pregnancy, almost every woman I interviewed recounted a similar story of one or another parent's resistance, rejection, and outright opposition to the whole idea. Once the alternatively conceived child was actually born, however, these negative feelings invariably dissipated. One woman told me that her parents had been totally against her having a baby on her own and that her father had stopped talking to her for the entire nine months of the pregnancy. Once the baby was born, however, the new baby quickly became their favorite grandchild. The mother explained that her baby was the favorite because unlike her siblings' children, her parents did not have to share her baby with another set of grandparents: he was all theirs.

The expectation of family support often figured prominently in unmarried women's accounts of their decisions to inseminate and was a recurrent theme in their descriptions of the childcare networks in which they were raising their children.

Yael in Jerusalem said:

My parents are very involved as grandparents, they love all their grandchildren. My sister-in-law and brother are also very supportive, and the cousins all play together on shabbat.

Etti in Beer Sheva explained:

Of course my family knows how Noa was conceived. They are very involved. My mother comes over almost every day to help me after work. My sister comes over. I spend shabbat with my whole family. They were thrilled when I had the baby.

Tamar also enjoys her family's support:

My mother lives in Jerusalem, but she comes at least once a week anyway, and whenever I have to go away my mother and father come to stay with Noam.

Family support was a more complicated issue for those women raised in traditional, religious homes, as was the case for Rita in Tel Aviv:

I discussed it with my father because he has to live with the decision in his community, which is very religious. He said: "I'm not happy, but I understand." My sister in Jerusalem is very observant and very supportive. I'm counting on lots of extended family support to bring up this child. I took all this into consideration. It doesn't make up for lack of father, I know, but it's something. My mother (who passed away) would not have had an easy time with this, but my father said that she would have understood because of my age. He himself would love another grandchild. He's not happy but he understands.

Friends and neighbors also played a valuable though more informal role in helping with childcare. This help was not unique to the children of unmarried women; informal childcare networks are widespread in Israel, where children generally enjoy a great deal of freedom. They run freely in and out of other people's homes, play together in communal playgrounds, and generally come and go as they please.

Clearly, unmarried Israeli women who have children through artificial insemination are not necessarily motivated by a desire to undermine traditional family ideologies or to raise their children outside regular, informal childcare networks; nor do they necessarily understand their reproductive agency as a threat to these ideologies or networks. On the contrary, unmarried women who have children participate in and depend on traditional families and informal childcare networks for emotional and practical support. Their reproductive choices are deeply embedded in a network of preexisting family and neighborly relationships; they are having children to express affiliation, to augment and to contribute to their extant families, conceived in both local and national terms, not to distance themselves from them.

In her ethnography titled *Families We Choose: Lesbians, Gays, Kinships,* Kath Weston describes how gay men and lesbians are using reproductive technology to innovate kinship in San Francisco in order to create chosen families. Weston contends that as gay people claim their rights as reproductive beings, the families they create challenge the traditional monopoly that heterosexuality has maintained over reproduction. Weston shows how reproductive technology is used to create new kinds of families in which biological relatedness is simultaneously the basis of, and the model for, new forms of family relationships that do not necessarily depend on genealogical referents.

Weston's model helps illustrate very different dynamics in the Israeli context. I suggest that unmarried women in Israel, both heterosexual and lesbian, who get pregnant via artificial insemination are not overtly interested in challenging the traditional monopoly that heterosexuality has had on reproduction; nor do they wish to create families that do not depend on genealogical referents. The social consequences of their reproductive choices are much less ambitious in their origin and much more profound in their result: for what they have done is to reveal inadvertently the ways that heterosexuality and marriage have never had a monopoly over reproduction in the Jewish imagination; in the Jewish imagination it is Jewish children born to Jewish mothers who have a conceptual monopoly over reproduction, regardless of how they are conceived.

In his book *The Policing of Families: Welfare versus State,* historian Jacques Donzelot describes the symbiotic relationship between the family and the state in eighteenth-century Europe, whereby the state actively worked to preserve the integrity of an idealized family unit by absorbing those who threatened to destabilize it, while the family actively worked to create good citizens for the state through proper socialization of its future participants. That description helps illuminate further the ways unmarried Israeli women and their artificially conceived, fatherless children are integrated into their natal family networks. Through this integrative social practice, which was universal among the women I interviewed and observed, unmarried Israeli women who have conceived children via artificial insemination can be understood to preserve the honor and prestige of the traditional family at the same time that they comply with the dominant ideology of the family as the center of social life.

In sum, the fact that children conceived with anonymous donor sperm and born to unmarried women are integrated into existing family networks is one more indication that these children are understood to be "ours," in the broader national context. These alternatively conceived children are not understood to be solely the product of individual choice, but are understood to be the product of family relationships. This understanding is reinforced by the fact that these children are conceived with Jewish donor sperm. Moreover, this donor sperm, although anonymous, has been explicitly "matched" with the mother's ethnicity, or the presumption of her ethnicity based on her "colors." The child's integration into particular Jewish families can be thus further enabled by the imagination that, in genetic terms, he or she is "one of us."

Stage 8:
Postnatal Concerns (Narrating Absence)

Unmarried women who conceive children via artificial insemination must innovate a counterdiscourse for the absence of a father. The challenge of explaining the paternity of a child born through anonymous donor insemination manifests itself on two levels: how, when, and what to tell the child; and how, when, and what to tell those the child encounters. Every mother I interviewed had anecdotes about these encounters with friends, relatives, or strangers, and I also experienced these tense social moments.

On one occasion, I attended the first birthday party of a girl in Jerusalem who was conceived with anonymous donor sperm, and the only word that the child could say was "Abba!" (Daddy). Her mother had invited all her friends and relatives from all over the country, and the little girl would toddle up to each one of them and say, "Abba!" Some people picked the child up and said, "Yes! Abba!" to her; others clearly felt uncomfortable and just smiled nervously and ignored what she was saying. There seemed to be a tacit understanding that no one was going to confront the awkward social gap that was being played out in front of them; indeed, no one seemed to have any idea how to confront it.

On another occasion, I was taking a walk with a mother and her two-and-a-half-year-old daughter in Jerusalem, when we encountered two elderly women sitting on a bench. The women beckoned to the child, and she went running up to them and began to show them how she could count to ten. The elderly women patted and encouraged her, and then one asked her, looking at me and her mother, "and where's Abba? Where's Abba?" The little girl looked back at her mother in utter bewilderment; she had not yet been told the circumstances of her conception, and the idea that she should have an "Abba" seemed completely foreign to her. The mother scooped up her child, and we walked away, leaving both her daughter and the elderly women somewhat perplexed.

On yet another occasion, I went with an unmarried mother and her son to visit the boy's grandmother in Haifa. The grandmother was very close to her grandson, but she had not been told how he was conceived; the mother felt that it was none of the grandmother's business. After a large lunch, the mother went to take a nap, leaving me, the grandson, and the grandmother at the table. The grandmother, perhaps sensing that I knew something she did not, began to tell me what a lovely grandson she had. She had no idea where her daughter found such a lovely child, but he was certainly lovely, wasn't he; where did I suppose she found him? I assured her that the child was lovely and left it at that. The grandmother persisted, though somewhat obliquely, to try and ask who was the father of her grandson.

The challenge in these social moments is how to represent the paternity of a child conceived with anonymous donor sperm in a socially acceptable way. Clearly, the discomfort in these encounters comes from the fact that these instances of reproduction are still comparatively rare, and so an uncomfortable silence flows into the space that some form of cogent kinship explanation will one day occupy. This explanation has not yet been innovated, because there is not yet a language in Israel that allows these origin stories to be easily told. Interestingly, three women found relevant metaphors about paternity in non-Jewish sources.[17] Two were living in mixed Jewish-Arab neighborhoods in Haifa, and one was a convert to Judaism.

Nomi explained:

> In Arabic, Santa Claus is called "Baba Noel." When Yuval was two and a half, an Arab friend asked her "su issim aba" (who is your father), and Yuval said, "Baba Noel." For a long time, that's what Yuval would say when anyone asked her who her father was.

Tsvia said:

> I was talking with my friend who's a devout Muslim about inseminating, and he wanted to justify what I was doing by looking back in history. He said that according to Islam, Jesus Christ was born without a father, God was the father, like Christians believe. But also you could say that Shmuel Hanavi was born with God's intervention, because Hannah became pregnant by praying, though she had a husband. You

could even say Itzhak was conceived that way, with the help of God. My friend said that insemination is in the hands of Allah. If God wants you to get pregnant, you will. So in a way, God is the father.

Vardit, a forty-two-year-old office worker in Jerusalem, said:
I'm a convert, I grew up as a Catholic. When I told my parents back home that I was inseminating, they accepted it much more than they would have accepted me sleeping with someone. My father said it's sort of like immaculate conception.

Normalization through Narration

I was very interested to know how unmarried mothers tell their children about the circumstances of their conception. Certainly, on a psychological level, one's "origin story" is a crucial factor in one's development. It is important to understand how the absence of fathers is being explained to those for whom it has the most profound effect. Most women approached the subject with straightforward candor.

Nomi told the following story:
One time in the playground my daughter identified a male friend of mine as her father when her friends asked. And once, when an older child asked me if Yuval has a father, I began to explain that every person in this world has a father, but we don't have a connection with Yuval's father, and he doesn't live with us, then Yuval cut in and said, "Ima (Mom), stop the shit, I don't have a father."

Lana said:
For the last few months he hasn't talked about it. Now I tell him about all the fathers in the world. I used to not read him so many stories with fathers in them, I didn't find a way yet to talk about it. I want him to talk about it, to ask me.

Ruby on kibbutz said:
I wrote them a storybook that explains the whole thing, how I went to the doctor's office and how they were conceived. They never asked, "Where is Abba?" I told them Mommy felt it was better to get pregnant using a doctor. I told them it is better to have no father than a father who doesn't want you. My son came home yesterday after

playing at his friend's house and said, "I would rather be born in a laboratory than have X's father."

Hagit in Jerusalem said:
> I talked with the kindergarten teacher [*ganenet*] and I told her: Noa doesn't know and won't know her father. It's her information. I'm waiting to see what she will do with it, how she will cope with it.

Etti in Beer Sheva said:
> I don't know what I'm going to do. I know that things are going to be open. I'm not going to lie; it's her information. If she should find it necessary to lie, I'm going to find a way to let her lie. It's her right to be able to lie.

Rita in Tel Aviv said:
> I'm going to be honest. I'm not going to say your father went to Turkey and got killed. I'm going to say I wasn't married and I wanted a child very much. I'm hoping I won't have to dwell on it. I will say you have grandparents, cousins, aunts, and uncles who love you and who are family. I will say that our family just has a mother [*Ima*]. You can't lie to kids. We don't have a father [*Abba*], but we have other things. I will say, "We don't have a father, but we have an extended family and that's family too." There is no question that my kid's going to suffer from not having a father. But my sister said a wise thing: there are no perfect parents and there are no perfect kids, you just do the best you can. My kid will just have the problem of coming from a one-parent family. When my kid gets ready to get married, I'll have to tell him to go get genetic testing because I don't know who the father is and I'll never know. [*handwritten:* b/ screening + tracking]

Leah said:
> If strangers ask me who the father is, I will just say: "It's an issue I'd rather not discuss." My friends all know. I'm not lying to anyone.

Gabi in Tel Aviv said:
> I'm going to be as honest as possible, that's the best thing to do. I'm hoping my single male friends will fall in love with my child. It's hard to know about male role models. . . . I'll be happy if my male friends connect, hopefully they will be there. . . . Look, my childhood was not

easy, and I came from a two-parent family, but all you need is one empathic parent.

Chaya in Tel Aviv explained:

For sure, the kids will say, "You don't have an Abba." I will take my kid to a therapist. I told my therapist today that I would bring my kid in to see her starting at age three.

Sharon said:

I will just tell the child the truth: he has no father. The social worker suggested I say I really wanted a baby so I went to a doctor who helped me. But I didn't like that. I'll explain when he's old enough to understand. Before that I don't know.

Tali said:

I'm going to tell him that I really wanted a baby, so I went to the clinic where a very generous man gave his sperm specially so I could have him.

These excerpts indicate that unmarried mothers who conceive through artificial insemination generally explain their children's lack of a father in a rather open, matter-of-fact way. The tense social moments that often surround questions of paternity among families and friends is offset by the candor in these intimate mother-child moments. Clearly, though the language to articulate these familial bonds is still evolving, these efforts to develop coherent origin stories for these alternatively conceived persons represent important attempts to normalize autonomous conception by unmarried women.

Israeli Lesbians and Artificial Insemination

Israeli lesbians make the choice to get artificially inseminated according to a different set of constraints than their heterosexual counterparts. For them, state-subsidized artificial insemination is a remarkable opportunity to achieve motherhood while avoiding an unwanted physical relationship with a man. Although a full examination of the dynamics of lesbian life in Israel are beyond the scope of this discussion, as is a discussion of the social uses of artificial insemination by lesbians in other contexts, these issues are analyzed cogently in other sources.[18]

Like unmarried heterosexual women, Israeli lesbians must navigate through the Israeli insemination bureaucracy. The lesbians I interviewed all concealed their sexual orientation from the probing examinations they underwent throughout their quest for conceptions. This decision can be partially explained by their real concerns that such a revelation would disqualify them for treatment. Though discrimination on the basis of sexual orientation is not codified into any of the existing regulations regarding reproductive technology, the head of gynecology at Hadassah Hospital, Ein Kerem, indicated publicly that he would not allow lesbians to be treated at his clinic.[19]

Galit, a forty-year-old lawyer who lived in Tel Aviv with her female partner Netta, felt resentful that she had to lie about her sexual orientation:

> I had a big dilemma. Crazy, sick people have children, and no one tells them not to do it. Because the state is paying they can establish the criteria they want. I understand it practically, but not personally, because the interviewers are not impartial. No one is professional enough to really make such a decision. For example, if I had told them I was a lesbian, it wouldn't fly. No one can say they are a lesbian and get through the interview. The doctor asked me why I wanted to have a child, and I told him I hadn't found a husband, the clock was ticking, and I wouldn't find a husband in time. He accepted this and I was approved.

Miki, a lesbian in Jerusalem, said that she did not ask too many questions in her interviews with the doctor and psychiatrist, because she wanted to make a good impression and she wanted them to be sympathetic to her. She told the truth: that she was divorced, that both her parents were dead, that her sister did not have kids, and that she was thirty-seven years old:

> I didn't say anything to him about being a lesbian. I said to myself: "I won't say anything and if he asks I'll figure out what to say then." He didn't ask, I don't think it even occurred to him. To him I was a thirty-seven-year-old divorced woman and that was it. His attitude was:

"poor thing, she deserves a child." I just told him I was thirty-seven, divorced, and have had fertility problems. He asked if I had a *shutaf* [masculine for roommate] and I said no, because I don't have a "shutaf" I have a *shutafa* [feminine for roommate]. He asked what I was going to do that this child would not have a father. And I said it's a dilemma, it's a real problem. Instead of saying it will be okay, everything will be okay, I said it will be a problem. I said that after thinking about it, the pros and cons, all in the balance, I think it's better that there should be a child than that there shouldn't be. The whole thing took two minutes. I told him I was a journalist, he checked if I could handle being a single mother economically. Then he said: "I have nothing against your being a mother."

For Ora, a lesbian in Haifa, the sperm selection process was inhibited by her decision to conceal her identity as a lesbian:

The doctor in my clinic, the one who chooses the sperm, he was awful. He gave me the idea that he was doing me a favor by answering my questions. I felt it was unfair that he didn't give better answers. I wanted to know: Did they do testing or questionnaires concerning the mental abilities of the donors? How did they find out about donors' physical health, sickness in families, inherited problems, mental health, learning disabilities, etc.? These things really concerned me, but I didn't get any answers. The doctor didn't give me answers as if he didn't approve of me, as if he doesn't approve of the decision of the ministry of health to give artificial insemination to single women.

I felt I'm not in a position to argue or ask questions or express any disapproval of him. I felt as if it's not my right. Maybe it's my attitude, maybe if I didn't have to lie about being a lesbian at the beginning things would've been different, but I didn't feel I had the right to get answers. In any case, I have no idea about the donor, the doctor only told me that he is light and Ashkenazi like me. The doctor told me the donor was a student, as if he was giving me information he shouldn't have [she imitated him by growling out the information].

That lesbians felt the need to present themselves as heterosexuals is one measure of the lack of social acceptance they feel in Israel. Most of the women I interviewed understood this subterfuge as an expedient form of self-protection that would allow them to achieve their goal of getting inseminated in Israeli clinics without confronting individual prejudice that may prevent their receiving treatment. In most cases, this kind of subterfuge did not seem to be experienced as a serious compromise of self, Tal Yarus-Hakak's case being the notable exception.[20] Yarus-Hakak's bold decision to come out as a lesbian during her quest for insemination may influence other lesbians seeking artificial insemination to be more open about their sexual orientations. Until then, Israeli lesbians will continue to hide their sexual orientations from those who may be prejudiced against them.

Like their heterosexual counterparts, Israeli lesbians often receive financial, emotional, and childcare support from their natal families. This support is somehow more poignant for the lesbians I interviewed, however, since it often acts to heal the rupture that sometimes occurs when lesbians come out to their families.

Miki in Jerusalem explained:

Before the baby, my mother would not accept my lesbianism at all, she would not call or come to the house, she would not talk to my lover. When I told her about the pregnancy my mother was very disapproving. So I told all my other relatives so that they could provide support for my mother, so that they could help her to accept it. Once the baby was born, my mother changed completely. It is her first grandchild, and now she comes by all the time, baby-sits, and even brings presents for my lover's biological son.

Miki's experience was echoed by Galit:

We don't say "lesbian" to our parents. Of course they know about the baby, but I don't know how much they know about what is between me and Netta. They know we live together. My father said he doesn't want to know what's between us. He knows that we have the same will, like a couple. We have two bedrooms, they know what they want to know and we don't press it. I told him slowly about the child. I spoke to him and he knows that I am "Ima" (Mom) and Netta is "Imele" (Mommy). At first, Netta's mother didn't call herself Grandma, but now she says Tal has two moms and one grandmother. Slowly they accept it. My brother is more spaced out. I have no idea what he knows or not. I told him that if something happens to me I want Netta to raise the child. Netta has a brother too, she spoke to her sister-in-law, they know. They know they have a new cousin, not in blood, but if they want, they have.

In addition to their natal families, Israeli lesbians are increasingly finding support from other lesbian mothers; this is particularly true for lesbian mothers who live in large, urban centers. Galit and Netta, for example, were part of a growing network of lesbian mothers in Tel Aviv. Shortly after my interviews with them, they appeared on an Israeli television special as "happy lesbian mothers" who had conceived their daughter through artificial insemination. They were very anxious about appearing on television; not only did they not consider themselves lesbian rights activists, they were not "out" to many of their friends and family members. Since Israel is such a small country, appearing on Israeli television as a lesbian was tantamount to announcing their sexual orientation directly to the whole country.

They told me that they had agreed to appear on the show in order to raise public awareness about children of lesbian mothers so that their daughter would encounter less hostility and ignorance as she came of age in Israeli society. To them, appearing on the show was perceived as an effort to make the world a safer place for their child.

I spoke with them after the show was broadcast, and they said they were astonished by the positive feedback they had received. Childhood friends called them and expressed their support; distant family members invited them to visit, and neighbors stopped them on the street and introduced themselves. The only negative responses they received, they said, were from members of the lesbian community who felt that they were propagating stereotypes about the importance of having children. Certainly, no generalizations can be made about general attitudes toward lesbians in Israeli society based on the responses Galit and Netta received to their television appearance, but the positive response they received could herald an evolution in popular attitudes toward lesbianism in Israel. It is possible that one reason for the positive response that Galit and Netta received was the fact that they foregrounded their identities as mothers, rather than as lesbians, in the television program, and, as we have seen, being a mother, whether married or unmarried, is the most valuable cultural identity for a woman in Israel.

Unmarried Religious Women and Artificial Insemination

Artificial insemination remains a relatively rare choice among unmarried religiously observant Jewish women in Israel for whom traditional families are still the preferred frameworks for conceiving and bearing children. Nevertheless, some unmarried religiously observant women are choosing to conceive via artificial insemination. I interviewed only three, all of whom identified themselves as "modern orthodox." They were all of Ashkenazi descent, they were well educated, gainfully employed in "secular" occupations, and voted for the National Religious Party, which is the main political representative body for modern orthodox Jews in Israel. I managed to speak briefly with one unmarried ultraorthodox woman who explained how she had asked her rabbi whether it was permissible to get pregnant via artificial insemination, and he told her it was a very complicated issue and suggested she consult a matchmaker.

It would seem that unmarried religious, or traditional, Jewish women of Sephardi or Mizrachi origin are unlikely to seek out artificial insemination as a reasonable alternative to childlessness. Perhaps this is due to popular beliefs among Jews of Sephardi and Mizrachi origin that reproduction is something a woman does not take into her own hands and does not seek to accomplish independently (Sered 1992). Or perhaps I was simply unable to locate religiously observant Sephardi or Mizrachi women who were pursuing pregnancy via artificial insemination.

The motivations and experiences that lead unmarried religiously observant women to artificial insemination seem to be similar to those of their heterosexual secular counterparts: they preferred to have a child within a traditional family, but when that option failed to materialize they took matters into their own hands.

Rina, a thirty-eight-year-old teacher in Jerusalem, explains:

> I always thought I had all the time in the world, I had lots of arranged
> dates with men, it was always a given that I would have a child, why
> wouldn't I? I come from a large, warm family, I never even considered
> alternative family structures. I'm religious, my family is very religious.
> I started thinking about artificial insemination three years ago. The
> dates I had were okay, but I was putting too much pressure on them
> and it wasn't fair. I kept wondering whether the guy was going to give
> me a child. I remember the day exactly: December 1, 1994. I spoke
> to my gynecologist and told him I thought about having artificial
> insemination.
>
> Listen, I think it's best for the child to have a father; I still think the
> nuclear family is the best option. I asked two men I knew if they would
> agree to father my child without having a relationship, and they both
> said no, they wouldn't do it without having a relationship with the
> child. So I finally decided to do artificial insemination.

Sarah, a forty-year-old modern orthodox woman in Jerusalem, considered adoption instead of artificial insemination:

> If I had adopted a child the gossip would have been: "what a *tsadikes*
> [righteous person], she's single and she adopted a child." If I get preg-
> nant and have my own baby out-of-wedlock, the gossip will be "she
> had a child on her own: she's a whore."

In a recent survey of Halakhic literature on the subject of unmarried women and artificial insemination, Devorah Ross (1998) concludes that there is no Halakhic basis for forbidding unmarried
women from pursuing pregnancy via reproductive technology. The
two main Halakhic problems with anonymous donor insemination
using Jewish donor sperm are:

> 1. the problem of *yichus* (knowing one's parenthood), which is not,
> per se, a Halakhic problem, but is a concern, for it's important to
> know your lineage. A child who does not know his or her paternity is
> called in the Talmud, a "shtuki" (Tractate *Kiddushin* 4a).
>
> 2. the problem of incest; for, as in all cases of anonymous artificial
> insemination with Jewish donor sperm, a child so conceived could

[handwritten margin note: Orthodox Jewish Law concerns]

grow up and unwittingly marry a half-sibling. Ross explains that these concerns can be effectively circumvented by using non-Jewish donor sperm (see chapter 3).

Though Ross persuasively demonstrates the Halakhic flexibility regarding unmarried women's reproductive agency and makes an excellent case for non-Jewish sperm as a procreative substance in such cases, deliberately having a child out-of-wedlock remains severely discouraged in religious and more "traditional" Jewish communities. This opposition emerges out of more amorphous, though no less powerful, social concerns about preserving social norms.

David Golinkin, an Israeli conservative rabbi, specifically outlines these concerns in a rabbinic legal opinion (*responsa*). As a conservative rabbi, Golinkin's responsa has limited influence in Israel, since only orthodox rabbis are invested with state power and jurisdiction over family matters. Nevertheless, his argument is worth mentioning, since it is one of very few published articles on the subject.[21] Golinkin acknowledges the absence of Halakhic prohibition against artificial insemination for unmarried women and yet argues that it poses a dangerous challenge to the Jewish family as the basic and enduring unit of the Jewish people.[22]

Golinkin's opposition to the practice was echoed in my conversations with an orthodox rabbi in Israel. I said to him that since there was no Halakhic problem with the status of the child born to an unmarried woman, it seemed that rabbis should approve of artificial insemination for unmarried women. He replied:

> Maybe, but it is very unlikely. This is very taboo; no rabbi would make it public if he allowed a single woman to get artificially inseminated, he would not let it be known that he authorized the use of artificial insemination for a single woman. The holy family is still the most important thing . . . and she is not obligated to procreate, remember, the obligation to procreate falls only on the man.   ✳

So I said, "But a rabbi *could* say that a single woman can use artificial insemination, since there is nothing to prohibit it Halakhically." He replied, "Or not, or not." The absence of a clear Halakhic prohibition to the practice makes a coherent orthodox rabbinic response to this question somewhat elusive.

It will be interesting to see whether the rabbinic evasion and resistance to this question will one day be translated into official rabbinic opposition to the practice; for if rabbinic opposition develops, it could directly affect the current regulations regarding access to reproductive technology. And if formal rabbinic opposition to artificial insemination for unmarried women does develop, state support for it could become more limited; it could be understood as an unintended social effect inadvertently created by the swift adoption of the ministry of health regulations concerning this issue.

Interestingly, it is exactly this concern about inciting rabbinic resistance to the provision of artificial insemination for unmarried women that prevented me from gathering definitive statistical information about the number of unmarried Israeli women who are pursuing conception in this way. After repeated attempts to access this information at the ministry of health, an inside source finally told me that no such information exists; no official records are kept on how many unmarried Israeli women use artificial insemination. Nor do the fertility clinics keep statistics on the number of single women getting pregnant via artificial insemination. In response to my queries about these statistics at individual clinics, I was told by doctors and nurses that not only did they not keep these figures, they could not possibly hazard a guess as to the numbers.

One cogent explanation for this curious silence, provided to me in confidence by a fertility doctor I had become close to, intimated that Israeli fertility doctors do not want to risk the publication of such statistics because that may provoke formal rabbinic condemnation of the practice. "The less said about this phenomenon the better it will be for the fertility doctors and for the unmarried women who seek artificial insemination," he told me. In fact, he continued, I would never succeed in getting any statistics about the number of single women receiving artificial insemination, because the doctors are afraid that if the orthodox rabbinical establishment finds out just how many women are receiving artificial insemination, they will do all that they can to limit single women's access to the treatment. He told me that the issue was a "Pandora's box" (*kuvsa Pandora*) that no one wanted to open out of the fear that the Rabbanut will move to prevent the practice. I asked him to explain why the Rabbanut would be so incensed, since the children born to unmarried mothers are not *mamzerim*. He explained that the Rabbanut is concerned about preventing future incestuous marriages. Since no records are kept on the paternity of children born to unmarried mothers conceived via anonymous donor insemination with Jewish sperm, incestuous marriages could take place between people conceived via artificial insemination and their paternal siblings to whom they are unknowingly related. In addition, the rabbinate could act to prevent the practice of artificial insemination for unmarried women on the grounds that it is socially undesirable and undermines the nuclear family, à la Golinkin.

Thus, my inability to gather statistical information about this phenomenon was not because I was unable to gain access to extant statistics; doctors deliberately do not keep records about those born with donor gametes so that the Rabbanut will have nothing to find if they decide to search. This way the Rabbanut will not be able to make lists of stigmatized children who were born through artificial insemination with unknown donor sperm and whose marriage prospects may be limited. For, the Rabbanut already maintains "mamzer lists" of those born of illicit sexual unions that they check before they perform marriages in order to make sure that they are not unwittingly marrying mamzers and nonmamzers.

In sum, though there is no clear Halakhic prohibitions against unmarried women and artificial insemination, it is clear that among religiously observant Jews, who hold more conservative beliefs about the traditional Jewish family and its central importance to the continuity of Jewish life, the nuclear family is still largely understood as the only appropriate framework for reproduction. Unmarried religiously observant women are availing themselves of the opportunity to conceive children via reproductive technology, though one can assume that they are doing so in significantly smaller numbers than their secular counterparts and with greater attention to Halakhic concerns.

Artificial Insemination and Loss

Finally, the following three poignant stories suggest an additional contour to the conceptual terrain that defines autonomous motherhood in Israel. For the women described below, the decision to reproduce via artificial insemination does not evolve "naturally" along a continuum of reproductive choices but stems from a larger sense of loss or from a sense of responsibility to the Jewish family conceived more broadly. Their desire to conceive babies via artificial insemination is a response to circumstances that are particular to the Israeli context. These stories vividly illustrate how the individual's desire to reproduce overlaps with the collective's desire to overcome tragedy; and reproduction as a response to tragedy is one of the most prominent characteristics of Israeli pronatalism.

Olga

Olga is a divorced woman from Kiev who immigrated to Israel as part of the wave of Russian Jewish immigration in the early 1990s. She came with her only son Yuri and settled in Jerusalem, where she found work and an apartment and began to make a life for herself and her son. One Sunday morning, in February 1996, Yuri boarded the local number eighteen bus to go to work. Twenty minutes later the bus exploded in the middle of the city, killing Yuri and many other people. This was one of a series of terrorist attacks that struck Jerusalem and Tel Aviv in winter 1995–96. Olga, then forty-three years old, was distraught over the loss of her son. Not only was his senseless death unbearable for her, she said that now she was left totally alone, without any family whatsoever. In the succeeding months, as part of her grieving, she decided that the only thing that mattered to her was to have another child. Since she was forty-three and had no time to lose, she went to the fertility clinic at Hadassah Hospital in Jerusalem and began receiving hormonal treatment to hyperstimulate her ovaries in preparation for artificial insemination with anonymous donor sperm. This was the only way she could go on living, she said.

Talya

Talya was a forty-year-old woman who lived in Tel Aviv. She invited me to spend the day with her and her three-year-old son. She was born in Israel, to Czechoslovakian parents who immigrated to Palestine in 1941; their entire families were killed in the Holocaust. We spent the day watching her son Benny play in the park next to her house. As he played in the sandbox, slid down the slide, and interrupted us repeatedly, she told me about her decision to get pregnant using anonymous donor sperm. She was married for eight years to a man who was infertile. She was thirty-six years old when they divorced, and it was then she decided to have a child via artificial insemination. She admitted that "on an unconscious level" the fact that her parents were Holocaust survivors, and that she was an only child, had something to do with her desire to get pregnant. Her parents "lost their whole world, their whole families were killed by the Nazis. They raised me with the message that you can disappear tomorrow, a total fatalism." Benny is named after her father's father who was killed at Auschwitz. I asked if her parents were happy that she had a child. "They have never been happier," she said, "to them he is a continuation, and it is irrelevant to them how he was conceived."

Nurit

Nurit is a thirty-eight-year-old lawyer whose husband Uri was killed while patrolling the Jordanian border on reserve duty. They had been undergoing infertility treatment at the time of his death and, as part of their treatment, had frozen several embryos comprising their reproductive genetic material. Nurit was distraught over the loss of her husband but saw the embryos as a source of great promise: she said that through the embryos, her husband lived on. Half of the embryos had recently been implanted in her womb, but the pregnancies did not last. She was very anxious that she would run out of embryos without conceiving Uri's child and then would have to use anonymous sperm. She said she was prepared to use donor sperm if she had to, and said she would name the child Uri if it was a boy.

Conclusion

Through the voices of these unmarried women, we witness extraordinary efforts to innovate responses, negotiate strategies, and create narratives that make sense of these unprecedented journeys to achieve conception and become autonomous mothers. Their efforts are reinforced not only by state policies that permit unmarried women to pursue pregnancy via artificial insemination but also by family, friends, and fertility clinic staff, for whom the desire to become a mother is thought to be entirely natural and deserving of assistance, technological and otherwise. Motherhood itself remains understood as a deeply natural desire and goal, despite the extraordinary technological measures necessary to achieve it. The cultural importance of motherhood thus becomes reinforced through unmarried women's use of reproductive technology at the same time that the meaning of motherhood has become transformed. Now that Israeli Jewish women can conceptualize motherhood as an ambition independent of marriage, it can become a goal in and of itself.

In Israel, shared assumptions about the importance of motherhood, the imperative of reproduction, and the acceptable status of children born to unmarried women converge to create new stages that lead to the reproduction of Jews. We have seen how the children conceived via artificial insemination and born to unmarried women inherit the same cultural, religious, and social identity as those born to married women. We have seen how these children are embraced as "one of us" in equal measure to children conceived and born in the traditional way, both by their families and by the Jewish state, which has created the conditions for their conception. In sum, the choice of unmarried women to get pregnant via artificial insemination does not threaten to destabilize foundational assumptions about kinship among Jewish Israelis, for these foundational assumptions are grounded in rabbinic notions of kinship that do not delegitimate children born to unmarried women. Certainly, this choice may be understood as a less desirable constellation in which to achieve conception, hence the imposition of social controls that limit the accessibility of these procedures to women over the age of thirty, but it is not a choice that runs contrary to one of the most central goals of the state: the reproduction of Jews.

- nuclear family way more desired
- continuation of family lines

In US.
- fertility treatments are expensive,
little to no funding for it,
demonstrates central goal of
America: limit reproduction to
the upper class

2

Not *Mamzers:*

The Legislation of Reproduction and the "Issue"
of Unmarried Women

By using reproduction as an entry point into the study of social life,
we can see how cultures are produced (or contested) as people imagine
and enable the creation of the next generation, most directly through
the nurturance of children . . . [for] reproduction is bound up with the
production of culture.—Faye D. Ginsburg and Rayna Rapp,
Conceiving the New World Order

To set the stage for the following social analysis, I begin with a
discussion of the Nahmani case, a highly publicized social and legal
drama that captivated the Israeli public imagination throughout the
early to mid-1990s. Though quite substantively different from the
Baby M case in the United States, the Nahmani case functioned in
the Israeli public imagination in much the same way: as the public's
introduction to the controversial ethical and social dilemmas represented by surrogacy and the new reproductive technologies. Unlike
the Baby M case, in which the surrogate mother sought custody of a
child she had gestated and given birth to, Ruti Nahmani was fighting
a legal battle to win custody of embryos that, if successfully gestated
by a surrogate mother, would be raised by her alone. In this way, the
Nahmani case triggered a public debate that functioned as something of a referendum not only on surrogacy, but on the legitimacy of
single motherhood achieved via reproductive technology.

As the Nahmani case was being played out in public as an ongoing high profile news story, Israeli legislators, rabbis, and fertility
specialists were working behind closed doors to hammer out recommendations for the appropriate uses of reproductive technology, rec-

ommendations that came to be known as the Aloni Commission Report. The simultaneity of the legal developments in the Nahmani case, with its intense media coverage, and the work of the commission was seemingly coincidental. Yet I suggest that the Nahmani case played an important social role by effectively educating the public about surrogacy and related issues of assisted reproduction. More importantly, the case and the media coverage it generated helped garner public support for the use of these technologies by detailing the suffering of "poor, barren Ruti Nahmani" and her relentless quest for motherhood. Thus, by the time the commission had completed its report, and Israel's new surrogacy law was being prepared and passed through the Knesset (see chapter 5), the public already had a set of positive associations with reproductive technology and the concept of surrogacy; specifically, it already had reason to believe that surrogacy was a legitimate recourse for those suffering from infertility. Indeed, according to Dr. Shlomo Mashiach, a well-known fertility specialist in Israel, "The Nahmanis contributed a lot to the fight for recognition of surrogacy in Israel. They exposed their private story to make a public issue. As a result, very soon surrogacy will be legal in Israel." He added that if the couple had had enough money to hire a surrogate abroad — or if surrogacy in Israel had been legal — "Ruti would have a child today" (*Jerusalem Post*, 31 March 1995).

The Nahmanis' story begins with their marriage in 1984. Shortly thereafter Ruti Nahmani had a hysterectomy because of medical problems. In 1988 Ruti and her husband, Dani, decided to try and have a child through in-vitro fertilization (IVF) and subsequent embryo transfer into the womb of a surrogate mother in the United States. This was not particularly unusual. Until the legalization of surrogacy in Israel in March 1996, many infertile Israeli couples contracted surrogates through private agencies in the United States.

It was at this juncture that the Nahmanis initiated what was to be the first of many lawsuits. In *Nahmani v. the Minister of Health* (H.C. 1237/91), the Nahmanis sought health insurance coverage for these costly IVF procedures, which were to be done in Israel as a prelude to the subsequent surrogate mother arrangement in the

United States. They won their case, and their health insurance paid for the Nahmanis' IVF treatments in which Ruti's eggs and Dani's sperm were combined, resulting in eleven embryos, which were then frozen at Assuta Hospital near Tel Aviv.

In 1992, before the Nahmanis brokered a surrogacy agreement in the United States, Dani left Ruti and moved in with another woman with whom he has since fathered two children. Ruti Nahmani, then thirty-nine years old, wanted to go ahead with the implantation of the embryos in a surrogate mother in the United States. She asked Assuta Hospital to give her the embryos, but they refused on the grounds that her husband had not given his consent. At this juncture, she filed another lawsuit in the Haifa district court, arguing that the frozen embryos represented her last chance to become a mother; the court ruled in her favor. The judges said that since Dani Nahmani had initially agreed to the IVF procedures using his sperm, he could not withdraw his consent after the fertilization had occurred.

Dani Nahmani, in turn, appealed to Israel's Supreme Court, arguing that he had been denied the right *not* to become a parent. The court initially ruled in his favor, 4–1. The court said that the husband's consent is required at every stage of the IVF procedure. Justice Tova Strassberg-Cohen, writing the majority opinion, stated that "a man cannot be contractually forced to become a parent, since this would violate his fundamental human rights."

In her explanation of the majority's decision, Judge Strassberg-Cohen wrote:

> On a personal level, sympathy favors Ruti Nahmani; however, sympathy does not create a right. In the public realm, enforcement would be contrary to a person's basic rights, and therefore would not comport with the public good and with the proper legal policy on which we expounded above . . .
>
> The problems regarding the status of the child, the surrogate mother, the dependence on her agreement to transfer the child, the factual and legal conflict between the surrogate mother's and the genetic mother's status regarding motherhood, and the legal status of the child are complicated and not easily solved. All these are, undoubtedly, real

difficulties; however, if I thought that Ruti Nahmani had a right to force parenthood on Dani Nahmani by means of the judicial system, I would not see these difficulties as an obstacle to her attempt to realize her motherhood. . . . I do not accept the claim that Ruti Nahmani could become a mother by alternative means and is therefore not entitled to force the continuation of the process on Dani Nahmani. It is almost certain that this is her last opportunity to attain biological motherhood. It is necessary to take into account her age, her physiological state, the limited chances that a new fertilization will be successful, the necessity of enlisting a sperm donor (while she is still married), or to resort to the process of adopting a child that is not her own, the time factor, and the emotional and physical efforts involved in all of the above. All these factors render the alternatives inappropriate, and they are not on a level with the use of her own eggs, fertilized with her husband's sperm, in the course of their married life and ready for implantation. Therefore, if I thought that Ruti Nahmani was entitled to continue with the process against the will of Dani Nahmani, I would not view the aforementioned claim as an obstacle in her path.[1]

Judge Strassberg-Cohen's statement on reproductive technology as a legitimate means for "realizing motherhood" acknowledges that only the legal principle that paternity cannot be coerced prevented the court from allowing Ruti Nahmani to take extraordinary measures in order to have a child "of her own." There appears to be no question in Strassberg-Cohen's mind that the law ought to recognize that IVF and surrogacy are solutions to the problem of infertility. The law simply dictates that, as solutions, they must be applied without violating individual rights. Moreover, the court explicitly acknowledged that though Ruti Nahmani would effectively be the sole, single parent to any child born from the embryos conceived by her egg and Dani's sperm, this result was not a basis for preventing her from pursuing the surrogacy agreement as a strategy for becoming a mother. As Strassberg-Cohen states, "The fact that the child to be born would be raised by his mother, and that his father would have another family, is a widespread phenomenon in our era. Single-parent families are accepted in our society with understanding and are even granted various benefits" (74). In other words, the fact that Ruti Nahmani was denied the "right" to become a mother through the implantation of her and her estranged husband's embryos in an American surrogate mother had nothing to do with the legitimacy or illegitimacy of such extravagant reproductive measures, or with her status as a single mother. It had to do with legal equations regarding the right to become a parent versus the right not to become a parent. Legal discussion in this court opinion thus functioned to legitimize surrogate mother arrangements in principle, by allowing their role as reasonable solutions to infertility to eclipse the profound social dilemmas on which they are inevitably based. It also helped popularize the technological pursuit of motherhood for single women, a point I will return to momentarily.

After the initial ruling that her husband's right not to become a parent outweighed Ruti's right to become a parent, the Supreme Court later decided, in an unprecedented decision, to rehear the case with an expanded panel of judges on the basis that new reproductive technologies raise issues of significant social and ethical import that must be given extraordinary consideration. In a surprising reversal of its earlier decision, the court ruled that Ruti's right to be a parent is more important than the right not to father children and ruled that she should be given custody of the embryos. In the words of Judge Tsvi Tal: "The interest in parenthood is a basic and existential value, both for the individual and for society as a whole. In contrast, there is no value to the absence of parenthood" (*Jerusalem Post*, 13 September 1996). Judge Ya'akov Terkel concurred, explaining that "in this difficult decision, I chose life" (*Ma'ariv*, 13 September 1996). Many of the judges also noted that since women carry pregnancies, the decision to follow through with a conception should be up to them, not up to their husbands. That Ruti Nahmani herself was incapable of carrying a pregnancy was mentioned only to the extent that her inability to do so placed her in the category of disabled people, and disabled people should not be discriminated against on the basis of their disability.

The right to parenthood, and specifically to single motherhood, triumphed in the Nahmani case. Ruti Nahmani became somewhat of a popular hero in her single-minded pursuit of motherhood; when the Supreme Court reversed its decision in the case, the popular daily *Ma'ariv* devoted its first three pages to sensational coverage of "Ruti's Victory" (13 September 1996). The public's sympathy for her reinforced not only the rights of barren women but also the popular ideology that motherhood is the most important goal in a woman's life, regardless of her marital status (Shalev 1998).

The legal and philosophical questions raised in the Nahmani case are fascinating. Inter alia, can parenthood ethically be coerced? What is the nature of the right to be a parent? Are there limits to enforceability of personal contracts? A comprehensive examination of these and other questions, however, is beyond the scope of this discussion.[2] What I would like to draw attention to is that "sympathy" for Ruti Nahmani, and for her pursuit of assisted single-motherhood, continually entered into the legal and popular discourse about the case.

Ruti Nahmani's quest for motherhood was far from over, however. Though she was granted "custody" of the embryos, she still had to contract a surrogate mother to gestate and give birth to them. Dani Nahmani filed an appeal blocking his estranged wife's right to seek a surrogate without his consent (*Jerusalem Post,* 2 October 1996), and at the time of this writing the final outcome of the Nahmani case was still unknown.

The lack of any substantive discussion about the legitimacy of reproductive technology as a means to assist pregnancy in the popular discourse surrounding the Nahmani case reflects not only an unquestioned popular belief that childlessness is a pitiable state that must be "cured" by any means necessary but also popular attitudes toward reproductive technology in Israel and its positive role in realizing motherhood. The underlying implication is that if the technological means exist to assist motherhood, they must be employed. Motherhood is always and everywhere good, regardless of the extent of fertility treatment involved in achieving it, regardless of the fact that the Nahmani child would be raised by a single mother, regardless of the fact that for Ruti Nahmani to become a mother her frozen embryos would have had to be exported transnationally for implantation into a paid surrogate mother (the case came before the Israeli Supreme Court before the legalization of surrogacy in 1996).

Thus what we learn from the public discussions surrounding the Nahmani case is that the new reproductive technologies have come to be understood as legitimate pathways to pregnancy by Israelis and that these technologies are widely taken for granted as reasonable solutions to the suffering of childlessness. The complex social repercussions of contracting reproductive services — of extracting, freezing, and transferring reproductive genetic material — are submerged. The nation just sees "poor, barren Ruti Nahmani" and wants to make her a mother by any means necessary. And Ruti Nahmani reflects back to the nation an image so deeply embedded it is unquestioned: that motherhood is the deepest desire of all women and should be pursued at all costs.

Consent for the new reproductive technologies is all but universal in Israel, a pronatalist state where the despair of the barren woman has deep cultural roots. Indeed, one could argue that Ruti Nahmani's battle for motherhood echoes that of the biblical matriarch Rachel, who lamented: "Give me sons or else I am dead" (Genesis 30:1).

In the remaining half of this chapter I examine the evolving regulations that control access to the new reproductive technologies in Israel and suggest ways that these regulations create a framework for social and biological reproduction that both complements and competes with traditional Jewish marriage. I then examine the legislative dynamics that inform the cultural context in which unmarried women make the choice to become pregnant via artificial insemination.

I argue that the ministry of health regulations regarding new reproductive technologies, although designed to alleviate infertility among married couples and to assist the nuclear family realize its reproductive goals, in fact offer an additional, competing framework for procreation specifically because these regulations provide unmarried women access to new reproductive technologies. As instruments of the state, the regulations theoretically pose a threat to beliefs that marriage is the exclusive site of legitimate social reproduction and that the nuclear family is the only family structure through which Israeli citizens ought to realize their reproductive futures. Ginsburg and Rapp frame the pertinent question concisely when they ask: "Who defines the body of the nation into which the next generation is recruited?" (1995: 3). Because Jewish religious law on marriage and reproduction is that which lays the groundwork for these secular regulations, as it does in Israel, then Jewish religious law is that which defines the body of the nation, both in the corporeal and figurative sense. Yet the fact that Jewish religious law fails to delegitimate the children of unmarried women, and the fact that the state is actively supporting the reproductive agency of unmarried women, creates a conceptual space in which notions about the appropriate constellation of the family, let alone the Jewish collectivity, are undergoing radical transformation from within.

Judaism and Democracy: Where the Twain Meet

Israel is a secular democracy governed according to civil laws enacted by legislative assemblies in the Israeli Parliament (Knesset). It is also a Jewish state, with a legal system "strewn with laws in the field called personal status matters, which combine Jewish legal principles with modern legal principles."[3] The link between Jewish "heritage" and Israeli law was formally codified in a law known as the Foundation of Law (1980),[4] as well as other laws pertaining to personal status in Israel. As a result, some areas of Israeli law are explicitly informed by Jewish religious considerations and Halakhic legal opinions. For example, the Law of Return, Israel's immigration law, guarantees Israeli citizenship for any Jew who wishes to immigrate to Israel.[5] Spurred in part by the rabbinic control over these personal status issues, a contentious relationship has long existed between religious and secular factions in Israel.[6]

The chair of the Judiciary Committee summed up the Knesset's approach to negotiating this uneasy relationship thus:

> The (Human Dignity and Liberty) Law opens with a declaration that it is intended to protect human dignity and liberty in order to secure, in the Law, the values of Israel as a Jewish and democratic state. In this

sense, the Law states already in its first paragraph that we consider ourselves bound to the values of Israel's heritage and Jewish heritage, since a positive determination is explicitly set forth — the values of the State of Israel as a Jewish and democratic state. The Law defines a number of the fundamental liberties of the individual, no one of them being inconsistent with Israel's heritage or with the values currently acceptable in Israel to all the parties of this House.[7]

For reasons of political expedience and national ideology, then, the state is often pressed to take rabbinic concerns into account when drafting legislation concerning personal status issues. To ensure that "Jewish heritage" is effectively preserved, the boundaries of the Jewish collectivity must be effectively policed. The issue of reproduction is of obvious interest to those concerned with maintaining Jewish heritage in Israel, and Jewish religious understandings of kinship are therefore manifest in many secular Israeli laws regarding personal status. Nowhere is this more true than in the laws on marriage and divorce in Israel, which are not simply influenced by religious law but are constituted by religious law.

Legal History of Marriage and Divorce in Israel

The Palestine Order and Council of 1922 functioned as the legal framework of the British Mandate in Palestine between 1918 and 1947. In Article 51 it was decreed that all matters of and relating to personal status, including inheritance, adoption, alimony, succession, and marriage and divorce, were to be determined by religious courts. All other legal disputes were to be determined in civil courts; Jews were to be married according to Jewish custom, Muslims according to Islamic custom, and Christians according to Christian custom.[8] After the establishment of the state of Israel in 1948, the Rabbinical Courts Jurisdiction (Marriage and Divorce) Law was passed by the Knesset on 26 August 1953. In this law, Article 51 was rendered inapplicable, and all legal matters relating to personal status, besides marriage and divorce, became matters of civil law in

Israel; religious courts retained exclusive jurisdiction over marriage and divorce. The provisions of this law have not been amended.

It states, in part: "1. Matters of marriage and divorce of Jews in Israel, being nationals or residents of the State, shall be under the exclusive jurisdiction of the rabbinical courts. 2. Marriages and divorces of Jews shall be performed in Israel in accordance with Jewish religious law" (Rabbinical Courts Jurisdiction [Marriage and Divorce] Law, 1952–53, 7: 5713–1953).

Jewish law thus determines what constitutes marriage for Israeli Jews, who is eligible to marry whom, and the terms and conditions of marriage and divorce. By giving religious authorities jurisdiction over marriage and divorce in Israel, the secular government of a liberal, democratic nation-state established a fundamental dependence on Jewish religious law.

Jewish law only allows for marriages between Jews, a restriction that creates a variety of contemporary political and social dilemmas regarding the positive determination of Jewishness and, by extension, a Jewish person's ability to get married in Israel. These dilemmas arise when Jewish Israelis seek to marry converts to Judaism who may not have undergone conversions in strict accordance with Jewish law. They are also particularly salient when immigrants to Israel seek to get married, because their Jewishness is often called into question by the orthodox rabbinate, as was the case for many Ethiopian and Russian immigrants in the 1990s. These issues are similarly of concern to those Jews conceiving through assisted conception in Israel. It is crucial that Jews conceived in this way be considered marriageable according to the criteria of the orthodox rabbinate, otherwise they will not be considered full-fledged Jewish Israelis. Thus, marriageability, as defined by Jewish law, operates as an arbiter of social inclusion in Israel and as the fundamental basis for one's status as a full-fledged Jewish Israeli.

Certainly, any person born to a woman deemed Halakhically Jewish is considered marriageable, as is any Jew who has undergone an orthodox conversion. However, marriageability is a complex category in the Halakhic imagination, and there are some categories of Jews for whom marriageability is not so straightforward. Jews who were conceived in certain rabbinically proscribed, illicit sexual unions are not considered marriageable in the Halakhically normative sense; they are considered *mamzers* and are subject to a range of social stigmas. The forbidden unions that create mamzers are explicitly defined as either incestuous relationships between certain family members or as adulterous relationships between married Jewish women and Jewish men other than their husbands. These illicit sexual unions can be metaphorically replicated in Halakhically improper uses of the new reproductive technologies, as we will see in the following chapters. Moreover, there is significant rabbinic concern that children conceived with anonymous Jewish donor sperm will grow up and unwittingly enter into incestuous marriages with their half-siblings.

The mamzer's material rights to inheritance, maintenance, and so forth are not impaired. Where the mamzer is severely stigmatized is in the area of marital rights, for a mamzer is forbidden from normative marriage (except with another mamzer) for ten generations. In effect, any Jew (or his or her descendant) who was conceived in a sexual union that is rabbinically determined to have been adulterous or incestuous, is essentially unmarriageable in Israel. Indeed, the orthodox rabbinate in Israel maintains a blacklist of mamzers that they consult when asked to perform marriages between those for whom there is some doubt about their marriageability.

Interestingly, if we accept Kathleen Gough's claim, as restated by John Borneman, that "marriage has become the external form of an internal compulsion, namely a mother's need to legitimize her child" (Borneman 1996: 224), then we must recognize that unmarried Jewish women in Israel make reproductive choices free from this need to legitimize their children through marriage. For children born to unmarried Jewish women are *not* Halakhically considered "illegitimate," contrary to traditional common law and Euro-American notions of bastardy in which children born out of wedlock *are* considered illegitimate.[9] Moreover, unless an unmarried Jewish woman conceives a child with her brother, it is Halakhically impossible for an unmarried Jewish woman to give birth to a mamzer. Mamzers can only be conceived in incestuous or adulterous unions, and only married Jewish women can commit adultery according to Jewish law. Thus, children born to unmarried Jewish women are considered to be full-fledged, marriageable Jews. Although marriage certainly offers many social and cultural benefits in the Jewish tradition, the legitimization of children is not one of them. Marriage, then, is not the exclusive locus for the reproduction of full-fledged Jews. This fact of Jewish kinship is made startlingly literal in state regulations regarding unmarried women's access to new reproductive technologies in Israel.

Regulations Regarding Reproductive Technology in Israel

In Israel reproductive technology is regulated according to rules promulgated in the manner described by Bernard Dickens, an internationally known authority on medical ethics and law, as follows: "Regulation may be proposed by legislation not directly, but by the legislative appointment of an agency empowered to license or set conditions for the operation of assisted reproduction services" (1994: 328–29).

The administration of reproductive technology in Israel is determined by secondary legislation adopted by the minister of health and by administrative directives issued by the director general of the ministry of health.[10] The regulations regarding reproductive technology are not statutes that have been codified into law through parliamentary procedure but administrative guidelines that have the force of law and may be amended by the ministry of health.

The current status quo is widely considered to be temporary by experts in the field who anticipate that access to and control over reproductive technology may eventually be limited if formal laws are enacted by the Knesset. The status quo evolved out of the necessity to create functional legislation for a rapidly developing technology that doctors were quickly assimilating into their practices, both because of professional interest and because of enormous popular demand for fertility treatment. In a more considered legislative process, the orthodox rabbinical establishment could marshal its considerable

political influence to enact stricter controls over the uses of reproductive technology.

Making Jews for the Jewish State

The ministry of health regulations on medically assisted reproduction (1987, 1992), like the Marriage and Divorce Law (1953) are
informed by, and grounded in, traditional Jewish definitions of kinship as codified in Jewish law. Therefore both sets of rules share the
same assumptions about who is a Jew, who is marriageable, and who
is not, and what the parameters of *mamzerut* are, as defined by
Jewish law. Both sets of laws make the identical claim: to create legal
foundations for the reproduction of Israeli citizens who are full-
fledged Jews according to Jewish law. Where the ministry of health
regulations exceed the parameters for procreation implicit in the
Marriage and Divorce Law, however, is in their provision of access
to reproductive technology for unmarried women. Unmarried Israeli
women's right of access to new reproductive technologies was first
articulated in the Aloni Commission's Report on the Matter of In-
Vitro Fertilization.

The Aloni Commission Report was commissioned by the ministry
of justice in Israel. Published in 1994, this report, not unlike the
Warnock Report in England, the Waller Report in Australia, and the
Glover Report for the European Commission, was the result of a
government-sponsored investigation into the legal, social, ethical,
and religious issues implicated in the uses of reproductive technology, including surrogacy.[11]

The Aloni Commission "was asked to examine the need for legislation that would regulate the rights and obligations of the involved
persons, including the children-to-be, and to state its recommendations regarding any related matter it deemed appropriate" (1994: 5).
The document represents a formal attempt to examine the appropriate legislation of reproductive technology in ways that are commensurate with Jewish and Israeli law. It is perhaps no coincidence that
in matters as controversial as assisted conception, and in a country in

which religious law determines the parameters of procreation, the two dissenting opinions, taken together, are longer than the report itself. For a list of the report's contents see appendix C.

In the report the right to privacy is foregrounded as a guiding legal principle for the administration of the new reproductive technologies:

> The right to privacy is a fundamental right in a progressive society, and it is intended to protect the intimacy of a person's private affairs. This right does not, however, impose a duty on any public system to provide fertilization or genetic engineering services to a couple wishing to undergo these or similar procedures. Likewise, the right to privacy does not obligate the State to allow innovative reproductive or genetic engineering techniques which may injure the child-to-be or *prejudice the fundamental principles of society or delicate fabric of society*. (1994: 12, emphasis mine)

In subsequent passages the report continues:

> The Commission agreed that, as a matter of principle, there should be no interference with the right of access. In other words, *the right to receive fertility treatment should be granted to every person*. (Ibid.: 15, emphasis mine)

> The Commission also addressed the question of the relevance of marital status of the patients. The Commission is of the opinion that *a person is entitled to receive fertility treatment regardless of his or her marital status* and that patients have a right to privacy and intimacy in their personal lives. (Ibid.: 17, emphasis mine)

What the above passages reveal is that the Aloni Commission specifically suggests that an unmarried woman's right to become a mother through artificial insemination not only does not threaten "the delicate fabric of society," it is guaranteed as part of her basic right to privacy. This is crucial, for if a woman's right to realize her reproductive potential autonomously is understood as part of her package of individual rights bequeathed to her by the progressive society in which she lives, and if the state actively assists women in claiming their rights to reproduce alone, then the meanings of mar-

riage, reproduction, and the nature of the individual must be conceptually reconfigured. In other words, by reifying the individual's right
to reproduce, and by situating that right in the same domain as other
basic human rights, the commission constructs a secular legal foundation for reproduction that is in direct competition with the religious legal foundation represented by the Marriage and Divorce
Law. And yet the competition is not a straightforward one between a
legal system founded on enlightened concepts of individual rights
and a legal system claiming to mediate and legislate God's will, for
the reproductive capacity of unmarried women is not repudiated by
either system; it is supported and subsidized by the first, and is not
delegitimated by the second. Thus the reproductive agency of unmarried women represents a point of unusual consensus between legal systems that may otherwise conflict over legitimate frameworks
for reproduction.

The Politics of *Mamzerut*

In its deliberations about limiting access to reproductive technology,
the Aloni Commission also considered the threat of creating individuals who would be considered mamzers according to traditional
Jewish law.[12] The question was "whether there exists a societal responsibility to prevent, as far as possible, the creation of problems of
this type, even to the extent of restricting the right of access, or
whether the patients should be given full information regarding the
religious ramifications and be left with the responsibility of making
their own decisions" (1994: 19). The report concludes that "the right
of access should not be limited *a priori* due to the fear of *mamzerut.*
Rather, the patients should be provided with all pertinent information, and the decision left to their private discretion" (ibid.).

In his dissenting opinion to the Aloni Commission Report, Rabbi
Dr. Mordechai Halperin takes sharp exception to this view and explains "the grave significance of artificial creation of medically or
socially defective [*yeled pigum*] offspring." He objects to the "use of
medical technology to create severely socially disabled babies due to

the laws of *mamzerut*" (ibid.: 98). To militate against the conception of mamzers, Halperin recommends the establishment of a sperm donor directory in which the names of all sperm donors would be recorded. The directory would create the opportunity for rabbis to know the paternal identity of children conceived with donor sperm in order to prevent incestuous marriages between such children, the offspring of whom would be mamzers. For secular lawmakers the dangers of a registry, including possible stigmatization if it becomes known that a child was conceived with donor sperm, potential paternity suits from donors who seek to claim their genetic heirs, and other problems of disclosure, far outweigh the benefits; at the time of this writing, there was no official sperm donor directory in Israel.[13]

The majority opinion in the Aloni Commission, which states that concerns about mamzerut should be left to the individual, embodies the progressive understanding that reproduction is a private matter. Halperin's concerns about legitimizing individual access to reproductive technology in ways that create unmarriageable mamzers suggests a more traditional understanding of reproduction as that which is a matter of explicit collective concern.

Popular sentiment about mamzerut suggests that it is still a powerful stigma in Israel. "People are very superstitious in this country and they don't want their children to be called *mamzers*," a secular Israeli attorney explained to me. "There is lots of sentimentality about religion. It is an excommunication to say that your child can't marry. Even if you yourself would go to Cyprus to have a civil wedding, you can't make that decision for your child."

The threat of stigmatization is thus a powerful political tool, for by determining who is a marriageable Jew in light of the laws of mamzerut, the rabbinic authorities exercise implicit and explicit control over the creation of frameworks for reproduction. If and when state legislators formulate formal laws for the appropriate uses of reproductive technology in Israel, rabbis may use the threat of mamzerut to influence the parameters of this legislation in such a way that the potential for conceiving mamzers is minimized and the religious and social consequences for doing so, severe.

Like other secular Israelis, unmarried secular Israeli women are concerned about the Halakhic status of their children and do not want their children to be stigmatized as mamzers. Indeed, as my ethnographic data illustrate, unmarried women do not imagine that their reproductive decision to have a child out-of-wedlock will necessarily be reproduced in the next generation. On the contrary, they are concerned that their children be full-fledged Israeli citizens who have the opportunity to get married in their own country, even if they may resent the fact that marriage is controlled by the orthodox rabbinate. They are also concerned with preventing their alternatively conceived children from unwittingly entering into incestuous marriages. Some of the women I interviewed said they would ask their child and his or her prospective spouse to take DNA tests prior to marriage to make sure they were not conceived with the same genetic material. Others said they would ask the father of their child's prospective spouse whether he had ever donated sperm. Still others were anxious for the creation of a sperm donor directory that they could check to make sure their child was not entering into an incestuous marriage. These concerns were not significant enough to prevent them from seeking artificial insemination with anonymous donor sperm. They were voiced instead as manageable hurdles to be overcome in the future.

Unmarried Women's Reproductive Agency

The opinion of the Aloni Commission in support of unmarried women's access to reproductive technology is partially reflected in the ministry of health regulations concerning access to reproductive technology, which explicitly guarantee single women's right to receive treatment. The ministry of health regulations differ from the Aloni Commission's recommendation in that they attach intrusive restrictions to single women's right of access to these technologies. Thus, although the state legitimized and guaranteed that single women will not be denied right of access to reproductive technology simply because they are unmarried, the state retained for itself a form of control over single women's reproductive agency.

Restrictions on Unmarried Women's Right of Access to
Fertility Treatment

Psychiatric and Social Worker Evaluations The ministry of health
regulations originally required single women to be screened and approved both by a social worker and by a psychiatrist before they
were eligible for fertility treatment:

> Artificial insemination shall be given to single women only in special
> circumstances, only after the receipt of a psychiatric opinion as well as
> a senior social worker's report. (Ministry of Health Regulations for
> the Administration of Sperm Banks, 1992, regulation 19[b])

In February 1996 the Association for Civil Rights in Israel (ACRI)
filed a petition in the Supreme Court of Israel on behalf of Dr. Tal
Yarus-Hakak against the director general of the ministry of health.
The plaintiff challenged the ministry's regulations requiring unmarried women to undergo psychiatric evaluations as a prerequisite
to receiving sperm donation on the grounds that it discriminates
against women on the basis of their marital status. The petition
contended that there was no valid reason for

> 1) Why rule 19b of the rules regarding the management of sperm
> banks and the guidelines for artificial insemination, which the respon-
> dent enacted, should not be invalidated.
> 2) Why the respondent should not order the director of the fertility
> research center at Akiryah to give the petitioner a sperm donation
> without conditioning it on a psychiatric opinion and a senior social
> worker report regarding the petitioner.
> —Supreme Court of Israel. Jerusalem. February 2, 1996. (my trans-
> lation)

The petition made clear that Dr. Yarus-Hakak was a lesbian
mother who had been living with her female partner for seven years.
They already had two children who were conceived through artificial insemination, and Dr. Yarus-Hakak wanted to have a third
child. When she went to the fertility clinic, the doctor informed her
that because she was unmarried, she was required, pursuant to the

ministry of health regulations, to undergo both a psychiatric evaluation and an interview with a senior social worker.

The petition asserted that: "The above noted rule (referring to
regulation 19 (b) above) subordinates the right to become a parent
to the discretion of a psychiatrist and a social worker according to
whom it will be determined whether the petitioner and other unmarried women are suitable to become mothers. The rule thus infringes
the rights of the petitioner and other unmarried women to become
mothers." The plaintiff argued that the right to be a mother should
be understood as a fundamental right, irrespective of marital status.
The plaintiff also contended that: "The above noted rule also infringes the right of the petitioner and other unmarried women to
receive fertility treatments and thus violates their rights over their
bodies."

Reproduction is legally articulated in the petition as an individual
right, implicitly guaranteed as fundamental in the manner of all individual rights. Equal access to reproductive technology was demanded as a legal right on the grounds that marital status cannot be
a valid basis for discrimination. The plaintiff defined access to reproductive technology as included within an individual's right to
control her body, regardless of marital status.

In sum, the petition argued that:

> Rule 19b is invalid because it discriminates on the basis of personal
> status and sexual orientation; because it violates the basic rights of a
> person to become a parent, and his privacy, and his right to his body;
> because it is in excess of their authority; because it is set forth in
> secondary legislation and not primary legislation; because it is unrea-
> sonable, and because it is not publicly published. . . . Married women
> are not required to undergo any sort of examinations and are not
> subordinate to any sort of discretion as a precondition for receiving a
> sperm donation. This is apparently based on the assumption that a
> woman who is not married creates a doubt regarding her appropriate-
> ness to be a mother. Thereby the petitioner and other unmarried
> women are discriminated against on the basis of their personal status.

Here, as in the Aloni Commission Report, the right of access to
reproductive technology is articulated in terms of an unmarried

woman's right to privacy, dignity, and equality. Again, this is a radical notion, particularly in terms of Jewish tradition, for to entrench
the right to reproduce as an individual right, independent of any sort
of family construct, lays the legal framework for a profound social
reimagination of the nuclear family as a prerequisite for reproduction. If the state explicitly constructs reproduction as an individual
right, then the nuclear family becomes simply one structural option
for reproduction among many. And as soon as the nuclear family
ceases to be legally privileged as the locus for reproduction, the potential exists that it will cease to be socially privileged in other ways.

The ministry of health acceded to the demands in the petition and
agreed to cancel the regulation that required unmarried women to
undergo psychiatric evaluations as a prerequisite to receiving artificial insemination; the regulation that demands an evaluation by a
social worker remains, but is now required of all those seeking assisted conception, both unmarried and married. The liberal legal
principles that guarantee the right to procreate and the right to privacy were employed effectively here in defense of an unmarried
woman's claim that her right to reproduce is equal to that of a married woman. That the petitioner is a lesbian only emphasizes the fact
that secular lawyers understand access to reproductive technology to
be a fundamental human right, independent of marital or personal
status.

If the state supports the reproductive options of women regardless
of marital status, and if it helps enable unmarried women to achieve
their reproductive goals, then motherhood becomes assisted and
privileged independent of marriage.

No Donated Eggs for Unmarried Women   Unmarried women's access to IVF treatment in Israel differs from married women's in
another important way. Regulation 8(b) states: "If the woman to
whom it is intended to implant the egg is unmarried, a fertilized egg
will not be implanted in her unless the egg is hers and she has received a report from a social worker of a recognized department
which supports the woman's request. The report shall be in accordance with the director's guidelines" (Ministry of Health Regulations Regarding In-Vitro Fertilization, 1987).

In other words, unmarried women, unlike married women, are not entitled to egg donations. If an unmarried woman suffers from a form of infertility that makes her eggs unviable, then she is not entitled to treatment. As the regulations stand, a woman may not receive both an egg donation and sperm donation (unless of course she is being paid to do so in a surrogate motherhood agreement; see chapter 5). It would seem, then, that an unmarried woman in need of an egg donation must get married in order to be eligible for such a donation. This restriction is not condoned in the Aloni Commission Report:

> According to the Regulations, an unmarried woman has the right to receive IVF treatment and to donate eggs. An unmarried woman is not, however, entitled to receive an egg donation. . . . as aforesaid, the Commission considers that there is no room to restrict the right of access to infertility treatment, including the right to receive an egg donation, for the sole reason that the patient is unmarried. (1994: 41)

This restriction was challenged by Vered Weiss in 1996, when she petitioned the High Court of Justice for a repeal to the law in Regulation 8(b) that says an unmarried woman may not receive an ovum donation. In their 1996 decision on this matter, the High Court ruled that in the matter of Vered Weiss, her health fund would be ordered to pay for her fertility treatment, which includes ovum donation. The court's leniency in this case can be partially attributed to the fact that Vered Weiss would not be using donor sperm to conceive, but would use the sperm of her live-in male partner. The decision of the court is limited to this case, however; there is to be no change in the ministry of health regulations that limit the right to ovum donation to married women.

Conclusion

The introduction of new reproductive technologies into a traditional, pronatalist society in which marriage is exclusively controlled by religious authorities inevitably creates a complex social drama.

These technologies have the potential to challenge entrenched notions about the appropriate relationship between marriage and its role in reproduction. The Israeli case is remarkable in that efforts to legislate for the appropriate uses of these technologies have revealed unusual points of consensus between traditional Jewish law and progressive secular law. Most strikingly, both legal systems grant varying measures of reproductive agency to unmarried women.

The regulations regarding reproductive technology, and the unusual alliance between the secular and religious legal systems on which they rest, present a formal challenge to traditional understandings of the nuclear family, which is constituted through marriage, as the exclusive framework for Jewish reproduction. Even when these regulations are explicitly drafted to conform to traditional rabbinic understandings of relatedness, they force potentially subversive underpinnings of Jewish kinship reckoning to become explicit. We have seen how these dynamics have unleashed the reproductive agency of unmarried women.

The social and legal conditions that contribute to this phenomenon are overwhelming:

1. The children born to unmarried Jewish women, like the children born to married Jewish couples, are considered to be full-fledged, marriageable Jews according to traditional Jewish law.

2. The Aloni Commission Report, sponsored by the Israeli ministry of justice, explicitly articulates the rights of unmarried women to reproduce in the liberal language of the individual right to privacy.

3. The narrow areas of regulatory control that limit unmarried women's access to reproductive technology have been successfully challenged before the Israeli High Court of Justice.

The policing of the family is thus left to the conceptual imaginations of a diverse array of social actors, from orthodox rabbis to secular legislators to unmarried women themselves. Orthodox rabbis may object to the deliberate insemination of unmarried women out of concern for the protection of the traditional nuclear family, but their arguments have no legal foundation in religious law. The pronatalist state may attempt to control unmarried women's access to reproductive technology, but the same language in which it articulates its control has been successfully used to challenge that control, as it was in the petitions of Yarus-Hakak and Weiss. All these dynamics are taking place within a state that has an explicit interest in supporting policies and legislative actions that encourage the reproduction of Jews.

A number of questions arise here, among them: how long will it be before Israeli women assimilate more progressive notions of their autonomous rights to reproduce and thereby cease privileging marriage as the preferred location for biological and social reproduction? Will Israeli women's investment in marriage change if it is no longer the only way to have children? And what will marriage come to mean if it has ceased to be the exclusive locus of legitimate reproduction?

Technological intervention and Jewish conceptions of kinship conspire to challenge the notion that marriage is the only legitimate site of biological and social reproduction. As soon as the doctor's office can compete with the family as the locus of conception and as soon as conception moves out of the private realm and into the public, then the meaning of the family and its role in social reproduction must change, particularly when children conceived in the doctor's office do not threaten extant notions of relatedness and legitimacy. The nuclear family constituted through marriage becomes relative; it is no longer the only social location for reproduction, but one location among many. As soon as reproduction becomes unhinged from the nuclear family, and children are understood as the products of technological intervention as well as sexual relationship, then the whole notion that marriage is the natural, and indeed national, basis for kinship becomes exposed as a vulnerable social construct. Within a society where marriage is so deeply entrenched as a religious and divinely inspired institution and where it has been integrated as such into the secular legal foundation of the state, exposing it as a social construct may have particularly profound and subversive implications.

3

Jewish and Gentile Sperm:
Rabbinic Discourse on Sperm and Paternal
Relatedness

A number of years ago, a great controversy erupted among leading rabbinic decisors, a dispute which generated a totally uncharacteristic outburst of invective heat and partisanship in the Halakhic world. Scholars all over the world were astounded by the sharp tone and bitter disagreements engendered by a point of law, for generally the tone of rabbinic discourse is elegantly cordial, and the fine points of Halakha are disputed in a measured intellectual atmosphere. Not so with the question of permitting artificial insemination.—Alfred S. Cohen, *Journal of Halakha*

There is a blessing on all good things in medicine that help to bring another soul into Israel.—Rav Schach, in *Yediot Aharonot,* 19 November 1991

The intention of the creation of man is to be fruitful and multiply . . . anyone who does not engage in this, it is as if he spills blood.
—Tur, *Even HaEzer*

As an innovation in reproductive technology that has the potential to increase the number of Jewish babies, artificial insemination has obvious attractions to those legislating within a pronatalist religious system. At the same time, as a maverick technology seemingly without historical precedent, it poses enormous threats to traditional religious ideas about the relationship between sex, reproduction, and parenthood. In this chapter I explore Israeli folk-cultural theories of reproduction as represented by rabbinic argumentation about the appropriate uses of artificial insemination for the treatment of male-factor infertility in married couples.[1] These rabbinic debates connect to national imaginations of kinship because they help form the conceptual base for the state of Israel's regulations regarding reproductive technology. I want to understand how these "native theories of reproduction" (Schneider 1984), which I examine in the form of rabbinic responses to the questions posed by artificial insemination, are articulated and negotiated and how they compete for legitimacy in a religious world in which rabbinic authority is decentralized and nonmonolithic.

Anthropologists and rabbis ask remarkably similar questions about kinship; both try to understand the significance of sexual intercourse as it is related to pregnancy. Both try to understand whether parenthood is predicated on conception, on genetic relatedness, or on birth, and both try to understand how notions of biology tie in to cultural theories of reproduction. That rabbinic and anthropological questions overlap allows for one set of theories to be used to think about the other. The analytic tools of the anthropologist are thus well suited to an examination of rabbinic kinship beliefs, particularly as these beliefs become explicit through rabbinic disputation about the appropriate uses of reproductive technology. By looking at rabbinic discourse about these technologies in Israel, we can more fully understand Ginsburg and Rapp's assertion that "reproduction, in its biological and social senses, is inextricably bound up with the production of culture," instead of identifying kinship as something limited to the domestic sphere. In Israel, rabbinic discourse about reproduction is intimately linked with the production of culture.

To be sure, the vast majority of Israeli Jews are secular, and those who seek fertility treatment do not consult rabbis for guidance. But for those Jews who are religious, rabbinic authority is essential to their decision-making processes regarding the use of these technologies. Indeed, unlike their secular counterparts, orthodox Jews only seek out fertility treatments with explicit rabbinic guidance and in close consultation with rabbinic authorities. Many will only seek treatment in Israeli hospitals that operate under close rabbinic supervision. The problem for infertile orthodox Jews is that the new reproductive technologies have developed so fast, the reproductive possibilities they present so various, and the desperation of infertile people in a pronatalist society so great, that demand for access to these technologies has outpaced contemporary rabbinic efforts to shape Israeli state regulations regarding the appropriate uses of these technologies. As a result, many Israeli fertility clinics provide access to these technologies in ways that may be acceptable for most secular Israelis but that do not conform to strict Halakhic guidelines, that is, guidelines rooted in traditional Jewish law.

To safeguard themselves from the reproductive lawlessness they fear otherwise reigns in Israeli fertility clinics, orthodox Jews have constructed elaborate, independent frameworks for the administration of these technologies, frameworks that depend on close cooperation between fertility specialists, orthodox rabbis, and infertile orthodox patients.

A Jerusalem-based organization called PUAH (Poriyoot ve'Refuah Alpi haHalakah, "fertility treatment according to Jewish law") maintains these frameworks. PUAH is also, not coincidentally, the name of one of the biblical midwives who saved Jews from the Pharaoh's genocidal decree. PUAH acts as an umbrella organization for rabbinic advice and referrals regarding the new reproductive technologies. Among its many activities, PUAH sponsors regular meetings between fertility specialists and rabbis in order to familiarize rabbis with the latest developments in infertility treatment, provides information to infertile orthodox Jews, and trains orthodox *maschgichot,* or supervisors, to monitor all laboratory procedures in fertility clinics that involve handling reproductive genetic material, in order to ensure that there is no untoward mixing of sperm, eggs, or embryos. In addition, PUAH sponsors a committee of rabbinic advisers who meet regularly with officials at the ministry of health to develop policies regarding the use of reproductive technology that are consistent with Halakhic kinship norms.

Through these activities, PUAH performs an important function for orthodox Jews: it creates kosher conditions for the use of reproductive technology. It also performs an important function for non-religious fertility specialists by translating rabbinic concerns and provisos about these technologies into medical language, thereby ensuring that rabbinic theory turns into medical practice.

I begin with excerpts of my extended interviews with Aryeh, the office manager of PUAH, in order to foreground the cultural and political context in which rabbinic decisions about the appropriate uses of reproductive technology are being made in Israel. When I went to visit the PUAH office in Jerusalem, I put on a long-sleeved dress and stockings in order not to offend the sensibilities of those who lived in the orthodox neighborhood where the office is located. After much searching, I finally managed to find the office; it was a tiny little room cramped into the bomb shelter in the basement of a modern, stone-faced building.

Aryeh and a very pregnant secretary named Ruchama welcomed me and sat me down on the narrow little couch between their desks for what was to be the first of a series of interviews I conducted at PUAH. Aryeh was a young man, about thirty, and had a closely shorn beard. Ruchama was wearing a wig and a very modest dress, typical for an orthodox woman. They were very busy and gave me a glass of coffee and a huge folder filled with clippings about the organization. Aryeh said he would be with me shortly; he was busy on the phone, and I overheard him making referrals to rabbis, doctors, and hospitals. He had a few phone lines and carried on several conversations simultaneously. Ruchama was staring into a computer and typing very slowly. I read through the clippings, most of which were about the organization's successes in catching IVF "mistakes" before they happened.[2]

When he finally finished with the phone calls, Aryeh turned to speak with me; we were almost knee to knee, which seemed to make us both uncomfortable. Before I had a chance to ask anything, he started in with the questions: Am I Jewish? Am I married? Am I religious? He was less interested in what I was doing than who I was and why I was doing it. I told him that I was Jewish, was not married, and that I knew something about the religious world though I was not religious myself. Since I had already described my research project to him on the phone, he knew I wanted to ask him some questions.

I began by asking him to describe what PUAH does and how the organization works. He said that PUAH has contacts with all the doctors and all the *poskim* (rabbinic decisors). "At PUAH," he said, "we only deal with first-class rabbis. . . . PUAH is the middleman between the couples, the rabbis, and the doctors. We translate medi-cal language into Halakhic language and provide a bridge between the medical and rabbinic world."

I then asked him to explain what happens when an orthodox couple has fertility problems, how they find out what kind of treat-ment they can get, what is Halakhically permitted and what is for-bidden. Aryeh responded:

> There's no clear answer to any question; each couple needs a letter
> from two doctors saying that they are infertile before they can start
> treatment. The answers go generally according to *edah* (ethnic group)
> whose opinion you follow. The Sephardim, for example, go either
> according to R. Eliyahu or R. Ovadia. If someone comes without a
> *posek* [authoritative rabbinic decision maker] we find one who will
> make their life easier. You are supposed to go according to your posek,
> if you go by his opinion in other things, you have to go by his opinion
> in this (fertility treatment) as well. Not everyone has a posek, and
> those who don't should go according to a *beit din* (religious court
> made up of three judges), two against one decides. The thing is, each
> couple is its own world; we work on a case-by-case basis.

In other words, if an orthodox Sephardi couple has fertility prob-lems, they consult a Sephardi rabbi for fertility counseling, whereas an orthodox Ashkenazi couple would consult an Ashkenazi rabbi. These ethnic differences are important, for although these couples may share identical fertility problems, one couple may be permitted to use various forms of treatment that are forbidden to the other couple. Moreover, two couples from the same ethnic group, with the same fertility problem, may consult the same rabbi and receive dif-ferent permission for different kinds of treatment, either owing to differences in age between the couples, different mediating circum-stances, or other factors. As Aryeh said: "Each couple is its own world; we work on a case-by-case basis." It rapidly became apparent that though poskim are supposed to be interpreting God's law regarding the appropriate combinations of reproductive material, God's law seems to depend a lot on whom you ask and who is asking. In other words, the fact that reproductive technology presents an array of unprecedented procreative possibilities makes the rabbinic enterprise of constructing a culturally coherent response to these technologies, ostensibly an exercise in exegesis of traditional sources, as much an exercise in invention as it is an exercise in interpretation.

In my discussions with Aryeh I learned that PUAH is an actively pronatalist organization that is doing all it can to solve the infertility problems of orthodox couples. These efforts include counseling young childless couples about how to have sex effectively (some orthodox Jews remain childless not because of physiological problems with infertility but because they have entered into marriage with little knowledge about the mechanics of sexual intercourse), counseling for orthodox couples who are navigating the bureaucracy of fertility clinics, and ensuring that infertile Jews seek advice from rabbis known for their lenient attitudes toward reproductive technology.

I was surprised by how knowledgeable PUAH's rabbis seemed to be about the medical intricacies of fertility treatment. Whether they were dealing with questions of sperm procurement, artificial insemination, ovum donation, or a host of other questions, it was apparent that information about these technologies had been well circulated and carefully analyzed in the rabbinic world. Indeed, Aryeh told me that "now, we have answers to almost all the Halakhic questions that are raised by these procedures."

The Practical Nature of Orthodox Rabbinic Authority

It is important to understand that orthodox rabbis do not now, nor have they ever, constituted a monolithic decision-making body. They differ by ethnic group, educational tradition, regional background, and many other factors. Although some contemporary rabbis have greater followings than others, there is no living individual rabbi whose rabbinic authority is accepted by all Jews. Unlike papal authority, which is absolute, rabbinic authority is, by its nature decentralized, variable, yet binding.[3]

Orthodox rabbis make their decisions about Halakhic questions according to a plethora of criteria, both legal and spiritual. However, the general principles of Halakhic decision making are the same: when confronted with a novel problem, consult the traditional sources for precedents, give ultimate weight to biblical commandments, both positive and negative, consider previous rabbinic rulings carefully, and make a decision based on common sense and logical reasoning. In this decision-making process, pragmatic and moral considerations are to be considered as interrelated.[4] To be sure, contemporary Halakhic decision making should not be based exclusively on direct exegesis of the Bible. Instead, the Talmud and the classical legal authorities should be considered as the definitive legal sources for contemporary rulings.[5]

It is important to point out that a powerful motive behind the creation of new rabbinic rulings regarding reproductive technology is rabbinic concern for the survival of the Jewish people. Broadly, this concern means that innovations that are perceived to threaten Jewish survival are ruled against while innovations that are perceived to encourage Jewish survival are ruled for. Because reproductive technology offers the potential to reproduce more Jews, it is understood to be a positive tool for Jewish survival. Moreover, rabbis approach the Torah, as these sources are called in their entirety, with the belief that, by its divine nature, the Torah will provide an appropriate constellation of analogies from which to determine rulings about contemporary problems.[6]

Rabbis and Reproduction

Many orthodox rabbis have issued lenient rulings allowing for the use of new reproductive technologies. Their leniency rests on three basic principles:

1. These technologies aid in the fulfillment of the commandment to be fruitful and multiply (Genesis 1:28), considered an obligation of central importance in Judaism.

2. The childless couple is suffering, and because of the mitzvah to practice *g'milut hasidim* (lovingkindness), rabbis have argued that they are obligated to do everything they can to alleviate that suffering, and the new reproductive technologies offer a means to that end.

3. The principle of family integrity is extremely important in Jewish law, and to prevent the kind of serious marital difficulties that can arise in a childless couple, including the obligation to divorce after ten years of childless marriage, reproductive technology should be permissible, according to many rabbis.[7]

New reproductive technologies necessarily raise numerous Halakhic questions. For example, there are practical concerns regarding sperm procurement for purposes of artificial insemination.[8] How should sperm be collected in a Halakhic system that prohibits masturbation?[9] Can masturbation be allowed if it is for purposes of procreation?[10] Is masturbation allowed if the man does not use his hands or thinks about his wife as a means to arousal? How else can sperm be collected? Through coitus interruptus? Using a condom? Using a perforated condom? Through a postcoital test?[11]

When the infertility of the husband is insurmountable and third-party donor sperm is indicated for treatment, the Halakhic issues become much more complex.

Contemporary rabbis use ancient Talmudic and midrashic precedents concerning instances in which conception had been achieved without sex as a framework for their discussions about artificial insemination. These texts, which have been the subject of ongoing rabbinic reflection and interpretation for centuries, have assumed central importance for contemporary rabbis who seek to create cogent guidelines for using artificial insemination and other new reproductive technologies in ways that do not contradict traditional rabbinic understandings of relatedness. I discuss three principal traditional sources below, paying particular attention to rabbinic discussions about how paternity is constituted.

The principal source that establishes a precedent for present-day rulings on artificial insemination is found in the Babylonian Talmud, *Maseket Hagiga,* 14b–15a (traditionally believed to have been edited in the fifth century C.E.).

> Ben Zoma was asked: may a Kohen (Priest) marry a maiden who has become pregnant?[12] (yet who claims she is still a virgin). Do we (in such case) take into consideration Samuel's statement, for Samuel said: I can have repeated sexual intercourse without causing bleeding (i.e. without the woman losing her virginity) or is it perhaps that the case of Samuel is rare? He replied: the case of Samuel is rare, but we do consider (the possibility) that she may have conceived in a bath (into which a male has discharged semen: Rashi) and therefore she may marry a High Priest.

The simple meaning of this passage is that if a woman is impregnated accidentally by sperm in a bath, however unlikely, she is still considered a virgin and may marry a Kohen (a member of the priestly class). Kohanim are traditionally prohibited from marrying divorced or devirginized women. This interpretation introduces the theoretical possibility that conception and sexual intercourse may be considered independently, since in this important Talmudic case, conception was achieved absent sexual intercourse. It is therefore considered to be the first recorded instance of "artificial" insemination in the Jewish sources.

Contemporary rabbis have looked to this passage and the myriad interpretations of it to address a number of questions raised by artificial insemination, among them, can a Jewish man be permitted to donate sperm for a married Jewish woman other than his wife? And if so, what is the status of the child so conceived? Additional questions concerning artificial insemination with Jewish donor sperm include: If a Jewish man who is married but childless donates sperm and then subsequently dies, is he considered to be childless even though his sperm has successfully conceived children, albeit not with his wife? And if so, is his brother still obligated to marry his wife in order to carry on his name, commensurate with the obligation of levirate marriage (yibbum)?[13]

Perhaps the question that has generated the most heated rabbinic debate, however, is whether artificial insemination with Jewish donor sperm from a third party constitutes adultery. Many rabbis follow the reasoning in the Ben Zoma case to conclude that adultery is constituted by forbidden sexual relations, not by the act of conception, since the maiden in the bathtub remains a virgin even though she became pregnant. In other words, since the maiden remained a virgin even though sperm entered her womb, virginity must be contingent on sexual intercourse, not on conception. Therefore, it is possible to understand adultery in a similar way, as an illicit act not dependent on whether sperm has entered the womb but on whether sexual intercourse has occurred.

The implications for the contemporary rulings on artificial insemination are clear, for here is a Talmudic precedent that can be interpreted to mean that artificial insemination with third-party donor sperm does not constitute adultery, if adultery is understood as a physical act that occurs between two people, not as a biological act that occurs between a sperm and an egg.[14] Indeed, Rav Feinstein, one of the greatest rabbis of the twentieth century, followed this reasoning to suggest that a married woman who conceives a child through artificial insemination by Jewish donor is exempt from the punishment accorded the adulteress and may continue to have sexual relations with her husband (a woman found guilty of adultery is otherwise forbidden from sexual relations with her husband and may be divorced).[15] Feinstein's reasoning is corroborated by Halakhic definitions of adultery and incest in other contexts in which it is clear that adultery depends on whether the penis of a man enters the vagina of a woman in a sexual relationship specifically proscribed in the Torah (Dorff 1998: 68). These interpretations rest on considered distinctions between the physical and "biological" act of adultery. The question is whether the sin in adultery is confined to the physical act of intercourse between a married Jewish woman and a Jewish man who is not her husband, or whether it inheres in the resulting conception as well. Some rabbinic interpreters suggest that the physical act of illicit sexual intercourse between a married Jewish woman and a Jewish man who is not her husband is inseparable from the subsequent biological act of the sperm and egg that are thereby joined in conception. If this definition of adultery is applied to fertility treatments using Jewish donor sperm, then certainly a married Jewish woman's egg should be prohibited from achieving conception with sperm that has been procured from a Jewish man who is not her husband. The child so conceived would thus be conceived in an adulterous union and considered a mamzer.

Because of these overwhelming concerns about creating children who could be considered mamzers, in addition to significant concerns about creating the potential for incestuous relationships between people unknowingly conceived with the same Jewish donor sperm, there is unanimous rabbinic consensus that artificial insemination with Jewish donor sperm from a third party must be prohibited.[16]

Many rabbis, however, vehemently disagreed with Rav Feinstein's interpretation of this issue, among them Rav Teitelbaum, who ruled that the artificial insemination of a married Jewish woman with Jewish donor sperm does indeed constitute adultery.[17] To Rabbi Teitelbaum and others, the Ben Zoma precedent is irrelevant to cases of artificial insemination because in the Talmudic case, the woman was impregnated by accident.[18] In contemporary cases of artificial insemination, the woman deliberately chooses to be inseminated with the sperm of a man other than her husband, albeit with her husband's consent. Therefore, these rabbis hold that conception and sexual intercourse cannot be bifurcated in cases of artificial insemination by donor. A woman who consents to artificial insemination by donor is like a woman who consents to having sexual intercourse with a man other than her husband, that is, she is considered to have committed adultery and is therefore forbidden from having sexual relations with her husband.[19] That her husband consents to the donor insemination is irrelevant.[20] It is the a priori decision to achieve conception via artificial insemination that is considered to constitute adultery here.

The second traditional text that contemporary rabbis look to in order to answer questions regarding artificial insemination is a gloss of Rabbi Peretz ben Eliyahu of Corbeil (thirteenth century C.E.) to the *Sefer Mitzvot Katan*.[21] Rabbi Peretz states that a woman must be careful about lying in the sheets of a stranger:

> lest she be impregnated by absorbing the sperm from another man. Why are we not afraid that she become pregnant from her husband's sperm and the child will be conceived by a *niddah* (a menstruating woman)? The answer is that since there is no forbidden sexual intercourse, the child is completely legitimate (kosher), even from the sperm of another, just as Ben Sira was legitimate. However, we are concerned about the sperm of another man since the child may eventually marry his sister.[22]

Here the text addresses the status of a child conceived absent sexual intercourse by a woman who becomes pregnant from lying on her husband's sheets while she is in *niddah* (her ritually impure days before and after menstruation). Here the rabbinic question is: should a child conceived this way considered to be a *ben-niddah,* a child conceived during a woman's "unclean" days when sexual intercourse is prohibited? Rabbi Peretz ruled that the child is not considered to be a ben-niddah because though conception occurred, it was not achieved through sexual intercourse. The status of the child is therefore not tainted as if he were a ben-niddah because it is the timing of the intercourse, not the timing of the conception, that determines whether or not a child is ben-niddah. This interpretation seems to reinforce Feinstein's reading of the Ben Zoma case, for it suggests that stigmas born by children conceived in illicit sexual unions, be they mamzers or ben-niddahs, originate in the act of illicit sexual intercourse, not in the act of conception itself.

This text exemplifies an additional concern about artificial insemination. It introduces the possibility that a man may have one child by his wife and another through the accidental impregnation of a woman who lies on his "sperm-covered sheets." Two women could thus unknowingly conceive with the same man's sperm and give birth to children who have the same father; these children could grow up and unwittingly enter into an incestuous marriage. This possibility is referenced by contemporary rabbis to underscore the problematic nature of artificial insemination with third-party donor sperm. Even if it does not constitute adultery, it does create the potential for conceiving a child with unknown paternity who could someday commit incest with his or her half-sibling.

The third precedent that contemporary rabbis consult in their deliberations about the appropriate use of artificial insemination, and indeed which is mentioned by Rabbi Peretz above, is a midrashic source that relates the medieval legend of Ben Sira. In the legend, Ben Sira is said to have been conceived by the prophet Jeremiah's daughter in a bath. The seed was believed to have been Jeremiah's, who was coerced into emitting his seed into the bath by a group of evil men.[23] As a midrashic source (folkloric rather than legal), the legend of Ben Sira has disputed Halakhic significance. Some medieval authorities used this text to suggest that even though Ben Sira was conceived with sperm that Jeremiah emitted into a bath with no intention of conceiving a child, let alone with his daughter, Jeremiah is still considered to be the father of Ben Sira. Therefore Ben Sira is considered to have fulfilled his obligation to be fruitful and multiply.[24] This interpretation of the Ben Sira legend establishes a precedent for assuming a kinship link between a sperm donor and the child conceived with his sperm.

Such a link is not taken for granted in rabbinic debates about artificial insemination because genetic relatedness is not generally considered equivalent to sexual intercourse as a means of achieving conception and creating a child. Nor is genetic relatedness necessarily considered an ultimate determinant of relatedness in the rabbinic imagination. In fact, some contemporary rabbis suggest that a child conceived with Jewish donor sperm should not be considered to be related to the man who emitted sperm for his conception, since to them paternity is established through the sex act; it is not established by a genetic link. Rabbi Ben-Zion Uziel argues that "a pregnancy induced by artificial insemination, though it progresses normally and produces a child, lacks the natural basis for paternity — sexual intercourse — and is therefore 'artificial.' . . . a child born of artificial insemination by donor is like a child born of parthenogenesis, having no father at all" (Zohar 1998: 78). Or, as Rabbi J. David Bleich explains, "Halakha, or Jewish law, takes no direct cognizance of genetics as a significant factor in and of itself. . . . There is no support of which I am aware for the notion that genetic continuity is, Halakhically speaking, a *sine qua non* of parenthood" (1994: 45). One strand of rabbinic thinking would seem to suggest, then, that the act of sexual intercourse is the prerequisite not only for determining whether a child is a mamzer or a ben-niddah, but for determining whether a child has a father as well. To these rabbis, if sperm is emitted into a receptacle, even if it is for the purpose of artificial insemination, the full range of paternal rights and obligations is not initiated. Only a more limited form of paternity is established in order to identify the donor to prevent the possibility of future incestuous marriages between children unknowingly conceived with sperm from the same Jewish man.

Professor Avraham Steinberg, a pediatric neurologist at Shaare Zedek Medical Center in Jerusalem and winner of the 1999 Israel Prize, elaborates on the problematic nature of this issue thus:

> The basis for the solution to this problem (about the paternity of a child conceived without sexual intercourse) is found in the precedent set by the virgin in the bathtub (Ben Zoma). Most poskim believe a child born this way is considered to be the son of the sperm donor in all respects. But others say that he is the son of the sperm donor only when it makes the ruling more stringent and not more lenient (*l-homra ve lo l-kula*). That is to say, just in order to set up a legal fence to protect themselves from the situation of incest (so that he won't marry his sister from the same father) he is considered as his son, but he is not considered as his son regarding being his inheritor, and the mother is not exempt from *yibum* and *halitza,* and the donor has not fulfilled the commandment to "be fruitful and multiply." But we have found poskim who say that even in the instance of the virgin in the bathtub, the child so conceived is not considered the son in every respect, because of the doubt over the source of the sperm. Thus, in the case of sperm donation from husband to wife, when it is clear, the resulting child is considered to be the son of the father in every respect. (1975: 131) (my translation)

That artificial insemination engenders rabbinic debate over whether paternity is generated via the act of sexual intercourse or whether it can be initiated via sperm donation as well reveals intriguing rabbinic notions about the nature of Jewish paternity. Indeed, it would seem that Jewish paternity exists along a continuum, the determination of which is dependent not only on the physical fact of successful conception but on the temporal and spatial conditions in which Jewish sperm is emitted.

There is what could be called *full* paternity, which is the result of the positive act of emitting semen during sexual intercourse with the intention of fulfilling the obligation to "be fruitful and multiply." Full paternity initiates the whole host of obligations between father and child and fulfills the man's obligation to be fruitful and multiply. In turn, any child who has been conceived in this way is obligated to honor his parents and is entitled to inherit property from his father.[25]

Second, there is what could be called *partial* paternity, which is established if Jewish sperm in and of itself, when emitted accidentally or into a receptacle, achieves conception. Partial paternity does not initiate the whole host of obligations between father and child and is important to determine primarily in order to avoid potential incestuous relationships between siblings conceived with the same Jewish seed. It can also be important for determining a range of related obligations related to levirate marriage, such as yibbum, halitza, and so forth.[26] Partial paternity could be called "genetic relatedness" between a Jewish sperm donor and the child conceived with his sperm. Yet in rabbinic kinship cosmology, relatedness is not constructed using the grammar of genes.

Interestingly, some rabbis have argued that the establishment of full paternity is not solely dependent on whether sexual intercourse occurred, but can only be determined when it is known whether acts intended to conceive a child, either sexual intercourse or artificial insemination, were successful. These rabbis argue that if a child is successfully conceived in either way, then the act of emitting semen for artificial insemination, like the act of sexual intercourse, must be considered a positive act that fulfills the obligation to be fruitful and multiply. Moreover, the sperm donor in such cases should be considered the father in all respects.

Thus the intention to fulfill the obligation to be fruitful and multiply, and actions undertaken to realize that intention, could be understood as the basis for full paternity. Dr. Noam Zohar suggests that thinking about paternity in this way creates new ways of thinking about adoption in the Jewish context. Zohar argues that actions undertaken with the specific intention of becoming a father, such as adopting a child, should be considered to establish full paternity.[27]

Until the advent of reproductive technology, sexual intercourse was the sole means of realizing that fructifying combination of the intention to be fruitful and multiply and actions undertaken to fulfill that intention. Now, however, the ways to realize such intentions have multiplied. Conceptual innovations in rabbinic understandings of paternal relatedness are thus made possible, innovations that, remarkably, do not depend on genetic referents.

Anthropologist Sarah Franklin articulates a similar idea in an entirely different context:

> The Schneiderian view of kinship as a cultural system . . . foregrounds the importance of heterosexual intercourse as a means of establishing conjugality and procreativity. This, he argues, is because of the capacity for the "natural facts" of reproduction to operate as a sustaining symbol of the essence of kinship and marriage. Yet, in the context of achieved conception, the instability of this "dominant" cultural logic is exposed: the pursuit of conception through artificial means *can function equally well as a unifying goal.* (1997: 165–66) (emphasis in original)

Here Franklin articulates how Euro-American kinship thinking privileges heterosexual intercourse as the activity that determines parental relatedness because it functions to combine reproductive genetic materials, "the natural facts of reproduction." By virtue of this occasional outcome, heterosexual intercourse assumes an important symbolic role, for it comes to represent reproduction and regeneration. Franklin argues that the new reproductive technologies present a conceptual challenge to the symbolic importance of heterosexual intercourse because they introduce new ways to achieve the goal over which it always had an exclusive monopoly: the combining of reproductive genetic material. Franklin's argument thus mirrors Zohar's and other rabbinic interpreters who argue that the new reproductive technologies force a rethinking of the conceptual underpinnings of parenthood, since these technologies present possibilities for more innovative, and yet culturally coherent, routes to its establishment.

In sum, if the genetic material being combined artificially is that of the husband and wife, then Halakhic concerns about adultery, mamzerut, and the future possibility of incest between siblings who are unknowingly related are eliminated. Moreover, it is exactly these concerns — about adultery, mamzerut, and future incest — which make the use of Jewish donor sperm from a third party Halakhically prohibited. Problems of determining whether a sperm donor has fulfilled his obligation to be fruitful and multiply, problems in reckoning inheritance, and problems related to other traditional obligations between father and child exist in cases of both artificial insemination by husband and artificial insemination by Jewish donor. These problems exist because many rabbis have raised questions about the nature of paternity when it is not initiated through sexual intercourse with a woman but through technological intervention following ejaculation into a receptacle.

Halakhic Alternatives to Artificial Insemination with Jewish Donor Sperm

In-Vitro Fertilization and Embryo Transfer

Rabbinic questions regarding the permissibility of artificial insemination with donor sperm are fundamentally different from questions regarding in-vitro fertilization with donor sperm and embryo transfer, a technological procedure in which sperm and egg are combined in vitro and the resulting embryo is placed in a woman's womb or fallopian tube for implantation and gestation. Since the literal prohibition against adultery is derived from the biblical verse: "Thou shalt not implant thy *seed* into thy neighbor's wife" (Leviticus 18:20),[28] a clear Halakhic distinction can be made between the act of sperm being introduced into a woman's reproductive tract, which can be understood to be unequivocally prohibited, and the act of an embryo being introduced into her, for which there is no clear prohibition. In other words, the prohibition against adultery is only against putting "seed" in thy neighbor's wife; it is not against putting an embryo in her. Thus IVF and embryo transfer are preferred by some rabbis as a form of fertility treatment that do not violate the literal Halakhic precepts against adultery.[29]

Cloning

Cloning is not yet a viable reproductive option for human beings, but it has been already carefully examined by contemporary rabbis for its reproductive potential.[30] Although there are no Talmudic precedents that specifically forbid cloning, since it does not directly violate any specific Halakhic principles, there are no precedents that clearly permit cloning either, let alone conception accomplished without sperm. Cloning raises many questions about the constellation of relationships into which a cloned child would be born, among them whether a cloned child would be considered to have a father, since the clone would be conceived not only without sex but without sperm as well. Two hypothetical advantages of cloning are that it could not possibly be considered adultery, nor would it compel a Jewish man to masturbate in order to procure sperm, for cloning cells could be more readily obtained from other parts of the body. At present, these issues are entirely hypothetical, and few definitive rabbinic rulings on cloning for reproduction have been issued (see Broyde 1999).

Artificial Insemination with Gentile Sperm

In cases in which male-factor infertility is otherwise untreatable some rabbis prescribe artificial insemination with non-Jewish donor sperm. Artificial insemination with non-Jewish sperm raises an additional set of Halakhic concerns, and yet it also creates a separate set of possibilities.

First, non-Jewish sperm donation circumvents the Halakhic problem of sperm procurement for Jewish sperm donors; since non-Jews are not obligated to the same laws that Jews are, it is not of explicit rabbinic concern whether or not they masturbate.

Second, since Jewishness is conferred matrilineally, a child born to a Jewish woman is always considered to be a full-fledged Jew, regardless of whether the sperm with which the child was conceived came from a Jew or a non-Jew.[31] A child conceived with non-Jewish sperm does not have a Halakhic father, however, for in the Halakhic imagination, non-Jewish paternity simply does not exist for Jewish children.[32] Indeed, in traditional rabbinic sources, children born to different Jewish mothers from the same non-Jewish sperm are not considered to be related in any way; they may even marry because they share no substance.

Third, there are no adulterous overtones with non-Jewish sperm donations, for adultery is clearly defined as sexual intercourse between a married Jewish woman and a Jewish man who is not her husband. Artificial insemination with non-Jewish sperm is therefore incapable of conceiving a child who would be considered a mamzer. The question then becomes: can the rabbinic precedent that denies paternity to non-Jews post facto be transferred to a proactive stance that expressly permits the use of non-Jewish sperm to conceive children for Jewish couples who face male-factor infertility? The question could be asked somewhat differently: does a child conceived through sexual intercourse between a married Jewish woman and a non-Jewish man have the same status, that is, Halakhically fatherless yet Jewish, as a child conceived through the technological combination of a Jewish egg and non-Jewish sperm and gestated to parturition in a Jewish womb?

Most rabbis would argue that there is a fundamental philosophical difference between determining the status of a child born as the result of an unfortunate act, that is, sex between a non-Jewish man and a Jewish woman, and deliberately authorizing the insemination of a Jewish woman with non-Jewish donor sperm. Nevertheless, the inability of non-Jewish sperm to establish any kind of paternal relatedness or to exert influence on the identity of the child so conceived makes it an attractive alternative for assisted Jewish reproduction. Indeed, for some rabbis, it is the perfect kinship cipher; it is there and yet it is not there; it creates a child and yet it does not leave a trace of relatedness. For these rabbis, non-Jewish donor

sperm offers a socially practical and Halakhically acceptable solution to severe male-factor infertility; it procreates, but it does not reproduce. Marilyn Strathern's dictum that "a person can be procre-
ated without at the same time reproducing other persons" (1995:
356) would thus seem to be strikingly true in this case. Indeed the
rabbinic prescription for non-Jewish donor sperm is predicated on a
sharp differentiation between procreation and reproduction. Thus
non-Jewish sperm is in many ways an ideal substance for the assisted
reproduction of Jews, for it conceives Jews who would otherwise be
literally inconceivable.[33]

Non-Jewish sperm donation was cautiously supported by two of
the foremost rabbis of the twentieth century, who offered lenient
rulings for the use of non-Jewish sperm in cases of severe male-factor
infertility.[34] According to Rav Shlomo Auerbach:

> It is possible that according to the letter of the law, it is not forbidden
> to do this (artificial insemination with non-Jewish sperm) with a mar-
> ried woman. The child born of this insemination does not need con-
> version, for he is absolutely Jewish, with no suspicion of being a
> mamzer. He is not disqualified from the priesthood (i.e., his descen-
> dants may marry Kohanim), the woman herself does not thereby be-
> come disqualified from marrying a priest, nor is she turned into a
> prostitute; and if she is a priest, the child is like her.[35]

According to Rav Moshe Feinstein: "With the husband's permission
and in the case where the infertile couple is suffering considerably,
one may permit the use of artificial insemination by donor, but specifically with the sperm of a non-Jew."[36]

Rav Feinstein's lenient ruling was met with such intense opposition that he ultimately chose to modify it.[37] Indeed, the question of
whether it is permissible to use non-Jewish sperm to impregnate
married Jewish women has been hotly disputed for decades and not
all rabbis imagine non-Jewish sperm to be so benign. Indeed, to
many rabbis, the use of non-Jewish sperm is considered an abomination. According to Rabbi Amsel: "It is impossible that any good for
Israel can come from such impure sperm in which its pollution re-
sides eternally. Even though the son of a Jewish mother and a non-
Jewish father is called a Jew, he is disqualified and the pollution of his

father is in him."[38] For Rav Waldenburg: "It is superfluous to describe the ugliness and pollution of this thing, in addition to the terrible destruction and the spiritual and frightening desolation that these creatures would introduce into the house of Israel in general, and the individual households who do it in particular."[39] Rabbi Teitelbaum (the Satmer Rebbe) asks: "Why should we permit the admixture of other lineages to contaminate the pure lineage of the House of Jacob?"[40] According to Rabbi Halberstam (the Bobover Rebbe): "Only a child who has a ritually fit Jewish father can be considered holy and of good lineage and only a son like this inherits all the special powers of the Jewish father and the holiness of the family and the tribe and indeed all the holiness inherent in the Jewish people ever since their pollution ceased with the giving of the Torah."[41]

Clearly, non-Jewish sperm is not considered to be neutral to these rabbis. Its inability to confer paternity and to create paternal relatedness does not cancel out its ability to "pollute" the Jewish kinship that already exists. In other words, the fact that non-Jewish sperm has no positive value does not mean that it has no negative value. In their reasoning, it is the ultimate manifestation of negative value. These responses are not based on legal reasoning but reflect a stream of Jewish thought that can be traced from Yehuda Halevi's *Kuzari* through the Maharal of Prague to *The Tanya* by Schneur Zalman of Liadi and up to the twentieth-century writings of Rav Kook.[42]

If we return to my earlier claim, that rabbis who make rulings about the use of reproductive technology are motivated by a desire to ensure Jewish survival, we can see why the concept of non-Jewish sperm as pollution is invoked as a reason to prohibit its use.[43] For these rabbis, the very survival of the Jewish people is at stake. Thus they logically prohibit artificial insemination with non-Jewish donor sperm.

Non-Jewish Sperm in Israel

In my discussions with Aryeh at PUAH, I learned how non-Jewish donor sperm is prescribed by contemporary orthodox rabbis for treatment of severe male-factor infertility. He explained:

It's not that a rabbi will say *lehatila* (from the beginning) that it is okay to use non-Jewish sperm, you have to look at the big picture. If a couple comes and asks whether they should use Jewish or non-Jewish sperm for artificial insemination, the rabbi will tell them to use non-Jewish sperm, not because it's good, but because it's better than using Jewish sperm. And some of the couples are desperate, and you have to make sure that they do something good rather than bad. It of course depends on the rabbi; some rabbis will say, "We in our community are very stringent and don't permit these things," it's one thing. But if you have a rabbi who understands alternatives, who sees the bigger picture, there are solutions. Look, it depends on how you ask the question, it's a *mahkloket* (a rabbinic dispute). The answer you get depends on how you ask the question; if you come and say, "Is it okay to use non-Jewish sperm for artificial insemination," of course the rabbi will say no. But if you come and explain the situation and say you are going to use donor sperm, which is better, Jewish or non-Jewish, the rabbi will say definitely: "not Jewish." Also, you have to understand, there is the halahkic question and then there is the spirit of the halahkic question (*ruah ha'Halakha*). If it is *d-oraita* (derived from the Torah itself) then there is nothing you can do, but if it is *d'rabbanon* (derived from rabbinic interpretation) then you have more room to work with, you can be more flexible.

I asked Aryeh where they get non-Jewish sperm in Israel. He told me that PUAH imports frozen non-Jewish sperm from America. I asked him why they don't use Palestinian sperm from the local population, and he replied: "No one wants Arab sperm. It is not a question of racism, it is a question of what people want. The fact is, it might be different if there were not other options, but there are, and that's what people want."

Aryeh's analysis of the market demand for non-Jewish sperm was contradicted in an interview with Dr. Zuckerman of Beilinson Hospital:

There's no problem acquiring the sperm of a non-Jew here in Israel. . . . A non-Jew can be a Muslim, a Circassian, a Druze, a Northern European, anyone who's not a Jew. If we're speaking of a Muslim, there are

[handwritten marginal note:] And people want racism!

plenty. If you want a child with blue eyes, well, there are enough kibbutz volunteers and students from overseas who are here. We'll manage. By the way, the Arab community, which also, of course, has fertility problems, uses many Jewish donors, which is against their religion. But they are upset, they want a child, and they don't ask needless questions. (Devorah Shapira, *Ma'ariv*, November 1994) (my translation)

I asked the head of the so-called non-Jewish sperm bank in Afula, Israel, whether he accepts sperm donations from Palestinians, and he replied: "God forbid! We get it from the kibbutz volunteers!" When I asked him who are the volunteers, he said, "Mostly Germans, English, Scandinavians."

Certainly, these attitudes reveal interesting inconsistencies and ironies in Jewish attitudes toward non-Jewish sperm. When theorized as a cipher for Jewish kinship, it is understood by rabbis who are positively disposed toward its use in monolithic, undifferentiated though neutral terms. Yet when evaluated by individuals as a choice for potential insemination, a whole set of different assumptions about non-Jewish genetic substance come into play; assumptions that reveal not only a set of assumptions about the role of genes in reproduction but also clear biases for European, or "lighter," sperm. In this way, infertile orthodox Jews are not unlike infertile people all over Europe and the United States, whose phenotypic preference for lighter sperm has been well documented. The question is whether preference for "lighter" sperm is the only issue at work here. This question becomes more complex when one realizes that preference for one type of sperm over another is being made in the context of highly charged, often antagonistic relations between Jews and Palestinians in Israel. It is made even more complex when one realizes that Palestinian sperm is being rejected in favor of what is often sperm from kibbutz volunteers, many of whom are German; interesting, given the historical experiences of Jews with each population.

Clearly, the use of non-Jewish sperm is the subject of some contention, both socially and legally. In practice, the development of intracytoplasmic sperm injection ("micromanipulation"), whereby individual sperm are microinjected into oocytes under a high-powered microscope, has eliminated many kinds of male-factor infertility,[44] which has in turn decreased the practical need to use donor sperm altogether. With the advent of micromanipulation, the reproductive futures of men who suffered from low sperm motility or low sperm counts can be assisted if just one individual sperm cell can be located and successfully inserted into an oocyte.

Nevertheless, the rabbinic discussions surrounding the use of non-Jewish sperm are valuable for what they reveal about rabbinic attitudes toward genetic relatedness and its role, or lack thereof, in the construction of paternity. Moreover, these debates continue to have social consequences not only because they determine the status of thousands of Jewish children who have been born with non-Jewish sperm but because they form the groundwork for rabbinic conceptions of paternity more generally.[45]

Conclusion

The advent of reproductive technology has forced rabbis to make their beliefs about paternity, maternity, and the origins of Jewishness explicit in order to create rulings that harness this technology to preexisting Halakhic conceptions of kinship. This process allows us to observe how symbolic meaning is ascribed to bodily substance in the rabbinic imagination. Moreover, it allows us to see that in the rabbinic imagination, paternity can have a variety of coordinates. Some rabbinic precedents suggest Jewish paternity is established through genetic relatedness; others suggest Jewish paternity is established through the act of sexual intercourse. Some rabbis argue that Jewish paternity can be established through the intentions and actions of a man who seeks to fulfill his obligation to be fruitful and multiply, regardless of how he links intention and action. Still others argue that genetic paternity can be totally erased, if it was ever understood to exist, as is the case when non-Jewish donor sperm is involved in conceptions with Jewish eggs and wombs.

That these rabbinic beliefs about kinship are contested only serves to emphasize how responsive reproductive technology is to the cultural context in which it is deployed. There is nothing inevitable about the social consequences of assisted reproduction; it does not necessarily privilege genetic relatedness, nor does it necessarily privilege other forms of relatedness. What is so unexpected here is that the diverse cultural uses of these technologies have exposed the traditional anthropological constructions of Euro-American kinship, as defined by blood, to be somewhat rigid. Rabbinic notions of kinship, by contrast, grounded as they are in an ancient, albeit unique, religious-legal system, have proven surprisingly adaptable to this new world of reproductive options. In Israel the social consequences of assisted reproduction depend on the goals of those administering it, the flexibility of the conceptual tools in which relatedness is imagined, and the willingness of social actors to innovate the symbolic meanings of kinship.

4

Eggs and Wombs:

The Origins of Jewishness

The next time I see you, I want to see an embryo in your womb.

—An Israeli ultrasound technician to an Israeli woman seeking to get
pregnant through in-vitro fertilization

In this chapter I focus on eggs and wombs as the determinants of maternal, religious, and national identity in Israel. There is a direct correlation between the social construction of motherhood and the social reproduction of the nation, for when the dominant religious culture provides the conceptual groundwork for kinship, as it does in Israel, and when this same religious culture determines identity matrilineally, as Judaism does, then eggs and wombs are not only the variables that determine maternal and religious identity, they are the variables that determine citizenship as well; for Israel is a nation-state where the positive determination of Jewish identity automatically confers citizenship.

The origins of maternality become complicated with the advent of ovum-related technologies. By forcing the biological roles of maternality to fragment into genetic and gestational components, ovum-related technologies force a conceptual fragmentation of maternality as well. As soon as eggs can be surgically removed from one woman's ovaries and transferred into another woman's womb, unprecedented reproductive possibilities are created. Traditional beliefs about the origins of motherhood are thereby challenged, creating Halakhic dilemmas for contemporary rabbis who must scramble to develop conceptual and practical strategies for determining where maternity is located: in the genetic substance of the egg? In the gestational environment of the womb? Or perhaps in both? The restrictions regarding the appropriate pathways of exchange for ova and the consequences for beliefs about maternity are the subject of ongoing rabbinic contestation, and appropriate policies regarding ovum donation have not yet been definitively formalized.

In the first section of this chapter, I describe an Israeli fertility clinic in which sperm is processed and eggs are surgically extracted from women's ovaries and reimplanted in women's wombs as embryos. Here I contextualize the practice of reproductive technology in Israel by focusing on the specific ways that the Halakhic imagination of women's bodies exerts a practical impact on clinical protocol. I hope this vivid ethnographic description of the medical and laboratory procedures in which eggs and wombs are the operable variables will make them more conspicuous subjects of analysis in the second section of the chapter. In the second section, I analyze the interpretive dilemmas facing contemporary rabbis as they attempt to understand the Halakhic problems posed by ovum-related technologies. These rabbis explicitly consider eggs and wombs as independent entities with various contingent statuses and identities. I examine the construction of maternity in a context where the technological expertise of fertility doctors and the conceptual categories of orthodox rabbis are understood as dynamically juxtaposed. Rabbinic debates about eggs and wombs are not simply theoretical, nor do their consequences only reverberate conceptually. These debates, and their outcomes, explicitly determine the appropriate rules for the appropriate conception of new Jewish citizens.

To be sure, the conceptual fragmentation of women's bodies into eggs and wombs is clearly problematic. It threatens to dehumanize women and to promote an attitude that views their bodies as detachable parts that can be combined and recombined in order to create legitimate maternity according to rabbinic specifications. Indeed, the egg-related procedures that I describe have been the subject of much feminist analysis and critique, for in these procedures women's bodies are routinely anesthetized, surgically invaded, and otherwise intruded upon, all in the name of conceiving children (Corea 1985; Stanworth 1987; Spallone 1989; Raymond 1993). However, a feminist critique of these procedures, while highly instructive, is not my focus here.[1] I am more interested in how these egg-related procedures challenge rabbinic and folk-cultural understandings of maternity.

The Setting: A Jerusalem Fertility Clinic

I conducted fieldwork in a small religious hospital in Jerusalem where most of the patients were either ultraorthodox Jews or religious Muslims, though secular Jews and Christian Palestinians also went there for treatment. What made this hospital "religious" was that all treatments and procedures that took place in the hospital were performed with careful consideration of Jewish law. The hospital's amenities were quite basic: there was no gift shop, no patient lounge, no cafeteria. The waiting room for the women's clinic was an uncarpeted hallway with chairs lined up along the walls and a bookcase full of prayer books in the corner. In the women's ward, there were five or six beds per room.

I spent several months in the fertility unit, which is part of the Department of Obstetrics and Gynecology. There were two different fertility laboratories in the hospital. In the first, the lab workers accept sperm samples from people undergoing fertility treatment; they check sperm for motility and mobility (spermogram) and process sperm for inseminations (swim-up, Percol wash, etc.). In the second, which was located next to the operating room in the women's ward, they perform in-vitro fertilization and micromanipulation; they also prepare gametes, zygotes, and embryos for surgical and intravaginal insertion into the womb. There were two incubators in this laboratory to store embryos until they were transferred into women's wombs. Toward the end of my fieldwork a new freezer arrived, which allows them to freeze embryos at the hospital as well.

There were four principal lab workers who rotated between the labs. All were secular Jewish women, a fact that will become important as we learn more about the working conditions in this clinic.

Because this was a hospital where treatments and procedures were performed with careful consideration of Halakha, often under the auspices of particular rabbis, only married couples with fertility problems were eligible for treatment; unmarried women were not accepted for treatment. Moreover, all the fertility procedures were monitored by *maschgichot,* or Halakhic inspectors, who watch each procedure to make sure that there is no untoward mixing of sperm and eggs.

The maschgichot were ultraorthodox women who were paid a nominal hourly sum to sit in the lab and supervise the lab workers as they process the incoming sperm and eggs. A maschgicha was required to be present in each lab whenever any sperm or eggs were being processed. They received their salaries from the hospital itself, though they worked under the auspices of PUAH (see chapter 3).

In this clinic there were five principal maschgichot who rotated shifts; all but one were older orthodox women who had many children and grandchildren of their own; the fifth was a younger woman who was married without children. At various stages of my research, each of them asked me detailed questions about what I was studying, and they seemed to take a keen interest in the ethical and religious questions that these technologies raised. Their job, however, was rather simple. As one maschgicha put it: "We make sure that Lichtenberg and Silberstein don't get mixed up." Meaning, of course, that they make sure that Lichtenberg's sperm and Silberstein's sperm do not get accidentally mixed up by the lab worker who may inadvertently use the same syringe, pipette, or catheter to handle sperm as she transfers it between test tube and petri dish. For if Lichtenberg's wife's egg was inadvertently fertilized with Silberstein's sperm, and the resulting embryo was implanted in Lichtenberg's wife for gestation and parturition, then Lichtenberg's wife would give birth to Silberstein's baby. This would obviously give rise to numerous social, ethical, and Halakhic questions. The maschgichot, then, are keenly aware of the larger implications of their work. Indeed, one of them told me that what she does is "holy work" and is more important than what the doctors and lab workers do to achieve pregnancy.

I was very impressed with how well the maschgichot seem to get along with the lab workers, considering the fact that the maschgichot literally peer over the lab workers' shoulders all day long. Amazingly, there seemed to be little animosity bred from what would seem to be an annoyance; on the contrary, one lab worker said she felt there was a need for supervision. "Four eyes are always better than two," she said, "and we also don't want to make any mistakes." Over many months, I observed only one professionally related altercation between a maschgicha and a lab worker, when an impatient client demanded that his sperm be processed quickly, and the lab worker complied, even though there was no maschgicha present in the lab to monitor the procedure.

The maschgichot often spoke Yiddish among themselves, as is common for many Ashkenazi ultraorthodox Jews. One maschgicha always kissed the mezuzah as she walked in and out of the laboratory. She liked to tell me how all of this technology would only work if God Almighty wanted it to work. Another maschgicha told me, quoting the *Talmud,* that there are three partners in the creation of a child: Father, Mother, and God. I jokingly added the names of the lab workers to her list, and she replied seriously: "They are not partners, they are only envoys" (*Hem lo shutafim, hem rak shlichim!*).

That the maschgichot and the lab workers were all women seemed to create a common, albeit limited, realm of conversation that revolved around shared family and domestic concerns like children's birthdays, weddings, brits, food, recipes, haircoloring, or diets. Although these discussions formed the constant backdrop to the rather extraordinary procedures that were taking place, the lab workers and the maschgichot did occasionally engage in more theoretical discussions about current events, politics, or religion. At the base of their shared working lives was an overlap of interests: both the lab workers and the maschgichot wanted infertile people to conceive children. Their mutual interest in this outcome was apparent every time we heard that one of the patients had gotten pregnant or given birth. Daily news in the lab consisted of who had gotten pregnant or who had not, and everyone seemed to share the pleasure or the despair of the news equally, and equally personally. When one of the patients in fertility treatment would give birth, they would all say: "Mazel Tov! One of 'ours' gave birth!" Indeed, when one woman gave birth to twins at the age of forty-two, after twenty-two years of infertility, all the maschgichot and all the lab workers went to the nursery to see "our babies."

One could argue that the matrix of relationships that exists in these fertility laboratories can be imagined as a fictive kin network, for it is within these relationships that conception occurs. The social practice of assisting reproduction creates an intimacy between the lab workers and the maschgichot in which the social pressure to achieve legitimate conception overwhelms the ideological and religious differences between the participants.

The positive working relationships and easy coexistence between the secular lab workers and the religious maschgichot was also indicative of the ways medicine and religion were structurally enmeshed at this hospital. One of the most striking examples of this intersection was manifest in the fertility clinic's patient flowcharts, where next to the spaces for recording hormonal treatments, blood tests, temperature readings, and ultrasound results, there was a space for recording the date of immersion in the *mikveh* (ritual bath). Immersion terminates the woman's status as niddah, rendering her ritually pure and thus able to engage in sexual relations with her husband. This state of ritual purity is also a crucial Halakhic prerequisite to conception, so it becomes important for the timing of inseminations and embryo transfer procedures. Recording the date of immersion thus becomes an integral part of the medical considerations in fertility treatment.

The influence of Halakhic concerns on medical protocol was similarly manifest in the prescriptive use of perforated condoms, which allowed patients to collect sperm for analysis while symbolically fulfilling the commandment to be fruitful and multiply. Clearly, the practice of medicine at this hospital was everywhere dependent on and determined by the interpretative framework of traditional Judaism.

In the Operating Room

To observe procedures in the operating room, I was given a pair of blue surgical scrubs, a gauze hat for my hair, and plastic shoe coverings for my sandals. I was allowed to roam freely in and out of the operating rooms, and once it became known that I was interested in observing procedures, the doctors often made a point of alerting me to upcoming operations.

When I began the fieldwork, I spontaneously identified with the anesthetized patients whose bodies were being slit, probed, suctioned, and sewn up. Gradually, I began to identify more with the doctors and nurses, who approached their tasks with dispassionate and pragmatic efficiency. The switch in identifications was important because it enabled me to endure surgical procedures that were often not only visually disquieting, they were clearly emotionally debilitating to the patients, with whom I often spoke before and after their procedures.

I observed a range of operations during my fieldwork, from cesarean sections to laparoscopies to zygote intrafallopian transfers and various other procedures. After they got used to seeing me in the operating room during various operations, the surgical staff began to ask me to help during some of the more routine procedures, like the oocyte pick-up. I would carry vials of ovarian fluid from the operating room to the lab, or help wheel patients in and out on gurneys. I was happy to help, though the patients would often ask me questions as if I were a doctor or a nurse, which made me somewhat uncomfortable.

The Oocyte Pick-Up

In an oocyte pick-up, ova are surgically extracted from a woman's hormonally hyperstimulated ovaries. The operation is a necessary prelude to in-vitro fertilization and micromanipulation and lasts approximately thirty minutes. It is an outpatient procedure; no major incisions are made in the woman's body, and recovery is usually rapid.[2] At the clinic I observed this procedure innumerable times. There were always three medical professionals present: the doctor who performs the procedure, the anesthesiologist, who anesthetizes the patient, and the nurse, who sets everything up and carries the ovum-bearing vials from the operating room to the laboratory (unless she has her hands full, in which case this task is performed by the visiting anthropologist).

During the oocyte pick-up, the patient is fully anesthetized and lies on her back with her feet in stirrups, as in a gynecological exam. The procedure takes place in a darkened operating room, since eggs are sensitive to light. The doctor begins by inserting a phallus-shaped ultrasound probe into the patient's vagina. Attached to this probe is a hollow aspirating needle that the doctor uses to pierce the egg-bearing ovarian follicles; the aspirating needle must pass through the walls of the vagina to reach the ovary, which produces some minor bleeding.

The ultrasound image of the ovaries guides the doctor to the follicles and allows her to see when and what to pierce. There is considerable skill involved in successfully locating and piercing the follicles, and the doctors I observed all appeared to be very adept at this procedure. Certainly, one needs to know how to operate the piercing needle manually and how to identify follicles on the ultrasound screen correctly. It is not always easy to tell a cyst from a follicle; both appear as round, grayish blobs. When the doctor finishes, she gauges the thickness of the endometrium on the ultrasound screen, which helps her determine what form of embryo transfer to perform. There are three standard forms of embryo transfer: gamete intra-fallopian transfer (GIFT), zygote intrafallopian transfer (ZIFT), or intravaginal embryo transfer. The first two are surgical procedures, the third is not. To be sure, a host of considerations determine what kind of embryo transfer will be most effective, depending on the nature of the patient's infertility and the quality of her reproductive genetic material. For instance, a patient with blocked fallopian tubes would be unlikely to benefit from the ZIFT procedure, which involves the surgical implantation of zygotes into the fallopian tube with the expectation that the resulting embryo will drop down through the fallopian tube into the uterus.

The most significant difference between the oocyte pick-ups I observed was the number of eggs retrieved. All the women who undergo the procedure have taken hormone therapy to hyperstimulate their ovaries into producing an abundance of eggs. Younger women often respond better to the hormones, however, and generally produce more and better quality eggs than older women. Success in such an operation is measured in the number of eggs retrieved; the doctor does a thorough check of the ovaries after she has finished to make sure that she has denuded all the egg-bearing follicles.

One of the most interesting aspects of the oocyte pick-ups I observed was that "Jewishness" was manifest in the way the medical procedure itself was performed. The doctor in charge explained to me how she performs an oocyte pick-up in such a way as to avoid rendering the woman a niddah as a result of the procedure. For if in the course of surgically denuding ovarian follicles of their eggs, the doctor inadvertently causes bleeding from the uterus, the woman could technically be considered niddah, defined Halakhically as a woman who is bleeding from the uterus.[3] A woman in niddah is considered to be ritually unclean for purposes of conception, and she may not conceive a child until she stops bleeding, observes seven "clean" days when she refrains from sexual contact, and immerses in a ritual bath. Thus, if while undergoing an oocyte pick-up a woman bleeds from the uterus, some rabbis would say that she is forbidden from receiving the subsequent embryo transfer two days later, for the resulting child could be considered a ben-niddah (a child of niddah) with all the associated stigma.[4]

There is a vast rabbinic literature that discusses the various sources, causes, and consequences of women's uterine and vaginal bleeding. A full examination of these Halakhic issues and the various determinants of niddah is beyond the scope of this discussion.[5] Suffice it to say that despite the lack of consensus in the rabbinic world on whether surgical procedures that cause uterine bleeding can render a woman a niddah, the Halakhic concerns are substantial enough that surgical protocol has been designed to circumvent any possibility that a woman undergoing an oocyte pick-up or other surgical procedure would be considered ritually impure and therefore ineligible for the subsequent embryo transfer.

The doctor who performs oocyte pick-ups explained to me that she avoids extracting eggs that are positioned in such a way as to require her to pierce the uterine wall with the oocyte pick-up needle, even if this means that she has to forego extracting an egg or two. She will only retrieve eggs that she can reach by inserting the needle through the walls of the vagina and into the ovary, since vaginal and ovarian bleeding are not considered to trigger the status of niddah. Strategic and ethical complications are presented in cases in which the ovary is positioned awkwardly behind the uterus in a way that would require the doctor to pierce the uterus to gain access to the ovary. If a woman has undergone hormonal hyperstimulation specifically to have her oocytes removed, should they not be removed simply because there's a chance that removing them would cause uterine bleeding? Are the medical risks incurred by the ovarian hyperstimulation enough to justify the extraction of eggs in a way that may cause the woman to become ritually impure? In other words, are the medical risks associated with oocyte pick-up sufficient to warrant a more lenient definition of niddah, if it would allow the woman to get pregnant?

These decisions are made on a case-by-case basis by the doctor, the patient, and the patient's rabbi. The doctor tells the patient if there has been uterine bleeding during the oocyte pick-up, the patient may then tell her rabbi, and the rabbi will then determine whether or not the patient is permitted to undergo subsequent embryo transfer without her child being considered a ben-niddah.

Obviously, there is considerable room for playing with boundaries here; a doctor who is under administrative pressure to increase the number of IVF pregnancies in his or her unit may be less forthcoming about the source of bleeding during IVF procedures if he believes that his patients will get pregnant as a result of the procedure. A patient who has been undergoing extended fertility treatment may be less likely to volunteer information to her rabbi that may negatively impact her treatment. And a rabbi may choose to grant a *heter,* or special rabbinic permission, for a woman to receive treatment who has been suffering unduly from childlessness, even if the medical procedures have caused some form of uterine bleeding. What is interesting here is that traditional Halakhic ideas about purity and impurity based on rabbinic understandings of bleeding from the uterus are explicitly translated into surgical protocol.

The oocyte pick-up is not the only procedure that the doctor performs with the practical intent of observing the laws of niddah. When the patient is not undergoing in-vitro fertilization and is simply receiving artificial insemination with her husband's sperm, the doctor often performs two inseminations, one immediately before and one immediately following ovulation. There are two primary forms of insemination: intracervical insemination, in which the sperm is inserted in a catheter and placed at the mouth of the cervix; and intrauterine insemination, in which the sperm is introduced through the cervix and into the uterus. The second form of insemination often produces some form of uterine bleeding. Thus, if the doctor thinks that the second insemination is going to be more successful, based on her assessment of the ultrasound imagery of the follicle, she will be careful to make the first insemination intracervical as opposed to intrauterine. That way, the uterus is less likely to bleed, and the patient will be "clean" for the second insemination. If she thinks the first insemination will be more successful, she will do an intrauterine insemination, and if any uterine bleeding occurs she will tell the patient, and the patient may then ask her rabbi, who may or may not grant permission for the woman to undergo a second insemination.[6]

The doctors performing these procedures are often secular and have had to learn the practical indications of niddah in order to work with ultraorthodox patients. The doctor who runs the clinic explained that she had to become expert at determining whether bleeding incurred during these procedures originated in the uterus, the cervix, or the vagina, because the patient trusts her to tell her where the bleeding is coming from. Then, if the patient has a question about whether or not she is in niddah, she can go and ask her rabbi. In sum, it is the doctor's responsibility to tell the patient if there is uterine bleeding, it is the patient's responsibility to tell her rabbi, and it is the rabbi's responsibility to determine whether or not this makes the woman ineligible for subsequent fertilization.

Fertilization

The oocyte pick-up procedure does not end in the operating room. The actual isolation and fertilization of the oocytes occurs in the laboratory. The nurse brings the vials of egg-bearing ovarian fluid from the operating room into the lab and gives them to the waiting lab workers. The lab workers then pour out the blood-colored, egg-bearing fluid into petri dishes and check it for eggs by swirling the petri dishes around under the microscope. When the lab worker locates an egg (which is identified as a small round shadow inside a little cloud of biological material) she sucks it into a pipette and transfers it into another petri dish, which she puts into the incubator until the sperm is processed for fertilization. The maschgicha is present, of course, and she watches to make sure the lab worker does not inadvertently use a pipette or a syringe from a previous procedure, which may carry traces of someone else's reproductive genetic material. The oocyte pick-up does not require constant monitoring; it is the subsequent fertilization that must be carefully watched, for that is when sperm may be inadvertently mixed up. During an oocyte pick-up, the maschgicha just makes sure that the petri dishes are correctly marked with the patient's name.

Once the eggs are isolated, they must be combined with sperm as soon as possible. Eggs cannot be frozen, and they expire within several hours if they are not fertilized; once fertilized, the resulting embryo can survive in an incubator for up to three days, or it can be frozen, but at the time of this writing, the technology had not yet been perfected so that eggs, by themselves, could be readily frozen.

The method of fertilization has been predetermined by the doctor, depending on several factors, including the number of eggs retrieved in the oocyte pick-up, the age of the woman, and, most importantly, the quality of the husband's sperm. Either the eggs are fertilized "in-vitro," which means that sperm is placed on the individual egg with a syringe, or the eggs are fertilized through micromanipulation, whereby one individual sperm is isolated and inserted into an egg under a high-power microscope.

In-vitro fertilization appears decidedly low-tech in comparison with micromanipulation. From what I observed, it is not technically difficult to squeeze sperm out of a syringe onto an egg in a petri dish. It is considerably more difficult to manipulate the controls on an enormous high-powered microscope in order to inject an individual sperm into the cytoplasm of an egg.

I watched dozens of micromanipulation fertilizations. There was a video monitor attached to the micromanipulation machine that projects the image the lab worker sees under the microscope: egg and sperm at 400x magnification. The egg appears as a huge round disk, and the sperm is clearly visible as a tadpole-shaped cell. The lab worker operates dual controls: with her left hand she manipulates the egg and with her right hand, the sperm. She must position the egg, isolate a sperm cell, induct it into the micropipette, pierce the egg's outer coating, release the sperm into the egg's cytoplasm, and quickly withdraw the micropipette before the egg's cytoplasm begins to seep out. The outer coating of the egg is visibly elastic and surprisingly resistant to penetration, considering that the micropipette has a sharp, beveled point. In the words of one lab worker: "In in-vitro fertilization, the sperm does the work, in micromanipulation, we do the work for him." In both in-vitro fertilization and micromanipulation the ova have to be carefully aspirated under the microscope so that the cumulus that naturally surrounds them is removed in order to facilitate fertilization. After the eggs have been fertilized with sperm they are placed in the incubator.

The Morning After

Twenty-four hours after the eggs and sperm have been combined, through either in-vitro or micromanipulation, they are removed from the incubator and examined under the microscope; successful fertilization is determined according to whether a dividing cell is visible. This day-old dividing cell, or zygote, can be surgically introduced into a woman's fallopian tube through "zygote intrafallopian transfer" (ZIFT). A detailed description of one particular ZIFT operation is illuminating for what it reveals about the day-to-day functioning of an Israeli fertility lab as well as the public culture in which conception and impregnation takes place.

It is the day before the national elections, so the city is buzzing with preelection propaganda. "Netanyahu is good for the Jews" is the latest slogan, and when I arrive in the morning the lab workers and the maschgichot are debating whether or not it is racist. I arrived in the lab late, about 10 A.M. and thought I had missed all the interesting procedures, but it turned out I had arrived just in time for a ZIFT on a forty-four-year-old woman. I first stopped into the lab and greeted Netta, the lab worker, and Bracha, the maschgicha, who were respectively preparing and watching some of the ten intra-uterine inseminations they had done that day. I walked over to the operating room, past the ultraorthodox patients sitting outside in the sunshine, past the bookcase full of prayer books and psalm books that stands in the hallway, and went into the second labora-tory, which they call the ICSI (intracytoplasmic sperm injection) room, for this is where they do micromanipulation. Pnina, another lab worker, was doing micromanipulation on some eggs that had been extracted in an earlier oocyte pick-up while lab workers Idit and Beatrice looked on. Suri, the maschgicha, was saying psalms in the corner, her surgical gauze cap falling off the blonde wig she wore in order to keep her hair modestly concealed, as is customary for ultraorthodox women. They told me there was a ZIFT going on, so I quickly went and put on my surgical scrubs.

When I entered the operating room, the patient was lying on the table, anesthetized, and Dr. Benjamin was waving her sterilized hands in the air to dry them before she put on her operating gloves. Dr. Elchanan was there, as were two nurses, a Russian woman anes-thesiologist, and a tall assistant whose job seemed to consist of mov-ing equipment around. I stood at the head of the operating table and watched as Dr. Elchanan slathered brown sterilizing liquid over the patient's abdomen. They were talking politics as they prepared for the operation. One nurse said the country would go to hell if Bibi (Netanyahu) was not elected; Dr. Benjamin countered with some pro-Labor statement; the anesthesiologist chimed in with her theory about the peace process, until finally Dr. Benjamin said: "Okay, enough, let's get started!"

The ZIFT is performed using a laparoscope. First, Dr. Benjamin inserted a hollow needle through a small incision in the patient's belly button. Then she inserted a tube into the needle, through which she pumped carbon dioxide in order to expand the abdominal cavity. She then took an instrument I called the "puncher," which is a long steel tube that has a rotating blade in the middle, squeezed the belly button, aimed the puncher, and jabbed it quickly down through the belly button, making a larger incision. She inserted a surgical video camera, which is like an eye on the end of a flexible metal tube, through the hole she had made in the belly button and peered around at the patient's innards. The image from the video camera was simultaneously projected on a television screen. The uterus and other internal organs appeared all reddish, yellowish, and shiny; Dr. Benjamin pointed at a reservoir of blood sloshing around one of the ovaries, which she said had been caused by the oocyte pick-up the day before.

Once she became visually acclimated to the caverns and slopes inside this woman's body, she made another incision, this time lower, about two inches below the belly button. Looking at the TV screen I could see the top wall of the abdominal cavity get depressed, then depressed again as the doctor tried to jab the scalpel through the abdominal wall. As I saw the doctor's arm slip suddenly down out of the corner of my eye, I saw the knife simultaneously enter into the abdominal cavity on the television screen.

They drained the leftover blood from the oocyte pick-up using a suction device that drew the blood out through a tube and collected it in a plastic jar. The end of the suction tube got caught here and there on the fleshy insides of the woman's abdomen, like the end of a vacuum on a carpet, and had to be gently disengaged.

After the blood was suctioned out, Dr. Elchanan inserted metal tongs through the lower incision and began fishing around for the fallopian tube, which was hidden behind the bulge of the uterus. She grasped the fallopian tube with the tongs and gently pulled it out from behind the uterus. She then picked at the fallopian tube with the tongs until the fleshy, free-floating end of it was exposed; it looked like a mushy, wet lily. Once she located this part of the fallopian tube, Dr. Benjamin called for Idit and Beatrice (the workers from the lab) to bring in the embryos. Idit had already positioned the embryos in a long, thin, and pliable embryo-transfer catheter. Beatrice brought the embryo-transfer catheter from the lab and stood next to the operating table. She and Dr. Benjamin then fed the embryo-transfer catheter through the hollow rod that was inserted into the lower abdominal incision (the tongs had been removed) and down into the mushy end of the fallopian tube. Dr.

Benjamin then released the embryos into the fallopian tube and withdrew the embryo-transfer catheter. The ZIFT was completed. Dr. Elchanan quickly withdrew the hollow tube from the lower incision and the video camera from the higher incision, and began to sew up the patient.

Dr. Benjamin yelled to me in the middle of this ZIFT procedure: "Sue, is it nice? We're making her a mother!" With this comment, Dr. Benjamin made the connection literal between the medical realm of the operating room and the symbolic realm of kinship. She made explicit what was implicit, that this technology created a new way to make mothers, a new origin myth, as it were, for the beginning of motherhood. Mothers are now something that doctors make women into, as if the surgical implantation of zygotes into the fished-out end of a fallopian tube is now how mothers are formed. The technological creation of motherhood is what Dr. Benjamin was drawing my attention to here. "Is it nice?" she asked me, somewhat proudly.

Two Mornings after the Oocyte Pick-Up

Forty-eight hours after the fertilization, the dividing cell is no longer considered a zygote, but an embryo, and may be introduced into the woman's womb intravaginally through an embryo-transfer catheter. On one slow Friday, Dr. Benjamin brought a patient clad in her surgical gown into the lab before the embryo transfer and said, "Devorah wants to see her children." So one of the lab workers opened up the incubator, pulled out a few petri dishes with the patient's name on them, and showed them to her. Then Devorah walked into the operating room, lay down on the operating table, and waited to have her "children" inserted into her uterus.

This kind of intravaginal embryo transfer was performed without any anesthetic, just like a pelvic exam. The most commonly used catheter for this procedure is called the "tomcat" catheter, a small plastic tube attached to the end of a special syringe. The lab worker uses the syringe to suck the two-day-old embryos out of the petri dish and into the catheter. The nurse brings the syringe with the embryo-bearing catheter attached to it into the operating room and gives it to the doctor. The doctor places the catheter into the woman's vagina, up through her cervix into her uterus and releases the embryos. The nurse then brings the catheter back to the lab, where the lab worker checks it to make sure that all the embryos were successfully released. Sometimes the woman's cervix is too tightly closed to allow the tomcat catheter to be inserted. I was present during one embryo transfer when they tried three different kinds of catheters. As Idit was preparing the last catheter, she said: "If this doesn't work, she'll just have to swallow the embryos like a pill!"

The embryo transfer takes two seconds if all goes well, and there are no complications. The nurse yells the patient's name into the lab, the maschgicha checks and makes sure that the lab workers are preparing the catheter with the right woman's embryos, the nurse brings the catheter to the doctor, and then the doctor simply places the catheter inside the woman's womb and releases the embryos. No sexual connotations, no fanfare, just impregnation. The doctor wishes the patient good luck, the nurse wheels the patient back to the ward, where she lies in bed for a few hours, hoping the embryos "take." I often chatted with the patients as they lay there waiting to "conceive," as it were. Many had been through the procedure multiple times. We would chat about their treatment cycles, how much pain they were in, or what they were having for dinner.

Ovum-Related Technologies: Halakhic Concerns

The Halakhic questions raised by ovum-related technologies are similar to those raised by artificial insemination, and there is a similar distinction between questions concerning treatments in which the couples' own reproductive genetic material is at issue and questions concerning treatments in which donated reproductive genetic material is used.

The rabbis' central concern in cases of ovum donation is: Who is the mother? The woman who donates the egg, or the woman who carries the pregnancy and gives birth? These are important questions in a kinship system that determines religious identity matrilineally, and even more so in Israel, where the positive determination of Jewish religious identity automatically confers citizenship.

The Halakhic problem here stems from the fact that ova were not thought to exist in the traditional rabbinic imagination, and there are therefore no clear precedents for deciding this question.[7] Rabbinic arguments about the appropriate use of ovum donation are therefore arguments about interpretation. Yet on what basis is the discovered "fact" of the existence of ova to be interpreted? The problem is that the texts that rabbis look to as Halakhic precedents regarding ovum donation do not explicitly contain the objects of knowledge (ova) that must be interpreted. In an interpretive framework for which legal analysis depends on conceptual grounding in traditional texts, it is difficult to construct an interpretation of an entity that was not known to exist in those texts.

In light of this interpretive dilemma, some rabbis advocate an appropriation of biogenetic understandings of maternity as a legitimate guide for rabbinic opinion. To these rabbis, it is legitimate to decide that maternity is derived from the genetic substance of the ova.[8]

Others argue that it is the woman who carries the pregnancy and gives birth who should be considered the mother, following the traditional dictum that while paternity is established at conception, maternity is established at birth.[9] This interpretation suggests that maternity should be determined at parturition. Still others argue that a child born as the result of ovum donation should be considered to have two mothers, one biological and one gestational.[10] Finally, some rabbis suggest that any child conceived with an egg extracted from an ovary, fertilized in-vitro, and reimplanted in a womb should be considered to have no mother at all.[11] No rabbinic consensus on these questions has yet been reached, though the majority opinion holds that the woman who gestates the child and gives birth should be considered the Halakhic mother.

Some rabbis have developed particularly novel explanations of these issues.[12] For example, Rabbi Ezra Bick (1993) advocates discarding the biological model, in which men and women are understood to contribute genetic material equally to an embryo, and in its place resurrecting what he calls "the agricultural model," in which conception occurs when men sow the seeds in women's fertile soil.[13] In this model the roles of men and women are not parallel but complementary; men are the active donors of reproductive material and women are the passive receptors of it. According to Bick, the determinant of maternal identity is "the ground from which a human being springs," which he reasons to mean that the gestational mother is the Halakhic mother.

In another example of contemporary Halakhic innovation, Rabbi J. David Bleich suggests a different way of using Talmudic agricultural analogies to understand where maternal identity is located. Bleich suggests that ovum donation can be understood as a parallel to agricultural cases in which there is continued growth and development of grain, trees, or vegetables after uprooting, reimplantation, or grafting onto older species. In these cases Bleich suggests:

> If this analysis of these Talmudic questions is accepted as correct, the question of maternal identity of progeny born as the result of in-vitro fertilization of a donated ovum may be regarded as analogous. Maternal identity is established in the first instance by the production of the gamete. The question is whether that determination is also dispositive with regard to the identity of the fetus whose later physical development is attributable to the gestational host or whether the identity of the developing fetus is derived from its nurturer, viz. the host mother, in which case the child could be regarded as having two mothers just as, for example, a single grain of wheat may be in part "pre-omeric" and "post-omeric." Since the Gemara leaves the basic issue unresolved and, accordingly, rules that the stringencies of both possible identities must be applied, a child born of in-vitro fertilization, on the basis of this analogy, would to all intents and purposes be regarded as having two mothers. (1991: 87)

Bleich's interpretation, while suggestive and compelling, does not resolve questions concerning the Jewish identity of a child who, for example, is conceived with a non-Jewish egg but gestated within a Jewish womb, or who is conceived with a Jewish egg and gestated in a non-Jewish womb. According to Bleich, such a child would have two mothers, but it is still unclear which mother confers Jewishness.

This Halakhic crisis, whereby the determination of maternity has been so profoundly destabilized by the advent of ovum-related technologies, will undoubtedly continue to reverberate in Israel with unpredictable social consequences. It has not prevented the practice of ovum donation, however; the drive to reproduce, and the technological potential presented by ovum donation, seems to have superseded any desire to await conclusive rabbinic rulings on the subject, even among the ultraorthodox population. To be sure, as with artificial insemination, ultraorthodox Jews follow the opinions of different rabbis in this matter, and some rabbis are much more lenient than others when it comes to ovum donation.

Moreover, rabbinic disagreements over the determination of maternal identity in cases of ovum donation have not slowed the secular rush to create regulations that legislate the appropriate uses of ovum donation.[14] Nor have these disagreements and Halakhic ambiguities prevented Israeli Jews, both religious and secular, from using the eggs of non-Jewish women to create Jewish babies.[15]

I asked Aryeh, the office manager of PUAH, about the use of donated non-Jewish eggs to conceive Jewish children. He explained that for those rabbis who believe that maternal identity is determined at parturition, a Jewish woman can give birth to a Jewish baby even if the baby is conceived with a non-Jewish egg. Other rabbis, who believe in the genetic basis for maternal identity, suggest that a child born of a non-Jewish egg to a Jewish mother needs to be converted to "sanctify the people of Israel."[16]

I then asked Aryeh whether women in Israel were using donated non-Jewish eggs to get pregnant. He explained:

Yes, it is happening every day, though it is a *mahkloket* [rabbinic dispute]. I should take you to Herzliya to see all the non-Jewish eggs women are using. [Eggs] from Arabs, or from Turkish women and other women who come here for treatment. You see, it is ILLEGAL in Israel to sell an egg. Because it is an operation and no doctor wants to authorize an operation that is not necessary, that is just to sell the egg. So women who are undergoing treatment are asked if they will donate eggs; I could show you one hundred people on the waiting list.

Aryeh mentioned that non-Jewish eggs also enter the Israeli ova marketplace via the many foreign women from Turkey, Europe, and the United States who come to private Israeli fertility clinics, like the one in Herzliya, in order to receive treatment. These women come to Israel because the reproductive services available are on the international cutting edge of infertility research and development. In addition, fertility treatment is often cheaper in Israel than in other countries. These non-Jewish foreign women, like Jewish and non-Jewish Israeli women, are routinely asked to donate any surplus ova "harvested" during their own fertility treatments. To be sure, the exchange of ova is not unidirectional. Non-Jewish Israeli and foreign women who receive treatment in Israeli fertility clinics also receive donated ova from Jewish women. Christian Palestinian women who undergo fertility treatment are also potential sources for, and recipients of, ova, although religious restrictions prohibit Muslim women from donating or receiving ova, as we will see below.[17]

In 1999 Israeli newspapers reported that Israeli doctors were setting up a fertility clinic in Cyprus to meet this demand for ova and to circumvent Israeli regulations against buying and selling eggs for profit. In the Israeli-run Cyprus clinic, women from Russia and other countries would be flown to Cyprus, paid to have their ova harvested, and then flown out; infertile Israelis and other nationals who are prepared to purchase ova wait in Cyprus and buy these freshly harvested ova (*Ha'aretz,* 16 February 1999).

It is important to understand that the Israeli ova marketplace is a competitive one. There is an enormous shortage of ova and a long list of women waiting for a donation, not unlike the predicament of those waiting for organ donations. A prominent lawyer in Jerusalem explained that the fact that there is such a critical shortage of ova was one reason that the ministry of health regulations allow unmarried women access to fertility treatment. To enlarge the pool of available ova, which by law can only be extracted from women undergoing treatment themselves, unmarried women were allowed access to fertility treatment so that their unused eggs, harvested to solve their own infertility, could enter the ova marketplace, provided they consent to donate extra eggs harvested in their own treatments. Aryeh explains the demand for eggs from unmarried women: "The most ideal situation is to have eggs from an unmarried Jewish woman (not necessarily single, but widowed or divorced as well). But it is better to use a non-Jewish egg than a married Jewish woman's egg."

The eggs of unmarried Jewish women are considered the most desirable eggs for donation to married Jewish women for two reasons: (1) there is a widespread social preference for eggs that are considered to be genetically "Jewish"; (2) eggs that come from unmarried Jewish women are often preferred because they circumvent the Halakhic problem of gestating an embryo that is the result of an adulterous combination of a married Jewish woman's donated egg and the sperm of a Jewish man who is not the egg donor's husband. As we saw in the rabbinic discussions of artificial insemination in the previous chapter, such a child could be considered a mamzer, with all the associated stigma.

It would seem, then, that a Jewish egg does not just carry the religious identity of the woman who produces it, it contains her marital status as well, and as her marital status changes, so does the status of her eggs. The rabbinic imagination would thus appear to have very innovative ways for thinking about the status of ova, for if a married woman is divorced or widowed her eggs simultaneously seem to lose their status as married for purposes of determining whether an adulterous union of sperm and egg has occurred.

Two Egg Stories

The practice of egg donation in Israel seemed to have curious and unpredictable dimensions. Though I did not conduct in-depth ethnographic interviews on this subject, I conclude this section with two particularly unusual conversations about egg donation I recorded, one with a fertility specialist and one with a religious woman undergoing IVF treatment.

The Doctor　In an interview with the head of one of the fertility clinics in Israel, I asked how he decides to ask a woman for an egg donation.

I only do it if the conditions are right, if we've harvested over fifteen eggs in her oocyte retrieval and if she's under thirty-five years old, so that the risks for her are less. I only ask if she's a secular or Sephardi Jew or if she's Christian; I don't ask if she's religious Ashkenazi or Muslim, since they are specifically forbidden from donating for religious reasons. Also, I only ask in cases in which it will not lower a patient's own chances of getting pregnant. I tell her not to feel any pressure or threat, but if she wants to help another woman who needs an egg, she can do it. I take off all the reasons to feel pressured and tell them that it is fine to say no.

It is totally anonymous, the other woman won't know it is she who gave the egg, and she won't know if there is a pregnancy. I will tell the woman who donates if there is a fertilization, because this is important if there is a problem of male-factor infertility with her husband; at least she will know if her eggs are fertilizable and good.

I then asked how long it takes to receive an egg donation at his clinic.

There is a waiting list of over a year until you are eligible for one donation. If that donation does not lead to pregnancy, you are put back on the end of the list. When there is money involved, at Herzliya for example, it can take only two–three months. When ova become available, women on the waiting list are called. Who receives the ovum donation depends on who has been waiting the longest, whose husband is at home to come in and fertilize the ovum, and simply who is in the right place at the right time. Again, for ultraorthodox women, constraints are much more explicit. They may only receive ova from donors that are deemed legitimate by their rabbis.

I was interested to know whether egg donors receive any form of monetary compensation at his hospital.

Not at this clinic. In Herzliya, where there is money involved, they get some form of compensation, like a reduced rate on their next round of fertility treatment. Here, they just get to know that they helped another woman, and they also get to know if their eggs were successfully fertilized, which can be important knowledge for their own treatment.

I concluded by asking how many egg donations he successfully performs per year.

Only four or five. Also, you have to understand that ICSI [intracytoplasmic sperm injection] has cut down on the number substantially. Because in problems of male-factor infertility before ICSI, there would only be enough sperm to fertilize five or six eggs, the rest would be thrown away, so you could say to the woman: "The excess eggs are going to be thrown away, would you consider donating them." But now with ICSI, if you have seventeen eggs, you can certainly find seventeen live sperm to inject in them. And then you can freeze the embryos. So the motivation to give is less, because instead of donating them or throwing them away, now you can keep them frozen as embryos for yourself.[18]

It would seem that at his clinic, only secular Jewish women, Sephardic Jews, and Christian Palestinians are asked to donate eggs. Muslim women and religious Ashkenazi women are forbidden from donating their ova for religious reasons, though they may be eligible to receive egg donations under the specific guidance of their respective religious authorities.[19] Potential egg recipients are informed of the ethnic and religious identity of the egg donor and may refuse to accept an egg donation from a woman on those bases, or based on her marital status, depending on how her rabbi, priest, or sheikh rules on ovum donation. Moreover, the doctor made it clear that he only asks for eggs from women under thirty-five, since younger women generally produce more and better quality eggs than older women. These practices were in no way unique but seemed to reflect the standard procedure for asking for egg donations at Israeli fertility clinics. They are extraordinary not just because they reveal a sophisticated understanding of the different religious attitudes toward the appropriate use of third-party donor material but because they reflect the pragmatic assimilation and integration of these differences into standard medical practice.

The Patient   An additional account of the practice of egg donation, this time from the patient's perspective, reveals similarly unusual and irregular features of this experience in Israel. This story was told to me by a woman I met in the waiting room of one of the large fertility clinics in Tel Aviv.

The doctor told me I needed an egg donation. So we registered for one in August. This entailed sitting with the egg donation clerk and telling her what we wanted in an egg donor. We told her we wanted a short woman of Hungarian/Byelorussian origin, cute and smart. Like me. She wrote down our preferences: short, brown eyes, brown hair, Ashkenazi, and asked me for a photograph. I sent her a letter with the photograph and in the letter I wrote: "Dear X, enclosed please find a photograph as you requested. I see you as the matchmaker between me and the woman who will donate her eggs in order to help us create children in the future (with the help of God). I bless you to choose this woman with wisdom, understanding, and truth. You are doing very important work. Sincerely . . . ."

That was it except for the fact that the doctor encouraged us to bribe her with chocolates in order to get a donation faster. So my husband and I went and bought a square of chocolate that said "Toda" (thank you) on it. We also [bought] a box of nice fancy chocolates, which we decided to give her in the event that I got pregnant. Since then the chocolates have become something of a joke between us.

Insofar as the questions about the birth mother, she told us that if I got pregnant, I would receive all the information about the birth mother. The egg donor would also be informed that I became pregnant so that she will know about her own fertility. If we both have children (God willing) then we will be informed about that, too.

I took estrogen tablets for two months without any phone calls telling us to come in. Finally, on the twenty-first day of the third month she called and told us to come in that night. We called PUAH and requested a maschgicha to meet us there, you had to order a maschgicha there, it was a secular hospital and they weren't part of the regular staff. The maschgicha was a nice woman named Bracha, she is Hasidic and lives in Petach Tikva.

She met us at the clinic, they handed us the condom and instructed us in how to use it properly. Bracha waited until we returned from our conjugal relations, took the sperm and carried it to the laboratory and gave it to the technician. She stood there and watched to make sure that no other man's sperm snuck in with ours.

We went home and waited. The next day we called and were told that we had four fertilized embryos growing away. We returned on Sunday, again with Bracha present, to unlock the precious embryos from the secured strongbox where they were stored. She gave them to the nurse to carry into the room where the insertion took place. The doctor was totally matter of fact and relaxed. I lay on my back for an hour, and then we went home. Two weeks later I took the test and I was pregnant; I was thrilled. But then I had a miscarriage. It has been a long road. Finally, we came to see the doctor here, and it turns out I don't necessarily need an egg donation. So now they took some eggs out of me and hopefully this time it will work.

Clearly, the social practice of egg donation in Israel is not governed by strict regulations. These dynamics will become even more pronounced in the following chapter, in which we will see how far ovum entrepreneurs are willing to go to make these valuable procreative objects available. The intense market demand for ova in Israel, fueled by the overwhelming desire to have children, creates complex dilemmas for both infertile and fertile Israeli women.

Conclusion

Ovum-related technologies bring into sharp relief a question central to the conceptualization of kinship: Where do mothers come from? From surgical procedures? From the genetic material in ova? From the gestational experience of carrying a fetus? From the act of parturition? In a kinship system that determines religious identity matrilineally, and in a country that confers citizenship based on religious identity, these questions become even more profound: where does Jewish identity, the primary substance of Israeli citizenship, come from? Is it embedded in bodily substance? Or is it created in gestational environment? Does the incorporation of non-Jewish reproductive material into the bodies of Jews change the meaning of being an Israeli? Or of being a Jew? One would think that what goes into making the body is what goes into making the body politic. In this chapter, I have attempted to illustrate how reproductive technology makes these questions simultaneously explicit in the medical, Halakhic and political realms and how the answers overlap, collide, and remain unanswerable.

Even though ovum-related technologies provoke deep questions about the origin of Jewishness, the rush to utilize these technologies surges forward in Israel. Contemporary rabbis remain confident that proper exegesis of traditional texts will yield cogent answers to current and future reproductive dilemmas. For example, J. David Bleich (1991: 95) points to the Talmudic discussion in the Gemara, Tractate *Niddah* 23b in which the Talmudic rabbis presciently discuss how to determine the identity of a human embryo gestated in and born from an animal womb. Bleich observes that this text may function as a precedent for determining the identity of a human being born from an animal womb, a technological innovation that he acknowledges may soon become a real possibility.[20] The rabbinic questions here were (and may be): Is a human being born from an animal womb a person? Or is such a creature an artificial person, a "*golem.*" The Talmudic rabbis debated these and other related questions that were once wildly hypothetical and yet now may become pragmatic: if a genetically human creature is born to a kosher animal, can it be slaughtered and eaten? Or the converse, if an animal-like creature is born to a Jewish woman, is such a creature a Jew, since it was gestated in and born from a Jewish womb? Based on rabbinic discussions of these questions, arguments are made that a being's identity should *not* be determined by its distinguishing *physical* characteristics, characteristics that today we would consider to be manifestations of its genetic substance, but should be determined by the identity of the being in which it was gestated and from which it was born.[21]

Bleich argues that to circumvent such questions, contemporary rabbis must begin to recognize genetic substance as a codeterminant of identity, together with the traditional determinant parturition. He argues that a strict adherence to parturition as the sole determinant of identity will create these and other serious interpretive problems as reproductive technology advances.

Bleich is not alone in expressing rabbinic caution and concern about the appropriate uses of these technologies, nor is he alone in making cogent, Talmudically based arguments for reshaping Jewish kinship thinking in light of them. He is in the minority, however, in advocating for genetic and gestational codeterminants of maternity; the majority of contemporary rabbinic decisors continue to adhere to the traditional notion that parturition from a Jewish woman must be the sole determinant of Jewishness.

Though traditional Jewish texts contain a rich variety of relational and reproductive metaphors, one must wonder if these technologies may one day provoke a conceptual crisis where the Halakhic tools for thinking about relatedness are finally called into question, where the Talmudic precedents for establishing Jewishness are ultimately revealed as anachronistic, and where the technologies for creating persons are acknowledged as truly novel and without metaphorical resonance in the traditional sources.

5

Multiple Mothers:

Surrogacy and the Location of Maternity

On March 7, 1996, a bill legalizing surrogacy was passed in the Israeli Knesset, making Israel the first country in the world where surrogacy contracts are publicly regulated by a government-appointed commission. The law was the subject of much dispute between lawmakers, rabbis, feminists, and other interested parties, but the pro-technology, pronatalist among them prevailed. It is now legal to contract for the services of a surrogate in Israel, provided that the arrangement is administered in accordance with the law and approved by the public-private committee appointed by the ministry of health to oversee surrogacy agreements.[1]

Central to this legislation is the provision that unmarried Israeli women are to be specifically recruited into the ranks of would-be surrogates. As the advertisement on the following page illustrates, women who are single, divorced, or widowed are targeted by contracting couples, who are legally required to seek out unmarried women for the provision of surrogacy services.

In this chapter, I first examine excerpts of the new surrogacy law and the politicking that went into its construction. I then analyze the motivations of potential surrogates as they appeared in various print and TV media. I have chosen media representations from approximately July 1995 to July 1996, the year in which the ministry of health regulations outlawing surrogacy were nullified, the new law was passed in the Knesset, and the first surrogacy contracts were legally approved. This period is particularly interesting for what it reveals about the media's role in manufacturing public consent for surrogacy agreements.[2] I hope that by analyzing what motivates unmarried women to become surrogates, albeit through the methodologically problematic medium of media representations, we can

אם את
מעוניינת
להיות
אם פונדקאית
רווקה/גרושה/אלמנה
נא לפנות לטל' **867578** בערב

If you are interested in being a
surrogate mother: single, divorced
or widowed, please call: 867578 in
the evenings. — *Jerusalem Weekly*,
2 August 1996.

begin to understand how they conceptualize their task. I argue that
their voluntary participation in surrogacy arrangements rests on specific beliefs about the biogenetic basis for maternality, beliefs that
enable them to "carry embryos" that they do not consider to be
"theirs," since the law requires that the ova used in the surrogacy
agreement may *not* come from the surrogate mother. To be sure, the
economic desperation of many unmarried women who volunteer to
become surrogates surfaces repeatedly as a significant motivating
factor, as does their "altruistic" desire to "do a good deed." Nevertheless, I suggest that their particular beliefs about the biogenetic
origins of motherhood are essential to their willingness to participate
in these agreements.

Surrogacy has been the subject of much scholarly attention, both in
Israel and elsewhere. Legal philosophers have explored the plausibil-
ity of creating contracts for motherhood (Field 1988; Shalev 1989),
feminists have criticized the potential exploitation of women and
the dangers of commercializing motherhood (Corea 1985; Corea et
al. 1987; Spallone 1989; Raymond 1993), ethicists and other social
scientists have explored the impact of surrogacy on the family and
the psychological effects of surrogacy on all the parties involved
(Ragone 1994; Bromham 1995). Although these discourses on surrogacy are instructive and have informed much of my thinking on
the subject, I do not intend to comprehensively analyze surrogacy,
nor do I intend to present a comprehensive analysis of Israel's new

surrogacy law. My intention here is twofold: (1) to show how the practice of surrogacy in Israel depends on divergent concepts of relatedness and shifting understandings of the origins of maternality; and (2) to place the practice of surrogacy in Israel along an emerging cultural continuum that explicitly values the reproductive capacities of unmarried women, whether they are enabled to reproduce for themselves through legalized access to state-subsidized reproductive technologies (as we saw in chapters 1 and 2), preferred as egg donors for married Jewish women (as we saw in chapter 4), or paid to reproduce for others in surrogacy agreements, as we will see in this chapter.

Key Texts of the Embryo-Carrying Agreements Law

Chapter B of the Embryo-Carrying Agreements Law (1996) reads as follows:[3]

2. The implantation of a fertilized egg whose purpose is the impregnation of a carrying mother for purposes of transferring the child to be born to the intended parents will not be executed unless all of the following exist:

— 1. An agreement in writing has been made between the carrying mother and the intended parents, which was approved by the approvals committee in accordance with the provisions of this law.[4]

— 2. The parties to the agreement are adult Israeli residents.

— 3. The carrying mother:

a) is not married; however, the approvals committee may approve a contract with a married carrying mother if it has been proven to the committee's satisfaction that the intended parents have been unable, after a severe effort, to enter into an agreement for the carrying of embryos with a carrying mother who is unmarried.

b) is not a relative of one of the intended parents.

— 4. The sperm used for the IVF is that of the intended father, and the egg is not the carrying mother's.

— 5. The carrying mother is of the same religion as the intended mother; however, if all the parties to the agreement are not Jewish, the committee is entitled to deviate from the provisions of this clause in accordance with the opinion of the religious representative on the committee (of that religion).

The law stipulates four main conditions for the practice of surrogacy: (1) all applications for surrogacy agreements must be approved on a case-by-case basis by a public-professional committee, (2) the surrogate and the contracting couple must be of the same religion,[5] (3) the sperm used to conceive the child must come from the husband of the contracting couple and the egg must come either from the wife of the contracting couple or from a donor (in other words, the surrogate's own genetic material may not be part of the conception), (4) every effort must be made to find a surrogate who is an unmarried woman, either single, divorced, or widowed. Only after a "severe" effort is made may a married woman be considered as a surrogate.[6]

These provisions were designed to limit potential rabbinic legal problems about the status of children conceived and born as the result of these agreements. They represent the outcome of prolonged political wrangling by orthodox rabbis and secular lawmakers who were closely involved with the drafting of this legislation.[7]

Knesset member Yossi Katz, head of the Subcommittee on Labor and Welfare, explained the political nature of these efforts in an interview with the *Sharon Area Local Newspaper* that appeared on January 19, 1996, two months before the surrogacy bill finally passed the Knesset. Katz explains why he met with the Chief Sephardi Rabbi Bakshi Doron to discuss the surrogacy bill:

> I was afraid that the law would not pass the Knesset. Like what happened when MK Yael Dayan brought the bill in front of the Knesset requesting equal rights for gay couples and it was struck down, I am afraid they will also not pass this bill. I am not a sucker; I don't want to bring the bill in front of the Knesset subcommittee and hear their applause, only to find that when I bring the bill in front of the whole Knesset it won't pass because of the religious parties. In areas where there is a religious sensitivity, I prefer to take into account all

points of view. We are talking about a very important law that will create the solution for tens of families that want children; surrogacy is their solution. In order to pass the bill with a majority, it has to speak not just to liberal groups, it cannot arouse controversy among the ultrareligious. You have to have a path in the middle, and I hope we have found that way. (my translation)

It is clear from Katz's remarks that orthodox rabbinic opinions of surrogacy were explicitly considered as part of the political process of drafting the legislation. This is not to suggest that the Embryo Carrying Agreements Law represents rabbinic consensus about the legitimacy of surrogacy, or that the final version of the law met with universal rabbinic approval. On the contrary, opposition to the law was fierce, particularly among many rabbis who saw its swift parliamentary approval as the result of political maneuvering by interested parties who pushed for the passage of the law regardless of the social and Halakhic consequences. In fact, many rabbis remain opposed to the whole surrogacy phenomenon. The final draft of the legislation, which states that a married woman may be contracted as a surrogate, came under particularly vehement criticism from the former Chief Sephardi Rabbi, Rav Eliyahu:

This Surrogacy Law should not have come into this world at all. Let me just take the law as it exists in front of me: "It is possible that in extenuating circumstances the surrogate may be a married woman." This is a disgrace to the people of Israel. The rabbi who approved this committed a sin; it is adulterous, promiscuous, and licentious.

So what if they exerted pressure on rabbis? The rabbis should have withstood the pressure before the elections. It explicitly says that the committee requires two doctors, etc., and a religious person. Who is this religious person? Where is the Chief Rabbinate? At least this religious person should be someone approved by the Chief Rabbinate!

As to the question: Is a woman who receives an ovum the mother in all respects? The answer is yes. The child belongs to the carrying mother. If a surrogate mother is a non-Jew or a mamzer, so the child is a non-Jew or a mamzer, the carrying mother determines the status of the child. A married woman may not donate ova nor may she be a surrogate mother!

To those who are considering using a surrogate, don't do it! Sarah, Rivka, Leah, and Rachel, our matriarchs, were all infertile, and they gave birth with God's help. So all you infertile men and women out there, pray to God Almighty and you will get a son or a daughter, don't contract a surrogate mother. And you should all have as many children as you can, which will speed the coming of the redemption.[8]

Despite the condemnation of Rav Eliyahu and other prominent orthodox rabbis, the Embryo Carrying Agreements Law must be understood as legislation that was explicitly crafted to accommodate Halakhic concerns about the status of children conceived and born as the result of these agreements. That the surrogate is ideally unmarried is a concession to rabbinic concerns about the status of a child born to a married surrogate mother. Many rabbis could consider a child born to a married surrogate mother to be a mamzer (a child conceived in an illicit sexual union), and such a child would be subject to severe social stigmas. The illicit sexual union at issue here is that between the contracting husband's sperm and the *womb* of the carrying mother. Many rabbis contend that if a married Jewish woman were to carry an embryo conceived with a Jewish man's sperm other than her husband's, the act could be considered equivalent to an act of adultery between a married Jewish woman and a Jewish man who is not her husband, even if the conception did not involve the surrogate's ova, took place outside the body, and was not achieved through sexual intercourse. As such, it is an act that would have direct consequences for the status of the child so conceived and gestated. By legislating that unmarried women must be sought as surrogates, these rabbinic concerns about the potentially adulterous nature of surrogacy contracts are effectively circumvented.

That the would-be surrogate must be of the same religion as the contracting wife reflects a concession to a different rabbinic concern about the status of the child conceived in a surrogate mother agreement. We saw in chapter 4 that there is an ongoing rabbinic debate about whether genetics, gestation, or parturition is the significant determinant of maternity; this question is obviously very important in Judaism where identity is determined matrilineally.[9] At present, the majority of orthodox rabbinic decisors agree that the woman who gives birth to a child determines its religious identity. Therefore, most rabbis rule that the surrogate mother is considered to be the Halakhic mother of the child. Thus if the embryo conceived with the genetic material of a Jewish couple is gestated to parturition in a Jewish womb, the child is considered to be Jewish, because the womb in which it grew and from which it was born was a Jewish womb. By contrast, if the embryo of a Jewish couple is gestated to parturition in a non-Jewish womb, the child is not considered to be Jewish.[10] Hence the preference for Jewish surrogate mothers.

By requiring that the surrogate must be of the same religion as the contracting couple, secular legislators accommodated the predominant rabbinic belief that the surrogate mother is the Halakhic mother of the child conceived and born in a surrogate-mother agreement. That way, the Halakhic relationship between mother and child, which acts to transfer Jewishness from mother to child, could be effectively safeguarded for the purposes of reproducing a Jewish child who would in turn be raised by a Jewish couple.

The whole enterprise of legalizing surrogacy arrangements raised profound ideological questions about authorizing an arrangement intended from the outset to create a child for purposes of subverting parental relationships considered immutable by Halakha. Specifically, secular lawmakers were confronted with the question of whom they were going to deem the mother of the child pursuant to secular law. The specific ideological question here was: if the surrogate is considered the mother according to Halakha, can she be divested of that status by means of secular legislation authorizing surrogacy agreements?

Despite the absence of Halakhic precedents that allow for the transfer of parenthood in secular legal terms, Israeli legislators created a new mechanism for the creation of parenthood when drafting the Embryo Carrying Agreements Law; this mechanism was called an "order of parenthood" (*tsav horut*) and was innovated specifically to allow these agreements to go forward.[11] Legal parenthood is defined in the law as "an order regarding the guardianship of the intended parents over the child and the existence of a parental relationship between them."[12]

It is impossible to know what kind of behind-the-scenes maneuvering went on regarding this question or the other profound questions involved in the legislation of surrogacy agreements. What we have before us is the final version of the law, in which it is expected that the contracting couple will be issued a "parenthood order" upon the birth of the child. The law states:

Upon the birth of the child, the child will be in the custody of the intended parents and the responsibilities and obligations of a parent toward a child will be incumbent on them. (Chapter C [10a])

Within seven days after the date of the birth, the intended parents will submit a motion for the issuance of a "parenthood order"; if the intended parents do not submit a motion as stated, the social worker will submit a motion by the means of the representative of the attorney general. (Chapter C [11a])

Upon the issuance of the parenthood order, *the intended parents will be the parents and the sole guardians of the child and it will be their child for all purposes.* (Chapter C [12a], Abra Siegel's translation; emphasis mine)

Something very interesting was accomplished in the passage of these rules. Halakhic conceptions of maternality and the origin of relatedness, so crucial to the provisions that the surrogate mother be unmarried and "of the same religion" as the contracting couple, have been suddenly submerged. The surrogate mother's status as the Halakhic mother has been curiously elided. Thus it would seem that a Halakhic, "naturalistic" definition of motherhood is assumed to be operational while the fetus is gestated and born (and while its identity as a Jew presumably forms), but within a week of parturition, a secular, legalistic definition of motherhood takes over, allowing the contracting mother to claim custody of the child.[13] What emerges here is an expedient tension between two contradictory legislative notions of the family: in Jewish law, the family is a natural construct in which statuses and identities cannot be changed by legal means, whereas in secular "Euro-American" law, and its Roman antecedents, the family is a legal construct that can be reconfigured through the use of legal fictions. In other words, in the Jewish legal system, once a mother always a mother; under secular law, mothers are only mothers if the law says so. This tension thus creates a remarkable legal dynamic: not only is the surrogate's womb rented in Israeli surrogate-mother agreements, the Jewishness of her womb is rented as well, since it is only by renting a specifically Jewish womb that the organic ability to confer Jewishness can be legally accessed.

We have seen how secular lawmakers were willing to incorporate Halakhic understandings of relatedness in order to appease religious Knesset members and garner their political support for the new law. However, one must conclude that this legislative sleight of hand, in which Halakhic definitions of the origins of maternality are simultaneously recognized and not recognized, was designed to ensure the reproduction of full-fledged Jews in surrogacy agreements.

Public Discourse on Motivations

The legal inconsistencies that inform the legislation of surrogacy agreements seem to be of little concern to potential surrogates. Prior to January 1998, potential surrogates were overwhelmingly represented in Israeli public discourse as economically disadvantaged free agents, motivated by the desire to help others and make money at the same time.[14] In January 1998 the Israeli media reported that the first surrogate to be contracted under the new law had a cesarean section in her eighth month in order to remove twin babies she had gestated after an extremely physically and emotionally debilitating pregnancy. A barrage of public concerns about surrogacy suddenly emerged in the media, which raised doubts about the ethical basis for surrogacy and called for a reexamination of the new legislation. The government's response was to shield subsequent surrogacy agreements from such intense media scrutiny. The practice of surrogacy continues, but it is simply concealed from the glare of the media spotlight.[15]

Rent the Womb to Feed the Children

In Israeli news articles on surrogate motherhood, the surrogate's economic motivations were often foregrounded as motivating factors. In an article for the "Sharon Area Local Newspaper" (19 January 1996, my translation) the reader is introduced to ZH, a divorced woman from Herzliya who recently advertised her desire to be a surrogate. "What caused her to do it?" the reporter asks.

> She has 20 NIS ($6) in her wallet until the end of the month, and she has 35000NIS ($1200) of debts. She owes thousands of shekels to the bank, the kindergarten, the supermarket, and for city taxes. . . . "In short," the woman says, "I thought surrogacy could help me get my life together. In order to get out of the mud that I am in today, I would need to work two or three years in hard conditions, and it doesn't bother me at all to be pregnant and give birth. I thought that if it goes easily, why not? To me, it is like someone who rents their car, I rent my womb, and then cut the connection. Now I work outside the house a lot and my children suffer; with surrogacy I will earn more money and be able to be at home with my children."

In a similar article (*Ma'ariv*, 10 July 1996), the potential surrogate is described as a divorced thirty-four-year-old woman from the center of Israel with two small children. The woman explains her economic motivations for becoming a surrogate as well as her "altruistic" desire to help a couple in need:

> I came to this decision out of financial motivations. I was married for four years. Already after the first child I thought about getting divorced. My husband worked on and off, and whenever he got his salary he wasted it. I went to work in a factory. We lived with my parents and it was difficult. My first motivation was financial; I have to worry about the future of my children, I want to give them a good education and a warm home, and I don't have the means. I initially thought about it as a financial solution, but after I met Tova [the contracting mother], I immediately agreed. Afterward we became friends,

and now I am doing it with all my heart. . . . Besides that, I have two small children at home that are mine, and I am doing everything, including being a surrogate, out of concern for them.

In an August 1995 article in the popular women's magazine *L'Isha*, we meet Zehava, a divorced woman from Petach Tikva who has already had two children of her own. Again, financial need and altruistic motivations are foregrounded:

> I want to be a surrogate, because it's a *mitzvah* [good deed] and because of the money. $10,000 is a lot of money for me; I am not afraid of pregnancy and there is no doubt that I will give up the child, because it is clear to me that he is not mine at all. Besides that, I have experience separating from children, because my children were put up for adoption and I have no connection with them.
>
> I don't want any more children because I don't have the means to raise them. I think that I could be a surrogate two or three times. I already met with a couple from the north of the country. The wife has no womb, and I really want to help them. We decided we'll start working on it as soon as surrogacy becomes legal. . . . the decision is that I will do the medical examinations and at every stage of the pregnancy I will show them the results, and she will be in the delivery room with me and will receive the baby immediately.

Finally, the desire to become a surrogate in order to transform one's economic, and indeed social, reality is perhaps most starkly represented in the following article, "Daughter of a Rabbi Wants to Be a Surrogate" (*Yediot Aharanot*, 19 January 1995).

> The drug-addict daughter of a well-known rabbi in Ashdod has a unique idea about how to get out of the downward spiral of drugs. This twenty-nine-year-old woman, who owes about $50,000 in debts, is prepared to be a surrogate in return for money. The money that she will receive she will use to pay back her debts and to recover from drugs. "I am prepared to be a surrogate in return for money, and before I am a surrogate I will use the money to get off drugs. After I give birth and I receive all the money I will pay back my debts and begin a new

life. If I am not able to be a surrogate I will stay in the world of drugs and crime," so says the woman.

These women clearly articulate economic need as a motivating factor in their decision to be surrogates. It is interesting to note that unmarried women with children, who are often more economically vulnerable in any event, are preferred as surrogates by many contracting couples. Their fertility is proven, and it is assumed that they can anticipate their physical and emotional reactions to pregnancy. In addition, unmarried women with children are considered to be more "reliable" surrogates, that is, more likely to honor the contract and give up the child after birth.[16]

It is extremely unlikely, however, that surrogacy represents any kind of long-term solution to the economic impoverishment of the women who contract to be surrogates. The sum of money that a surrogate receives for "carrying an embryo" is determined by the government-appointed commission and is currently fluctuating between ten and fifteen thousand dollars. Moreover, would-be surrogates are legally prohibited from receiving any more money for their services than that recommended by the government-appointed committee. Indeed, owing to the widespread concern that the legalization of surrogacy would lead to its commercialization, payment to the surrogate is legally articulated in terms of "compensation."[17] This wording effectively criminalizes payments to surrogates that exceed the sum determined by the government-appointed commission. If the surrogate receives, or is offered, a sum higher than that determined by the approvals committee, both she and the contracting couple are subject to a prison term of one year.[18]

By "compensating" instead of "paying" her, the surrogate is not privileged to receive the benefits of freedom of employment legislation, which allows market competition to set prices. Interestingly, surrogacy centers that act as brokers between surrogates and contracting couples, by making connections between the two parties and providing counseling and other forms of support, are covered by freedom of employment legislation. They may charge as much as they like for their services. By regulating the sum of money given to the surrogate, and by keeping that sum so relatively low, the government-appointed commission thus effectively ensures that surrogacy remains an affordable, "middle-class" solution to childlessness.

"It's Not My Child"

The desire to become a surrogate in Israel is informed not only by economic and so-called altruistic considerations but also by certain specific beliefs about the origin of maternal relatedness. Although a would-be surrogate's economic reality may motivate her to enter into a surrogacy agreement, her understanding of the origin of maternal relatedness, specifically her belief that the child she gestates is not "hers," is crucial to her willingness to participate in such arrangements. If the law did not specifically proscribe the use of the surrogate's genetic material in the conception of the embryo, one could assume that financial considerations might nevertheless override concerns about maternal relatedness if her genetic material was used, but such an assumption is merely speculative, given the legal prohibitions against this practice.

In interviews with potential surrogates and contracting couples as they appear in Israeli public discourse, it seems that neither group privileges Halakhic understandings of relatedness over biogenetic understandings of relatedness. In these narratives we repeatedly hear both the surrogates and the contracting couples emphasize that because the egg used to conceive the embryo gestated by the surrogate does not come from the surrogate herself, the resulting child does not belong to the surrogate, it belongs to the contracting couple.[19] As one potential surrogate explains: "I already know that it will be their child, not my child. I am just putting their child in my womb. The child will have his father and his mother, he is not from my egg and not from the sperm of my partner, it's not my child" (*Ma'ariv*, 10 July 1996).

Similarly, zh in Herzliya explains what happens when people call and answer her advertisement about being a surrogate:

First of all they ask me about my origins, and I don't understand why that interests them. The embryo will be conceived with an egg and sperm that are not mine, and I will not have any genetic influence on the pregnancy. What scares me is when people call and ask me to donate my egg. To use my egg for a pregnancy means to put MY child up for adoption, and I am not prepared to do that. An embryo conceived with the egg and sperm of a couple that grows in my womb is very distant from me, and that's the purpose . . . the egg and the sperm will not be mine, and I will just give my womb to rent. It's exactly like giving my child to a babysitter to take care of: she feeds him and takes care of him. So what? Does a babysitter think that the child is hers just because she gives him food and takes care of him?

The reporter then asks her what she will tell her own children: "I will tell them that there is egg and sperm, and a woman needs space in her stomach in order for a child to develop. And there are some mothers who can't contain in their stomachs the development of the egg and sperm, and I have the ability. I will tell them that the baby is not ours, and what I give birth to does not belong to the family" ("Sharon Area Local Newspaper," 19 January 1996).

This common perception that "ownership" of children can only be established through genetic relatedness was again reinforced in a March 1996 broadcast of the popular TV program, *The Yael Dan Show*. Yael Dan interviews a would-be surrogate named Rosa, a well-dressed blond woman who looks to be in her mid-thirties. She tells a sad tale of her immigration to Israel at the age of sixteen from the Caucasus Mountains; her ensuing marriage to a man who beat her, raped her, and tried to set her on fire; and her subsequent divorce. Rosa has two daughters from this marriage and describes her desire to be a surrogate as a desire to do a mitzvah and to redeem the suffering she and her children suffered at the hands of her violent ex-husband. "For what do we bring children into the world?" she asks, "so that it will be bad for them? No! So that it will be good for them!" Rosa explains that she would "love and caress a child that she carried in her womb, like someone who received something very valuable to guard, knowing that she would give it up at the end, that it wouldn't be hers. . . . I understand that it is something that will be with me for a few months and then it will be gone, shalom. Like a boarder in my house, like a boarder in my body." It is interesting to note that the Hebrew word for surrogate is "pundakit," which also translates as "innkeeper." Rosa's description of the fetus as a "boarder in her body" emerges directly out of the very language in which surrogacy is articulated in Israel.

In the August 1995 article in *L'Isha,* one husband, Eli, explains: "The sperm and the eggs are mine and Ilana's, it will be our child in every way. We just want to use the services of a womb that we don't have." In the same article, Galit explains that she and her husband "are not asking for the donation of sperm or eggs, everything is ours. We just don't have a human incubator for our embryo."

In an article titled "My Womb, Her Baby" a would-be surrogate in the center of Israel says that the idea of becoming a surrogate appeals to her because she is looking for work she can do at home while she takes care of her two small children. She says she considers surrogacy "pregnancy without ego, because the pregnancy is not mine." In response to the reporter's question, How can you give up a baby that grew in your womb? she says: "It is exactly this question of the ability to choose which differentiates us from animals. When I make a child for someone, I know from the beginning that *it is not mine*" (*Ma'ariv,* 21 July 1996, emphasis mine).

In these narratives we see how both surrogates and contracting couples articulate beliefs that suggest that genetic inheritance is the determining factor in the creation of parent-child relationships. The belief in biogenetic relatedness as the ultimate determinant of kinship is crucial for the practice of surrogacy in Israel. Not only does this belief allow surrogates and contracting couples to rationalize their actions in the accepted terms of authoritative scientific discourse, it is politically expedient in that it paves the way for the practice of surrogacy by helping normalize the notion that unmarried women are reasonable women and will make reasonable surrogates. To practice surrogacy, popular suspicions about the motivations of the would-be surrogate must somehow be mitigated. What kind of woman would give up her "own" child? What kind of woman would give up a child to whom she gave birth? Isn't there something "unnatural" about such a woman? The fact that biogenetic relatedness is emphasized in popular discourse on the subject helps allay public fears about the surrogate as a dangerous and suspicious character whose participation in a surrogacy agreement threatens conventional notions of motherhood. As long as the child she gives birth to is not considered to be "hers," then all the troubling implications of a mother who enters into a contract to sell her baby can be made invisible. Surrogacy depends on a curious contradiction: the extraordinary measures that an infertile couple takes to realize their "right" to have a child of their own, and the ideology of the nuclear family on which these measures implicitly depend, are enabled by the mandated erasure of the "natural," and in this case Halakhic, bond between a mother (the surrogate) and her child. But if the child she gives birth to can be conceptualized as not "hers," then these troubling aspects of surrogacy can be minimized.

That surrogates and contracting couples imagine maternal relatedness in terms that are explicitly contradictory to rabbinic beliefs on the subject is evidence of the dynamic coexistence of competing kinship cosmologies in Israel. Thus the dominant Halakhic belief that maternity is determined by parturition and the "secular" belief that maternity is determined by biogenetic relatedness can be seen as two halves of a rather extraordinary conceptual whole. The social practice of surrogacy in Israel depends on the intersection of these complementary understandings of the origins of maternal relatedness.

Shellee Colen's term "stratified reproduction" illuminates an additional dimension of surrogacy in Israel, for it helps explain reproduction as a social phenomenon in which some reproductive futures are privileged over others.

By "stratified reproduction" I mean that physical and social reproductive tasks are accomplished differentially according to inequalities that are based on hierarchies of class, race, ethnicity, gender, place in global economy, and migration status and that are structured by social, economic, and political forces. The reproductive labor — physical, mental and emotional — of bearing, raising, and socializing children and of creating and maintaining household and people (from infancy to old age) is differentially experienced, valued, and rewarded according to inequalities of access to material and social resources in particular historical and cultural contexts. Stratified reproduction, particularly with the increasing commodification of reproductive labor, itself reproduces stratification by reflecting, reinforcing, and intensifying the inequalities on which it is based. (Colen 1995: 78)

We can see how the social practice of surrogacy in Israel is indeed "stratified" according to various inequalities; specifically, inequalities of economic class and marital status. The ability to pay for surrogacy services has been translated into a legal entitlement to parenthood in the new law. The fact that contracting couples are inevitably wealthier than would-be surrogates emphasizes and reproduces these class-based inequalities. In addition, the fact that unmarried women are prohibited from contracting surrogates emphasizes a different order of inequality embedded in the new law: that between married and unmarried women. It is the unmarried woman who is targeted by this legislation as the one who should reproduce for the married woman. This unidirectional flow of reproductive services from unmarried to married Jewish women, then, is one way that the reproduction of the traditional family is given privilege in the legislation of these technologies in Israel.

What is interesting, however, is that although the parental rights of the surrogate may be denied, the parental rights of unmarried women as a social category are not. We have seen how the reproductive futures of unmarried Israeli women are specifically valued in legislation regarding access to reproductive technology. Thus, although the reproductive features of unmarried women are explicitly valued by the state, they are valued, and indeed assisted, differentially according to a range of factors, including most importantly economic class.[20] What differentiates unmarried women who are recruited into surrogacy agreements from unmarried women who choose to have children via artificial insemination are significant economic inequalities. In other words, some unmarried women are encouraged to reproduce for others while some are encouraged to reproduce for themselves. Although class-based differences between and among unmarried women in Israel determine how the state envisions their reproductive futures, the point is that their reproductive futures are envisioned by the state, in both conceptual and practical terms.

One could argue, then, that in the pronatalist drive to reproduce via reproductive technology in Israel, a strange reliance on the bodies of unmarried Jewish women is being constructed. These bodies, these Jewish wombs, these sources of Jews, as they exist in the pronatalist Jewish state, are being put to reproductive work. The state makes extraordinary provisions to recruit unmarried Jewish women into the ranks of those who reproduce; whether they reproduce for themselves or for others, they reproduce Jews, and by reproducing Jews they are reproducing citizens. Thus the reproductive future of the unmarried woman is valued, whether she be a surrogate, an egg donor, or an autonomous mother.

That the bodies of unmarried women are understood as reproductive resources in these pronatalist efforts to reproduce Jews has disturbing implications. An article in an Israeli newspaper describes a so-called entrepreneur in Beer Sheva who stated that now that surrogacy was legal in Israel he was exploring the possibility of "exporting" Israeli surrogates to infertile Jewish couples abroad, especially in the United States, where one can command high rents for Jewish wombs ("Womb for Rent," *Yediot Aharanot,* July 1995). According to this would-be womb merchant, infertile Jewish couples will pay high prices not just for Jewish surrogates but for Jewish eggs as well, a product he is also eager to provide. In chapter 4 we learned how the demand for ova in Israel has been met with the creation of an offshore ova market in Cyprus.

The potential for an international black market in the reproductive capacities of women is troubling at best, for if it is true that where there is a demand, there will inevitably be a supply, the reproductive capacities of women both Jewish and non-Jewish, married and unmarried, may be exploited in both the local and international marketplace. Such services may have particular appeal to those concerned with the Halakhic status of their children, who know that they can conceive Halakhically kosher Jewish babies with non-Jewish eggs and unmarried Jewish women's wombs. Jewishness is a scarce commodity, and until the advent of reproductive technology it was a commodity that could not be bought, sold, or transferred at will. Moreover, it is a commodity that has specific importance for the determination of citizenship in the state of Israel, where all Jews, as defined by those who are born to a Jewish mother, are guaranteed citizenship.

It seems, then, that the advent of the new reproductive technologies, and the attendant fragmentation of maternity into commodifiable components, may ensure that some form of motherhood is a social inevitability for all Jewish women in Israel, married or unmarried. These forms of motherhood emerge from shifting notions of how motherhood is constituted and where it is located.

To be sure, these shifting notions of motherhood are bound to collide, for their complementarity rests on a fragile intersection of motile beliefs. For example, it will be interesting to see what happens the first time a surrogate contracted under the new law has second thoughts about the agreement and wants to keep the baby she has gestated, for Halakha will be in her favor, whereas the secular legislation will not. Such a legal battle might pit orthodox rabbis, and even some feminists, against secular lawyers in a drama over conflicting ideologies of the origins of relatedness.

In this chapter I have demonstrated how Halakhic concerns regarding surrogacy, concerns that were overtly politicized and directly affected the final draft of the Embryo-Carrying Agreements Law, overlay economic conditions and secular beliefs about relatedness in such a way that the practice of surrogacy has been practically and conceptually enabled in Israel. The Israeli practice of surrogacy shows how competing conceptions of kinship can be willfully deployed, manipulated, and juxtaposed in the ongoing political struggles to construct the parameters of reproduction. Here again, the bodies of unmarried women and the beliefs of orthodox rabbis intersect and overlap to create an alternative legal framework for the reproduction of Jews.

6

Consequences for Kinship

The anthropological project of identifying how biological processes are constituted in cultural forms received a great deal of analytical attention in the 1990s (Strathern 1992a, 1992b, 1995; Ginsburg and Rapp 1999; Franklin 1997; Franklin and Ragone 1998; Rapp 1990). A central goal of these efforts has been to illuminate the conceptual link between reproductive models and cultural knowledge. Marilyn Strathern examined these links in the context of public debates surrounding the new reproductive technologies in Thatcher's Britain. She argued that changes in reproductive medicine and the choices afforded by new reproductive technologies necessarily affect how Euro-Americans think about kinship, and when thinking about kinship is affected, a whole set of cultural assumptions is destabilized. Central to Strathern's conceptualization of these issues is her supposition that "cultural life is lived through constant displacement of knowledge."

> We move between contexts, draw analogies, forget this in order to concentrate on that, extend our vision and, above all, return to previous positions again. Often what is displaced is only over the horizon, there to be recovered. But there is a special effect that arises from the desire to make known or explicit facts otherwise assumed to be foundational. The displacement effect of uncovering assumptions, of making the implicit explicit, sets off an irreversible process. The implicit can never be recovered and there is no return to old assumptions, displacement becomes radical. (Strathern 1995: 347)

I agree with Strathern that the social uses of new reproductive technologies sets off an irreversible process that has unintended social effects. Yet I argue that this process does not necessarily displace a culture's foundational assumptions about kinship. I suggest instead that this irreversible process has served to reinforce and entrench the foundational assumptions of Jewish kinship thinking, rather than to destabilize them, as Strathern suggests is inevitable when the new reproductive technologies are deployed in a Euro-American context.

Are Jews Euro-Americans?

To untangle Jewish ideas about kinship using Strathern's conceptual framework, we must first interrogate the term *Euro-American* as it appears in Strathern's work, and indeed in the work of others (Franklin 1995, 1997; Van Dyck 1995) as a term that characterizes certain ways of thinking about kinship. Strathern explains:

> The epithet is meant to highlight the cultural specificity of the kinship system that is most immediately affected by the new reproductive technologies, although they are by no means confined to it. The system is found across North America and Northern Europe but it is not tied to locale, though it may be tied to class or to the late-twentieth-century "classlessness" or apparent cosmopolitanism afforded by communications technology. It also once contributed to a larger world view that saw social relationships as built up after the facts of nature. (1995: 350)

According to Strathern, there are three criteria for establishing the "Euro-Americanness" of a kinship system. The first concerns whether a particular kinship system is affected by the new reproductive technologies. The second concerns whether the kinship system in question is found across North America and northern Europe, though it is not strictly "tied to locale." The third concerns whether this kinship system "contributed to a larger world view that saw social relationships as built up after the facts of nature."

Certainly, the Jewish kinship system, if such a thing can be said to exist in a monolithic sense, is immediately affected by the new reproductive technologies. And certainly, a significant population of Jews lived, and continue to live, in northern Europe and North America, though Jews are certainly not bound to these locales. Therefore, are Jewish ideas about kinship Euro-American in the sense that they are grounded in notions of biological relatedness? Or, do Jewish beliefs about kinship, like their Euro-American counterparts, assume that biological relatedness is logically prior to social relatedness? (Schneider 1984). In other words, did the spatial proximity to "Euro-American" culture, and the attendant "world view that took natural facts as a domain for scientific investigation . . . and that provided kinship with a symbolic basis in nature" (Strathern 1995: 350), leave their marks on Jewish conceptions of kinship as they unfolded in the diaspora? By framing this question in spatial terms, I reference traditional ethnographic discourse, which relies on spatial boundaries to delineate its objects of study. The emphasis on spatialism, however, is inherently problematic when undertaking Jewish ethnography. Jonathan Boyarin comments: "The space in which Jews exist cannot be neatly delineated on the map, and they are still primarily defined, both internally and externally, as a minority wherever they live" (1992: 61).

The ethnography of Jews in Israel fits more neatly into the traditional ethnographic genre of studying spatially bounded populations than does the study of Jews in America and Europe. Jews in Israel are the majority population and live within well-defined boundaries; indeed, Boyarin makes it clear that studying Jews in the diaspora is a fundamentally different enterprise from studying them in Israel. Yet the spatial boundaries of the Jewish collectivity in Israel are relatively recent; the rabbinic and folk cultures in which Jewish ideas about kinship percolated over the centuries had no such boundaries.

Moreover, the sources that contemporary rabbis use as their interpretative frameworks for understanding relatedness in the age of reproductive technology were codified in second-century Palestine and then interpreted all over Europe and in various parts of the Arab world over hundreds of years. Rabbinic, and by extension popular Jewish thinking about kinship, therefore inevitably reflect many different influences, including so-called Euro-American influence.

In addition, given the diverse locations and customs of Jewish communities and the decentralized nature of rabbinic authority, multiple and often contradictory popular opinions about these matters have always simultaneously coexisted, competed, and conflicted with each other. Indeed, Jewish beliefs about kinship reflect diverse folk and rabbinic ideas about conception, pregnancy, birth, and the origins of Jewishness.[1] These beliefs are manifest in everything from rabbinic laws concerning the determination of maternity, paternity, and the legal construct of the family to Jewish mystical tracts on the origins of human life to Jewish folk rituals for enhancing fertility, etc. In addition, Jewish beliefs about these matters have always been informed by coexisting discourses. For example, not long after the ovum was scientifically identified in the sixteenth century, its role in reproduction gradually begins to be cited in rabbinic responsa concerning conception and birth.

The belief that Jewishness is transmitted through the matriline stands out as one that has enjoyed particular consensus among Jews, regardless of their place of origin or degree of religiosity. And yet even this belief has been confronted with its own set of challenges in the twentieth century, whether by the Reform movement's codification of paternity as a codeterminant of Jewishness, by ongoing debates about "Who is a Jew" in relation to Israel's immigration policies, or by the conceptual challenge presented by ovum-related technologies, which fragment maternity into genetic and gestational components.

That Jewish beliefs about kinship are shifting and contested does not, in itself, differentiate them from Euro-American beliefs about kinship, tenets that necessarily shift, overlap, and diverge as well. Moreover, by opposing Euro-American and Jewish ideas about kinship, we should not make the assumption that these ideas are necessarily distinct. Jonathan Boyarin points out that it is important to understand that patterns that are authentically Jewish are not necessarily uniquely Jewish (1992: xviii). In other words, Jewish ideas about kinship can be authentic at the same time that they may bear the conceptual imprint of Euro-American kinship thinking.

These kinds of methodological problems reveal the conceptual limitations inherent in a broad-based moniker like *Euro-American*, for as much as there is a need for such a generalizing concept, such a term inevitably rests on a set of assumptions that does not adequately account for the beliefs of significant populations that share the spatial conditions for which it purportedly speaks. In this way, such a term is reminiscent of *Judeo-Christian,* the other generalizing concept often applied to attitudes "in the West." What I am trying to draw attention to here is that these terms rarely account for Jewish particularities, but instead function as shorthand references for concepts and beliefs particular to Christian Europe.

With full recognition of the methodological problems inherent in such a comparison, it is nevertheless instructive to posit a significant point of tension between these two broad sets of beliefs, "Jewish" and "Euro-American"; that is, their differing conceptual frameworks for imagining kinship, particularly their differing assumptions about genetic relatedness and its role in establishing kinship.

Strathern suggests that with the advent of the new reproductive technologies in the Euro-American context, "nature" has become eclipsed and its ability to serve as a field of metaphors for culture has been destabilized. Nature has not disappeared in the contemporary era of reproductive technology, according to Strathern, but "its grounding function has. It no longer provides a model or analogy for the very idea of context" (Strathern 1992a: 195). The new reproductive technologies and the Euro-American "enterprise" culture in which they are deployed have turned nature into an anachronism; it no longer exists as an idiom unto itself but has become context-dependent. Once it *was* the context, it was the field from which metaphor emerged; now nature has simply become flattened into a market concept that depends on the consumer's invocation of it in order to come into being. This conceptual shift is profoundly de-stabilizing to Euro-American beliefs about kinship, where kinship has been understood "as a fact of society rooted in facts of nature," or as that which connects the domains of nature and culture (Strathern 1992b: 16–17).

Indeed, Strathern explains that before this shift, "kinship was re-garded as an area of primordial identity and inevitable relations. It was at once part of the natural world that regenerated social life and provided a representation of this relationship between them" (Strathern 1992a: 198). By contrast, in this post-nature era, Sarah Franklin explains that "the important symbolic conjunction of conjugal

and procreative activity and the equally important opposition between acts undertaken for love and those undertaken for money are
breached" (Franklin 1995: 336). The conceptual consequences of
this shift are severe: Euro-Americans will no longer imagine themselves to be the "natural" product of human relationships but as the
embodiment of consumer choice enacted in a market context. For
choice is the hallmark of the new, technologized marketplace in
which reproductive decisions can now be made. And once we understand children to be the products of choices, the foundational authority of nature as the groundwork for kinship will have eroded.

While kinship is being destabilized in Euro-America, what havoc
are the new reproductive technologies wreaking on Jewish ideas
about kinship in Israel? Does "nature" play a grounding function for
Jewish conceptions of kinship in the same way Strathern claims it
does for Euro-American conceptions of kinship? And if so, is the
confrontation with new reproductive technologies having the same
dislocating effect? Or do Jewish beliefs about kinship emerge from a
different set of foundational assumptions that are somehow more re-
silient to the conceptual challenges posed by new reproductive technologies? Moreover, does Euro-American enterprise culture have an
Israeli counterpart that is similarly significant in determining a new
groundwork for Jewish kinship thinking?

First, it is important to point out that Strathern herself has persuasively argued that the nature-culture opposition must be understood as Eurocentric (Strathern 1980), and indeed others have argued that it is an opposition that has changed and evolved over time
and is not static (Jordanova 1980; Bloch and Bloch 1980). Nevertheless, in order to understand whether the new reproductive technologies destabilize Jewish beliefs about kinship, we can first ask
whether the opposition between nature and culture is a salient one in
Jewish kinship cosmology.

Unfortunately, a full analysis of the intellectual and spiritual di-
vergences between Judaism, Christianity, and the Jewish and non-
Jewish cultures of Western Europe is beyond the scope of this discussion. But if we understand Strathern's concept of "nature" to be
synonymous with a set of beliefs that privilege genetic relatedness as

the ultimate and determinative form of relatedness, then we must recognize significant differences between Euro-American and Jewish beliefs about kinship. For knowledge of genes and their role in reproduction does not necessarily translate into Jewish belief in genes as the ultimate determinants of relatedness. Indeed, if we accept rabbinic kinship cosmology as a codified description of Jewish beliefs about kinship, and if we look to this cosmology as it is made explicit in contemporary debates over the appropriate uses of new reproductive technologies, it is clear that within rabbinic cosmology genetic relatedness does not enjoy the same position of conceptual authority that it does in Euro-American thinking. On the contrary, genetic relatedness is a considerably more plastic category in rabbinic thinking about kinship; it can be conceptually erased, made invisible, or otherwise reconfigured.

New Directions for Fictive Kinship

Nowhere are these dynamic notions of genetic relatedness more vivid than in the rabbinic prescription of non-Jewish sperm and eggs for infertile Jewish couples. Indeed, one could argue that the rabbinic prescription of non-Jewish genetic material for the conception of Jews suggests a new meaning for the Euro-American term *fictive kinship*. Rather than denoting the social process of fabricating relatedness where there is no biological basis, here the term can be used to denote the social process of fabricating nonrelatedness where there is a biological basis. The meanings of the words *fictive* and *kinship* are thus turned on their heads. This process reinforces, in a very literal way, the familiar Euro-American axiom that genetic relatedness is only one trope of genealogical discourse. Yet it is the only process of which I am aware in which the absence of belief in genetic relatedness is proactively embraced for the conception of kin.

What emerges here is a remarkable counterdiscourse about the significance of genes and their role in establishing relatedness, a discourse that stands in direct opposition to dominant Euro-American beliefs that biogenetic material is the ultimate determinant not only of kinship but of everything from personality to sexual orientation to self. It is not that contemporary rabbis deny the existence of genes or their role in communicating important biological information, it is simply that they interpret the meaning of this information in selective and, one might say, self-serving ways. Thus, contrary to Strathern's claim that "no one denies that being an actor in the process of conception establishes a relationship" (1995: 352), it would seem that in rabbinic kinship thinking, being a genetic actor in the process of conception does not necessarily establish any kind of relationship. Moreover, the "denial" of knowledge about genetic paternity and maternity in fact has important social uses. And it is not just the denial of knowledge about genetic paternity and maternity that is remarkable here, it is the denial of the need to know.

The denial of the need to know about genetic paternity is strikingly manifest in the social prescription of anonymous donor sperm for unmarried Jewish women seeking to get pregnant via state-sponsored artificial insemination. Here, as with the rabbinic prescription of non-Jewish donor sperm, the biological role of sperm in procreation is certainly understood, and yet the specific identity and origin of sperm is conceptualized as irrelevant to Jewish reproduction.

What is remarkable here is that these rabbinically and socially prescribed inseminations are taking place within a larger socioreligious cosmology in which "paternity is a concept, the meaning of which is derived from other concepts and beliefs" (Delaney 1986: 495). In other words, what Delaney calls the "cultural logic" of monogenetic, single-source creation is a meaningful part of the cultural cosmology here: Jews after all, are the original monotheists. However, it would appear that they are what could be called matrilineal monotheists.

The difference between the model of paternity that Delaney claims is at work among the Turkish Muslims she studied and the models of paternity that have been made literal in these Jewish/Israeli uses of new reproductive technologies is that the male role in reproduction in the latter case seems to be exclusively generative, not creative. We have seen how anonymous donor sperm, both Jewish and non-Jewish, is being used to generate Jewish children, but at the same time, it is not understood to create Jewish children. For we have seen

how the majority of orthodox rabbinic decisors agree that the creation of a Jewish child can only be accomplished via gestation in, and
parturition from, a Jewish womb.

It is important to understand that Jewish kinship thinking is neither exclusively cognatic nor exclusively lineal. Although Jewish kinship terminology mimics the kinship terminology in the cognatic
Euro-American system, in that children are recognized as the offspring of parents whom they call mother and father and to whom
they are considered to have equal obligations (as in the biblical commandment, Honor thy father and mother), at the same time Jews
have a communal status that is explicitly inherited through the matriline, and which is therefore independent of the individual identities of those individuals designated as parents. Matrilineal inheritance in Jewish kinship reckoning is limited, however, in that it fails
to confer special rights, roles, privileges, or obligations beyond the
designation of descent group status. Indeed, although descent group
status is conferred through the matriline, the filiative tie with the
father is clearly recognized, as in the customary inheritance of patrilineal last names or in the invocation of the father's name during
various rituals, from the circumcision ceremony to the traditional
call to the Torah reading. In addition, the traditional importance of
knowing one's "yichus," or genealogy, continues to retain conceptual force for many Jews.

Given the complex nature of Jewish kinship thinking, it is illuminating to juxtapose Jewish models of reproduction and Trobriand
models of reproduction (the Trobrianders, like the Jews, figure kinship through the matriline). Annette Weiner argued that reproduction for the Trobrianders was not simply a biological process but a
cultural achievement (Franklin 1997: 58). Indeed, though Jews certainly do not share beliefs about paternity or models of conception
with the Trobrianders, they may think about reproduction in certain
similar ways. Sarah Franklin explains Weiner's thinking on the subject thus:

> She (Weiner) demonstrated that the reproduction of the *dala* identity,
> of the matrilineage, is an "integral and complementary part of the
> processes of human reproduction and reproduction of social rela-

tions" (1979: 329). This is because cultural identity, which is the crucial difference between a Trobriander and a mere biological person, is primarily achieved through kinship, through the establishment of a person's position in relation to their ancestry, their matrilineage, their clan, their parents and their siblings. In sum, the establishment of kin ties is the establishment not only of cultural identity but of humanity among the Trobrianders. (Franklin 1998: 59)

If we substitute "Jews" for "Trobrianders" in the above paragraph, a compelling and, one might argue accurate, description of Jewish beliefs about kinship emerges. Like the Trobrianders, Jews also believe that reproduction is not simply the sum of its physiological facts. It is a complex process that depends both on the cultural meanings ascribed to physiological facts and on the constellation of relationships into which a child is born. Reproduction for Jews then, like reproduction for the Trobrianders, is a cultural achievement. It is not imagined simply as a biological process that creates human beings, it is imagined as a cultural process constitutive of humanity. Moreover, in rabbinic kinship cosmology, it is a cultural achievement that depends primarily on the gestational capacity of Jewish women, not on the "seed" of the male "founder-father" (Delaney 1986).

Retro-Paternity

If uncertain paternity is the hallmark of a simple society, then the Israeli social uses of anonymous donor sperm, both Jewish and non-Jewish, could be understood as a certain kind of postmodern primitivism. For the social recognition of the biological fact of paternity, what Louis Henry Morgan saw as the proverbial dawn of civilization, is being effectively denied. Certainly, Israeli social actors do not deny that the biological fact of paternity exists, but the uses of reproductive technology in Israel reveal a tacit agreement among the rabbinical establishment, the state, the medical profession, the women who are getting inseminated, and their husbands (if they are married) to deny the social recognition of genetic paternity. For unmarried Israeli women, it is important that the anonymous donor sperm being used most is donated by Israeli Jewish donors. The anonymity of the individual donor can thus be mitigated by the shared cultural and religious identity between donor and recipient. Similarly, for religious Jews who use non-Jewish donor sperm, the choice is made within a larger religious cosmology that denies paternity to non-Jewish men who conceive children with Jewish women.

On some level, all this cutting and pasting of conceptual kinship categories is something of a game, for even if Israelis erase social paternity in their practice of donor insemination, the dominant conceptual categories for thinking about paternity remain intact. What the cutting and pasting accomplishes, I hope, is a certain self-consciousness about the anthropological, and indeed the rabbinic, endeavor of mapping kinship, and indeed a certain self-consciousness about the thing we call kinship in and of itself.

The cultural uses of reproductive technology provoke a conceptual scramble to make coherent links between the social and biological facts of reproduction. That the biological facts of reproduction become so explicit, to the point that they are determined outside the realm of social interaction, means that all conjectures about the relationship between social and biological facts must be reexamined. For these conceptual models are based on structural certainties about the processes of reproduction, and those certainties are reflected in assumptions of coherence and stability in the relationship between social and biological facts, regardless of the particulars of that relationship. It is this coherence and stability that reproductive technology calls into question, for as we have seen, biological facts can be "erased," and social facts can be rearranged.

Sarah Franklin has argued that the new reproductive technologies are represented in Euro-American cultures as "natural science in service of the natural family" (1995: 328). It would seem that reproductive technology in Israel is being used to reproduce the "natural family" as well. The rabbinic conception of the "natural family" simply assumes different forms and has different structural underpinnings than its Euro-American counterpart.

Jewish kinship will not be enveloped by enterprise culture as long as the orthodox rabbinate continues to define the legislative framework for Jewish reproduction in Israel. Although much of Israeli social life is increasingly characterized by consumerism, the foundational notions of Jewish kinship remain intact because they are protected and controlled by rabbinic authorities invested with state power. Moreover, since reproduction is not conceptualized as a choice in Jewish law, but as an obligation, the infertile couple's decision to take advantage of the new reproductive technologies does not evolve out of a consumerist impulse but out of a compulsion to fulfill a divine commandment. From the perspective of Jewish law, infertile couples seeking to solve their childlessness with the aid of new reproductive technologies are not customers seeking services but people with a malady seeking a remedy. From the perspective of state regulations regarding reproductive technologies, unmarried Jewish women who seek artificial insemination are not imagined as consumers with the right to make choices about the individual characteristics of their sperm donor but as both reproductive resources for married infertile couples and as Israeli citizens with the capacity to reproduce Jews. The enterprising of Jewish kinship is thus held at bay.

The flexibility of Jewish kinship, however, is exposed. For the advent of new reproductive technologies has revealed curious and provocative loopholes within the rabbinic imagination of relatedness. These loopholes implicitly allow for and legitimate Jewish children conceived by unmarried Jewish women as well as by infertile Jewish couples who conceive children with reproductive genetic material donated by anonymous non-Jews. The social uses of new reproductive technologies in Israel thus simultaneously reveal and reinforce the foundational assumptions of Jewish kinship thinking, rather than displace them, as Strathern suggests is inevitable when these technologies are deployed in a Euro-American context. The whole project of Jewish reproduction thus becomes open to a diverse range of social actors for whom it was previously closed. By so doing, the project of Jewish reproduction is expanded in new and unexpected ways.

If genes do not create kinship, where does relatedness come from in the rabbinic imagination? I suggest that bodily experience between two Jewish bodies, either between a Jewish man and a woman during sexual intercourse, or between a Jewish mother and fetus during gestation and parturition, is the base line for establishing a relationship between persons in rabbinic kinship cosmology. For it would seem that in rabbinic debates about new reproductive technologies, bodily experience is consistently singled out as that which establishes a more significant relationship between persons than the simple combination of reproductive genetic material. And yet ironically, the conceptual significance of bodily experience between Jews is being eroded by rabbinic rulings regarding reproductive technology that explicitly legitimize the reproduction of Jews that is accomplished absent sexual intercourse.

Rabbinic enthusiasm for the new reproductive technologies has thus created an intriguing paradox. For while it reinforces the imperative to reproduce more Jewish bodies — a value of undisputed importance in a pronatalist religious system — it has unwittingly contributed to the conceptual disintegration of the significance of Jewish bodily experience, once a precondition for the creation of Jews.

The cultural meanings of this historical development are particularly disconcerting in light of Daniel Boyarin's argument that a central difference between Christians and Jews can be traced to early rabbinic and Christian attitudes toward the body (Boyarin 1993). For what are Jews when they are no longer that which has defined them as culturally and religiously distinct: individuals who are the celebrated products of sexual relationships? What does it mean that heterosexual sex, once a prerequisite for the creation of Jews, is no longer imperative for the project of Jewish reproduction?

Will rabbinic recipes for the appropriate combinations of bodily substance sustain the project of reproducing Jews? Or will the individuals so conceived and born be something other than Jewish? How long will the "ends" justify the means? And if the ends make the means irrelevant, what will the texture of Jewish life be like?

Conclusion:
Reproducing Jews and Beyond

The process of reproducing Jews via reproductive technology has revealed significant "facts" about where Jews come from. This process has sharpened our understanding of the Jewish grammar of personhood and has illuminated the rabbinic belief that genes are not privileged as determinants of relatedness; nowhere is this belief more in evidence than in the fact that Jews are now deliberately reproduced with non-Jewish genetic material. Indeed, since gestation and parturition are understood as the processes through which Jews come into being, the wombs of Jewish women, both married and unmarried, have come into focus as central to the enterprise of reproducing Jews.

In chapter 1, I delineated eight stages that illuminate the processes unmarried Israeli women go through on their way to autonomous motherhood. We learned how unmarried women negotiate the bureaucratic apparatus surrounding insemination in Israel, how they employ various rationalizations for their decisions to get pregnant via artificial insemination, and how they are motivated to motherhood for a variety of reasons. Their individual stories must be understood to echo the larger collective discourse about the cultural imperative to reproduce.

In chapter 2 we saw how secular legislation regarding reproductive technology, which is grounded in rabbinic beliefs about the origins of relatedness, has been constructed in such a way that marriage is no longer the only legitimate site for social and biological reproduction in Israel. Although the use of artificial insemination by unmarried women may come under rabbinic criticism and censure as a social practice, it does not violate rabbinic precepts of relatedness any more than the use of these technologies by infertile ultraorthodox couples. In other words, since marriage does not necessarily legitimate children in Jewish kinship cosmology, it is not necessarily a prerequisite to legitimate reproduction.

In chapter 3 I examined how rabbinic assumptions about relatedness are made explicit in rabbinic discourse. Rabbinic debates about artificial insemination have forced rabbinic conceptions of paternity to become explicit in such a way that paternity can now be actively strategized. The symbolic meaning ascribed to bodily substance, either Jewish or non-Jewish, thus becomes part of a "kinship puzzle" that can be fit together in order to reproduce Jews. This kind of rabbinic innovation has allowed thousands of infertile Jewish couples to produce Jewish babies who would otherwise be literally inconceivable. The fact that the somewhat synthetic nature of the enterprise of constructing kinship has been revealed, and indeed embraced, by orthodox rabbis suggests that rabbinic pragmatism vis-à-vis the new reproductive technologies works to reinforce the Halakhic imperative to be fruitful and multiply.

In chapter 4 I examined two spheres in which the fragmentation of women's bodies into eggs and wombs is practiced, both literally and conceptually: the daily workings of an Israeli fertility clinic and the rabbinic deliberations on ova donation. I examined the linkages between these two spheres by looking at how Halakhic concerns about purity as a prerequisite for conception are translated into clinical protocol. The literalization of the components of maternity in both of these spheres has created a new cultural site for intense and ongoing debates about the origin of Jewish identity.

The social meanings of the fragmentation of maternity resurface in the new surrogacy law, examined in chapter 5, in which competing notions about the origin of maternity are selectively employed in the practice of surrogacy. A range of contradictory beliefs about maternity exist in Israel today, beliefs that are appropriated and applied discriminately by various social actors in the overwhelming effort to reproduce Jews. What remains untransformed in the practice of surrogacy in Israel is the belief that Jewish babies are only born from Jewish wombs. The rabbinic idea that gestation and parturition determine Jewish identity is thus codified, and thereby entrenched, in secular legislation.

In chapter 6 I juxtaposed Jewish and Euro-American kinship thinking in order to illuminate conjunctions and tensions between the two. The analysis highlighted the different consequences the new reproductive technologies have on Jewish conceptions of kinship, as opposed to their Euro-American counterparts.

The uses of the new reproductive technologies in Israel create a series of complex social dilemmas. The fact that the reproductive futures of unmarried women are explicitly valued, that their motherhood is assisted regardless of their marital status, poses something of a quandary. The same technology that presents unmarried women with an unprecedented degree of reproductive autonomy at the same time exposes them to a host of arguably exploitative reproductive practices, from surrogacy to paid egg donation to the implicit coercion to motherhood. Moreover, although these technologies may be experienced as enabling on the personal level, since they allow unmarried women to achieve their individual goals of becoming mothers, they must also be understood as enabling on the collective level, for they create the conditions for the pronatalist state to recruit the maximum number of wombs into the project of reproducing Jewish citizens.

Looking toward the Reproduced Future

How Jews "come into being" (Delaney 1991) is made explicit and startlingly literal in orthodox rabbinic efforts to harness the new reproductive technologies to the task of creating Jews. The "cultural repertoire" for thinking about kinship that is available to Jewish Israelis today is quite vast (Strathern 1995). From the rabbinic social practice of mining traditional texts for coherent kinship metaphors, to the ongoing efforts of contemporary Israeli Jews, both secular and religious, to make sense of this technology while using it to realize their reproductive futures, there is a range of coexisting kinship ideologies from which to choose in the ongoing cultural effort to reproduce Jews. Although rabbinic conceptions of kinship may have the political edge over popular Israeli definitions of kinship, since these beliefs explicitly inform state regulations concerning the new reproductive technologies, neither of these conceptual fields are static or monolithic. Indeed, the rush to embrace reproductive technology in Israel has roused conflicting and contradictory kinship cosmologies that are invoked selectively by various social actors in their diverse desires to create Jewish children, either with the intention of reproducing the nation or simply with the intention of reproducing themselves. What Strathern calls "late twentieth century cultural logic" about kinship competes with Talmudic legends about relatedness in the contemporary state of Israel. Sometimes these kinship cosmologies overlap, sometimes they do not, but these cosmologies, and indeed many others, are applied and invoked expediently in the pronatalist state to reproduce Jews.

Appendix A

National Health Regulations (IVF) 1987

Translated from Hebrew by the author. After a brief explanation of terms, the regulations read as follows:

2.
a. No person shall take an egg from the body of a woman, fertilize, freeze, or implant it in the body of a woman except in a recognized department in accordance with these regulations.
b. The director (of the ministry of health) is entitled to establish forms that must be filled out for purposes of these regulations.

3. Eggs can be taken only for the purpose of fertilization and implantation after fertilization.

4. Eggs shall be taken only for whom the following conditions exist:
a. The patient is involved in medical treatment as the result of fertility problems.
b. A responsible doctor determines that the taking of an egg will advance this treatment.

5. No doctor shall fertilize an egg that was taken except with sperm that was intended in advance for fertilization, and that was received in accordance with the directives of the director, either from a donor, or from her husband, or from a sperm bank as stated in National Health Regulations regarding sperm banks.

6. An egg taken from a married woman will not be fertilized with donor sperm except with written consent of the woman and her husband.

7. The egg of a donor will not be fertilized with the sperm of the husband of the woman in whom it will be implanted without the advance written consent both from the wife and from the husband, and the egg was taken from a donor who has met all the conditions of regulation 4.

8.

a. No fertilized egg shall be implanted in a married woman unless it is hers or a donor's and was fertilized in accordance with these regulations.

b. Notwithstanding the aforesaid in subparagraph (a), if the woman to whom it is intended to implant the egg is single, a fertilized egg will not be implanted in her unless the egg is hers and she has received a report from a social worker of a recognized department that supports the woman's request. The report shall be in accordance with the director's guidelines.

c. If the woman who has the fertilized egg is widowed before it is implanted, the egg will not be implanted in her unless a year has passed from the time that the egg was taken and fertilized and a report is received from the social worker as stated in paragraph 1.

d. If the woman in whom it is intended to implant is divorced, and the egg is fertilized with the sperm of her former husband before the divorce, then the egg will be implanted only with receipt of the former husband's consent.

9.

a. An egg, including a fertilized egg, will be frozen for a period not to exceed five years.

b. If a request in writing is received from the wife and husband and certified with a signature with an authorized doctor, then the freezing period can be extended for another five years.

10.

a. An egg that is taken from a married woman who died will not be used.

b. An egg that is taken from a married woman whose husband dies can be donated with her consent.

c. When a fertilized egg is created from a sperm and egg of a married couple and one of them dies, then (1) if the husband dies, reg. 8B2 applies. (2) If the wife dies, the fertilized egg will not be used.

d. An egg, including a fertilized egg, that is taken from a single woman who dies will not be implanted in another woman after her death, unless the donor gave her consent to the donation of the egg before her death.

11.

a. A fertilized egg will only be implanted in the woman who shall be the mother of the child (later invalidated).

12.

a. A fertilized egg will not be implanted in a woman who is related to the egg donor.

b. An egg that was taken from a woman for donation will be implanted in another woman only if she gave her consent to donation.

13. No egg shall be implanted in a woman that was taken from a donor unless it was fertilized with the sperm of the husband of the woman.

14.

a. Every action involved in IVF as set forth in regulation 2 shall be done only after the responsible doctor has explained to all of the parties the significance of the actions and the consequences that are likely to result from it and receives the consent of each one individually.

b. Every action involved in the IVF of a married woman will be done only after receiving the consent of the husband.

c. Consent according to these regulations shall:

1. not be given to a specific person or re. a specific matter.

2. shall be given in writing in the presence of a doctor; however, a married couple's consent shall be given on one document.

15.

a. A recognized department that is engaged in IVF activities will not give out the information related to the identity of the sperm or egg donor.

b. The director of a recognized department will take all necessary steps to ensure proper execution of subparagraph (a).

Appendix B

Rules as to the Administration of a Sperm Bank and Guidelines for
Performing Artificial Insemination.

Translated from Hebrew by the author. An internal memo of the
ministry of health, November 13, 1992, Circular 34/92. From
January 1, 1993, prohibition on using fresh sperm. Chapter A provides a
brief synopsis of terms. This circular should be distributed to all doctors
in women's units and IVF clinics.

Chapter B: The Sperm Bank

Administration:

2. No person shall operate a bank except in accordance with these rules.

3.
a. No bank shall be operated except if the director has recognized it,
   and it must be part of a hospital.
b. Artificial insemination with donated sperm from a recognized sperm
   bank will be done in the following places:
   1. In a hospital in which there is a recognized sperm bank.
   2. In public clinics and departments that have fertility clinics.
   3. In recognized units for IVF.
c. No artificial insemination by a donor will be done in a private clinic.

4.
a. The bank will be operated by a certified doctor with a degree of
   expertise in one of the following specialties (and he must have
   undergone appropriate training): hematology, pathology, neurology,
   endocrinology, ob/gyn.
b. The bank will be operated in the department of a hospital in which
   there is a minimum of two doctors with expertise in the above areas.

5. Request for recognition of a bank will be submitted by the director
of a hospital to the office of health in whose region the hospital is
located, on a form in Appendix "a".

6. Conditional recognition: the director (of the ministry of health) is entitled to recognize the bank subject to certain conditions.

7. The responsible party and the director of the hospital in which the sperm bank is operated are responsible.

8. Receipt and selection of sperm donations will be done in accordance with paragraph 26.

9.

a. Files must be kept in three separate systems:
   1. A list of donors.
   2. A list of women recipients.
   3. A list of sperm.

b. The Donor Card will include the following details:
   Side A:
   — Personal data including numerical code.
   — Data for ruling out genetic diseases and hereditary illnesses.
   — Lab results including periodic follow-ups.
   — Results of physical exam.
   Side B:
   — Personal declaration and agreement to keep things private. Both doctor and donor will sign here.
   This card will be kept in a *safe,* and access to it will be by the treating doctor only.

c. Donation Recipient Card (Female)
   Side A:
   The personal data on the female patient and her husband, emphasizing the important physical and ethnic attributes for purposes of choosing an appropriate donor.
   Side B:
   A sequential list of the samples, by code, that will be used for inseminating the woman, by date. In the event that pregnancy ensues, this can be noted in the appropriate place. This card shall be kept separately from the woman's file, located with the treating doctor.

d. Sperm Card
   The Sperm Card will include the following details: it will be marked only with the code of the donor. This code will be noted on the semen test tube. Every sample will be checked and its results listed across the card only. In order to thaw it, the sample is checked

again, including if it results in pregnancy. The identification column is intended to indicate the location of the bank in which it is stored to enable its quick location.

10. Every sperm donation shall be kept in a separate test tube. And between each test tube there will be an appropriate separation.

11. On each test tube, no details shall be noted except the numeric code, or the identification number that refers to the semen card. This number shall be noted on each sperm sample that is submitted by the sperm bank to the doctor executing the insemination as set forth in paragraph 3(b).

12. The responsible party must refrain from receiving too many donations from the same donor.

13. The authorized party will keep in the bank the donor's consent form as set forth in paragraph 26 (5), in a separate enclosed department.

14. Access to the lists of a bank and the donor's documents will be allowed only to the authorized party or to the person he appoints in writing for purposes of these regulations.

15.
a. The director will appoint supervisors for purposes of auditing the banks.
b. The audit will be done by a staff of at least two supervisors, one of whom must have a specialist's degree as noted above.
c. They don't get to see lists of donors that would make them able to recognize donors.

Chapter C: Artificial Insemination

17. Artificial insemination will only be done by a certified doctor with a specialist's degree in ob/gyn or who is in his training for this degree.

18. The doctor may only do the artificial insemination after the woman has undergone a medical examination.

19.
a. Artificial insemination shall not be done with the sperm of a donor, either with the husband's or partner's sperm or alone, unless it has been determined that despite accepted medical treatments it has been determined that the woman is able to get pregnant from the husband or partner's sperm alone.

b. Notwithstanding the foregoing, artificial insemination shall be given to a single woman only in special circumstances, only after receipt of a psychiatric opinion as well as a senior social worker's report.

20. The doctor must ascertain that the woman is not pregnant when he performs the artificial insemination.

21. The selection of sperm in the case of artificial insemination by donor is in the hands of the doctor alone, without the interference of the couple and without their knowledge, subject to these conditions: — the doctor will refrain from using the sperm of a donor that is related to the recipient.

22. To the extent that it is possible, the husband or partner's sperm will be mixed with the sperm of the donor if the conditions stated in paragraph 19 exist.

23. The doctor must explain to the woman and her husband before performing the artificial insemination that there is no guarantee that the woman will get pregnant, or as a result of the fertilization give birth. Likewise, he must explain to them the likelihood of complications in pregnancy and birth and possibility of defects both physical and mental.

24.
a. In the case of artificial insemination with a donor, it is necessary to receive the consent of wife and husband in writing, for the performance of insemination, and the declaration of the husband that a child born as the result of artificial insemination will be considered in every matter like his natural child, including child support and inheritance and will bear the name of his family.
b. In the case of artificial insemination of single women, you must receive the consent of the woman.

25. The identity of the donor, on one hand, and the identity of the woman and her husband, on the other, are prohibited from being revealed, including to each one of them. Likewise, the identity of the donor will not be revealed to the child who is born as a result of this operation.

26. Sperm frozen or fresh will not be taken, received, or utilized from a donor if any of the following exist:
a. The sperm is not normal.

b. The donor did not undergo general medical examination prior, which includes a physical exam and tests for hepatitis B and C, and Tay-Sachs for all ethnic groups.

c. The donor is sick with a sexual disease, tuberculosis, infection in sexual organ or impurity in his sperm, or he has some sort of defect that is likely to harm the woman or the child born with his sperm.

d. The donor did not undergo an AIDS test, an HIV antibody test on the day that he donated the sperm, and an HIV exam six months after the first test, and positive result was received in one of the tests.

e. The donor did not give his consent in his writing on donor card side b for use of his sperm in artificial insemination.

27. If, before artificial insemination is approved for couples, a question arises as to their fitness, either mental, physical, social, or emotional status, the doctor will consult with an expert in the field of psychology.

28. The sperm of man who has been injured or is likely to be injured as a result of sperm production ability (cancer, radiation, etc.), that sperm will be stored for a period of five years . . . if written consent is provided.

Appendix C

Report of the Public-Professional Commission
in the Matter of In-Vitro Fertilization
Jerusalem, July, 1994

Official translated document of the Ministry of Health.

Table of Contents

Appendix D

Rabbi David Golinkin's *Tshuva* on
Artificial Insemination for Single Women
Responsa of the Va'ad Halakha of the Rabbinical Assembly
of Israel, Vol. 3, 5748–5749

Official translation of the Va'ad Halakha.

Question: A single woman (we shall call her Sarah) in her early thirties wants to conceive a child through AID (artificial insemination by donor). Is it halakhically permissible for a single woman to give birth through artificial insemination?

Responsum: We appreciate Sarah's sincere and human desire to bear a child, but after careful deliberation and examination of the sources we must rule that such an act is forbidden both halakhically and philosophically for the following reasons:

1. Jewish law and tradition forbid the unnecessary destruction of sperm. If Sarah were married, most authorities would permit AIH (artificial insemination by husband) because the sperm would not be wasted but rather used to perform the mitzvah of "be fruitful and multiply." But in the case under discussion there is not mitzvah involved because women are exempt from this mitzvah. Thus any Jewish donor, and most donors in Israel are Jewish, is wasting sperm unnecessarily, and while Sarah would not be guilty of any sin, she would be "abetting a sinner," which is forbidden by Jewish law.

2. More importantly, in most countries including Israel it is illegal to reveal the identity of a sperm donor. This creates a double halakhic problem. According to Samuel (Yevamot 42a), it is a mitzvah to know one's parentage, and in this case that is impossible. Furthermore, the Torah prohibits the marriage of a brother and sister (Leviticus 18:9). Since one portion of sperm can foster two hundred children and since the same

donors frequently return to the same sperm bank, there is a real possibility of a brother marrying a sister. In fact, such a marriage has already taken place in Tel Aviv, and in the United States a similar marriage was averted at the last minute by a doctor who revealed the couple's genetic link.

3. Theoretically, when the child grows up we could inform him of his father's identity in order to avoid incest. However, this is not possible because such a revelation is prohibited by law.

4. Four authorities permit AID if the donor is not Jewish because in such a case the child's halakhic pedigree follows the mother. Thus, halakhically there is no danger of incest. However, genetically there is still the danger of incest. Furthermore, it is hard to believe that Sarah would want to be impregnated with the sperm of a non-Jew in the state of Israel!

5. Lastly, this suggestion is objectionable for a number of ethical, philosophical, and social reasons:

a. The Jewish family has been the basic unit of the Jewish people since the days of Abraham. In the past twenty years the Jewish family has begun to disintegrate: divorce has skyrocketed, Jews are marrying late and are having fewer children, and homosexuality is on the rise. If we approve of this suggestion, we are in effect saying: there is no need for the Jewish family! A man does not need a wife, a woman does not need a husband, and children do not need two parents!

b. Many children from broken homes suffer from various psychological problems. But these problems were created after the fact. The proposed suggestion creates such a situation before the child is born! Furthermore, the child will suffer the additional stigma of being born out-of-wedlock and the tension of never knowing his father. It would be wrong to create a situation that is bound to lead to psychological problems.

c. Frequently in Judaism and in any society the good of the individual is superseded by the good of society. AID may help Sarah in the short run, but it will definitely harm Jewish society in the long run.

d. One of the purposes of marriage in Judaism is "to be fruitful and multiply." However, Jewish marriage has two other purposes that would not be achieved by this suggestion. The first is companionship and love between a man and a woman, which would obviously not be served by AID. The second is the holiness of kiddushin, which sanctifies sexual relations, the family, and Jewish society as a whole. Needless to say, this aspect is also missing from the proposed suggestion.

6. Thus AID for a single woman is prohibited by Jewish law and tradition. But what can be done to help Sarah? There are two halakhically acceptable solutions:

a. Rather than spending a considerable amount of money on AID, the money should be spent on a matchmaker or computer dating service. Matchmaking is a venerable Jewish tradition, which according to the Midrash has been God's main occupation since He finished creating the world.

b. If, after serious effort, Sarah does not find a husband, she can adopt a child. While this solution has some of the same pitfalls as AID, the difference is that here Sarah would be solving the problem of an unwanted child after the fact, rather than creating a problematic situation by design. Adoption is a new institution in Judaism, but the Talmud has already stated: "Whoever raises an orphan in his house is considered as if he had born the child."

Yet the natural Jewish solution is still marriage. We hope and pray that Sarah will get married in the near future and be blessed with the triple blessing of kiddushin: holiness, children, and companionship.

Appendix E

Embryo Carrying Agreements Law

(Approval of the Agreement and Status of the Child 1996)

Translated from Hebrew by Abra Siegel.

Chapter A: Interpretation

In this law

"The carrying mother" — the woman who carries a pregnancy for the intended parents.

"Intended parents" — a man and a woman who are a couple who contract with the carrying mother for purposes of having a child.

"Embryo Carrying Agreement" — an agreement between intended parents and the carrying mother according to which the intended mother agrees to become a parent by means of implantation of fertilized eggs and to bear the pregnancy for the intended parents.

"Recognized Unit" — A unit in a hospital or a clinic that the director general of the ministry of health has recognized in the official gazette pursuant to the terms that he has set forth for purposes of executing the medical procedures relating to in-vitro fertilization.

"Relative" — mother, daughter, grandmother, aunt, sister, maternal or paternal cousin, except for family member by adoption.

"Approval Committee" — a committee appointed by the minister of health pursuant to paragraph 3.

"Social worker and head social worker" — a social worker who the minister of labor and welfare has authorized pursuant to paragraph 20c for purposes of this law.

"Child" — a child born to a carrying mother as a result of performance of an agreement regarding the carrying of embryos.

"Parental relationship" — a system of obligations, rights, and authorities that exist between a parent and his child according to the law.

"Parental order" — An order regarding the guardianship of the intended parents over the child and the existence of parental relationship between them.

"Court" — family court (new law creates family court, which will concentrate family disputes in one place) and until its establishment, the district court.

Chapter B: Approval of an Agreement for the Carrying of Embryos

2. The implantation of a fertilized egg whose purpose is the impregnation of a carrying mother for the purposes of transferring the child to be born to the intended parents will not be executed unless all of the following exist:

— 1. An agreement in writing has been made between the carrying mother and the intended parents, which was approved by the approvals committee in accordance with the provisions of this law.

— 2. The parties to the agreement are adult Israeli residents.

— 3. The carrying mother (a) is not married; however, the approvals committee may approve a contract with a married carrying mother if it has been proven to the committee's satisfaction that the intended parents have been unable, after a severe effort, to enter into an agreement for the carrying of embryos with a carrying mother who is unmarried. (b) is not a relative of one of the intended parents.

— 4. The sperm used for the IVF is that of the intended father's, and the egg is not the carrying mother's.

— 5. The carrying mother is of the same religion of the intended mother; however, if all the parties to the agreement are not Jewish, the committee is entitled to deviate from the provisions of this clause in accordance with the opinion of the religious representative on the committee (of that religion).

3a. The minister of health will appoint an approval committee with seven members that will consist of the following: 1. Two doctors with the degree of specialist in ob/gyn, an internal medicine specialist, a clinical psychologist, a social worker, a public representative who is a jurist, a religious representative of the same religion as the parties to the agreement for the carrying of the embryos. The ministry of health will appoint a chairman to the approvals committee from among its members.

3b. The social worker will be appointed in consultation with the minister of labor and welfare; the public representative will be appointed in consultation with the minister of justice, and the cleric will be appointed with the consultation of the minister of religious affairs. The composition of the approvals committee will include a representation of at least three members for each type.

3c. The minister of health will appoint a substitute for the chairman among its members and a substitute for all the members of the approvals committee subject to the provisions of subparagraph 3b.

3d. The legal quorum in meetings of the approvals will be five members including the chairman.

3e. The decisions of the approvals committee will be made a majority of its members. The decisions shall be set forth in writing and shall be signed by the chairman.

3f. The meetings of the approvals committee will be closed and publications of statements made or submitted to them is forbidden, except for purposes of executing this law or in connection with a criminal investigation of an infraction pursuant to it.

4a. A request for the approval of an agreement for the carrying of embryos will be submitted to the approvals committee together with the following documents:

— 1. an offer for an agreement to carry embryos.

— 2. a medical opinion regarding the inability of the intended mother to become pregnant and to carry a pregnancy, or that pregnancy is likely to significantly endanger her health.

— 3. medical opinion regarding the suitability of each of the parties to the agreement, to the procedure.

— 4. A psychological evaluation regarding the suitability of each of the parties to the agreement to the procedure.

— 5. A psychologist or social worker's confirmation that the intended parents received appropriate professional counseling including the possibilities of alternative means to parenthood.

— 6. If the parties to the agreement have entered into a contract pursuant to a brokerage agreement for pay, the agreement will be submitted to the committee together with the details of the broker.

4b. The approvals committee will examine the documents submitted to it pursuant to subparagraph 4a, and listen to all the parties to the agreement; it is also entitled to ask the parties for additional material and to hear any other person as it sees fit.

5a. If the approvals committee is of the opinion that all the terms in paragraph 2 have been met, it is entitled after it has weighed the entirety of the facts indicated in the opinion, documents, and the statements made before it, to approve the embryo carrying agreement, or to approve it subject to certain conditions, if it is convinced that the following are all true:

— 1. All the parties have entered into the embryo carrying agreement with their consent and out of their own free will and with an understanding of its significance and its results;

— 2. there is no fear of harm to the carrying mother's health or to the welfare of the child to be born;

— 3. the embryo carrying agreement does not contain terms that harm or violate the rights of the child to be born or the rights of one of the parties.

5b. If the approvals committee has approved an embryo carrying agreement, the parties will sign it in front of the committee, and every change to the agreement requires the committee's approval.

5c. The approvals committee is entitled to reconsider an approval it granted if a significant change has occurred in the facts, the circumstances or the terms that form the basis of its decision, so long as the fertilized egg has not been implanted in the carrying mother in accordance with the embryo carrying agreement.

6. The approvals committee is entitled to approve terms in the agreement regarding monthly payments to the carrying mother to cover actual expenses involved in the performance of the agreement, including expenses for legal counseling and insurance as well as compensation for time lost, suffering, loss of income or temporary loss of ability to work for a salary, or any other reasonable compensation.

7. In-vitro fertilization and implantation of a fertilized egg will not be performed except in a recognized unit and on the basis of an embryo carrying agreement that has been approved as stated.

Chapter C: The Status of the Child

8. This chapter will apply to pregnancy and the birth of a child who is born pursuant to an embryo carrying agreement that has been approved in accordance with the provisions of chapter B.

9a. The intended parents and the carrying mother will notify a social worker as to the place of birth and the estimated date of birth at the end of the fifth month of the carrying mother's pregnancy. The notice will include the details that will be set forth in the regulations.

9b. Immediately upon the birth of the child and no later than twenty-four hours afterward, the intended parents or the carrying mother will notify the social worker about the birth of the child.

10a. Upon the birth of the child, the child will be in the custody of the

intended parents, and the responsibilities and obligations of a parent toward a child will be incumbent upon them.

10b. A social worker who will be selected for this purpose by the head
social worker will be subject to the provisions of subparagraph a, the sole
guardian of the child from the moment of its birth and until the issuance
of the parenthood order or until the issuance of a different order that
determines the status of the child.

10c. The transfer of the child by the carrying mother to the custody of the
intended parents will be in the presence of the social worker and as soon
as possible after the birth.

11a. Within seven days after the date of birth, the intended parents will
submit a motion for an issuance of a parenthood order; if the intended
parents do not submit a motion as stated, the social worker will submit a
motion by the means of the representative of the attorney general.

11b. the court will issue a parenthood order unless it is of the opinion,
after receiving a memo from the social worker, that the matter is in opposition to the best interests of the child; if the court is of the opinion as
stated it shall issue an order pursuant to paragraph 14.

12a. Upon the issuance of the parenthood order, the intended parents will
be the parents and sole guardian of the child and it will be their child for
all purposes.

12b. The parenthood order has no effect on the laws of prohibiting and
permitting matters of marriage and divorce.

13a. If the carrying mother has asked to withdraw her consent to the
embryo carrying agreements, and keep the child, the court will not approve this, unless it is of the opinion after receiving a memo from the social worker that there has been a change in circumstances that justifies the
withdrawal of consent of the carrying mother and this will not harm the
best interests of the child.

13b. After issuance of a parenthood order, the court will not approve
withdrawal of consent to the embryo carrying agreement as stated.

13c. If the court has approved the withdrawal of consent by the carrying
mother from the embryo carrying agreement, it will set forth in an order
the status of the carrying mother as mother and guardian of the child and
it will be her child for all purposes; the court is also entitled to set forth in
the order, provisions regarding the status of the child and its relationship
with its intended parents or with one of them.

14a. Where the court has not granted a parenthood order pursuant to paragraph 11b, and the carrying mother has requested guardianship of the child, the court will issue an order as stated in paragraph 13c, unless it is of the opinion after receiving the report of the social worker that this would be in opposition to the best interests of the child.

14b. Where the court has not issued a parenthood order pursuant to paragraph 11b, and the carrying mother has not requested that she be granted guardianship over the child, or the court is of the opinion that an order pursuant to subparagraph a is contrary to the best interests of the child, it is entitled to determine in an order any other provision regarding the status of the child as it will see fit under the circumstances.

15. Where the court has issued an order pursuant to paragraph 13 or 14, it is entitled to set forth a sum for the repayment of expenses to each of the parties of the embryo carrying agreement.

16a. An order pursuant to paragraphs to 11, 13, or 14 will be noted in a list which will be administered by a registrar who will be appointed by the minister of justice.

16b. The details of the listing and its nature will be set forth in regulations which the minister of justice will enact subject to the approval of the knesset labor and welfare committee.

16c. The provisions of paragraph 30 of the adoption of children law 1981, will apply to this matter subject to the necessary changes.

17. A hearing under this law will be behind closed doors unless the court sees fit to conduct it in public, however, the court is empowered to allow a category of persons (relatives?) to be present during part or all of the hearings.

Chapter D: Miscellaneous Provisions

18. There is nothing in this law or in an embryo carrying agreement that has been approved pursuant to it, which has any effect on a requirement under the law for informed consent to medical treatment or to prevent a carrying mother from receiving medical treatment or to perform a medical procedure according to her will, including the termination of her pregnancy pursuant to subchapter b in chapter 10 in the penal law of 1977.

19a. A person who implants a fertilized egg for the purposes of impregnating a carrying mother for the purposes of transferring a child not in accordance with the provisions of this law, or in connection with the performance of an embryo carrying agreement that has not been approved with the approval committee or contrary to the terms that were set forth, is subject to one year in prison.

19b. A party to an embryo carrying agreement or his agent who offers, gives, asks, or receives monetary or equivalent compensation, in connection with the performance of an embryo carrying agreement, which has not been approved by the approvals committee, is subject to one year in prison.

19c. A person who publishes without the permission of the court statements made in the meetings of the approvals committee or documents submitted to it or their names, identity, or any other matter that is likely to lead to the identification of the carrying mother, the intended parents, or the child, or the content of the embryo carrying agreement or documents submitted to the courts regarding these matters, is subject to one year's imprisonment.

19d. A person who transfers or receives a child without a social worker being present or not in accordance with a court under this law is subject to one year's imprisonment.

20a. The minister of health is in charge executing chapter b and he is entitled to enact regulations for its execution.

20b. The minister of labor and welfare is in charge of the administration of chapter C, and he is entitled to a consultation with the minister of justice to enact regulations for its execution.

20c. The minister of labor and welfare will authorize for purposes of this law, a head social worker and other social workers who will act in accordance with the instructions of the head social worker in general or as to a particular matter.

21. Changes to Other Laws:
In the Population Registry Law of 1965, after paragraph 20 insert; 20a. subparagraph a: when an order is given pursuant to the embryo carrying agreement law (approval of the agreement and status of the child 1996) the details of the registration set forth in the order will be registered in the Registry. (b) The minister of the interior is entitled to establish provisions in the regulations regarding the registration procedures including temporary registration until issuance of an order by a court.

22. In the Family Court Law of 1995 in paragraph 1, after clause 6(i), insert (j), "embryo carrying agreements law and status of child 1996."

23. In the national insurance law, consolidated version 1995 — in chapter c, in the title of subchapter d, instead of "the adoptive parents" insert "the adoptive parents and the intended parents." After paragraph 57, insert 57a; subparagraph a, in this paragraph — "Embryo carrying agreements law" . . . "intended mother — the insured according to chapter 11, or the wife of the insured according to chapter 11, who have received custody of a child as an intended parent, pursuant to the provisions of the embryo carrying agreement. (b) notwithstanding the provisions of paragraph 42, the provisions of subchapter b of this chapter will apply to an intended mother, subject to the necessary changes and adjustments set forth by the minister with the approval of the Knesset labor and welfare committee; . . .

Minister of Health
Ephraim Sneh

Minister of Labor and Welfare
Ora Namir

President   *Speaker of the Knesset*
Ezer Weizman   Shevah Weiss

Prime Minister
Shimon Peres

Notes

Introduction

1   The National Health Insurance Law (1994) provides universal coverage for all resident Israelis, both Jewish and Palestinian. However, while Jewish residents of the Occupied Territories are covered by this law, Palestinian residents are not. The law guarantees that every Israeli citizen has the right to receive healthcare and obligates health funds to accept all applicants as members and to provide them with a basic basket of services. For more information on the guarantee of subsidies for fertility treatment see appendix B of the National Health Insurance Law.

2   Abortion is subsidized for those under seventeen or over forty, in cases in which the pregnancies are the result of rape or incest, the pregnancy is considered life-threatening for the woman, or the fetus is suspected to be malformed physically or mentally. These regulations make it difficult for healthy women to receive abortions; those who seek an abortion and who do not meet the above criteria must have their cases reviewed and approved by a professionally appointed health committee and must pay for the abortion out of pocket.

   For an interesting discussion of abortion legislation in Israel and its social effects see Amir and Navon 1989: 13–69.

3   Indeed, according to traditional Jewish law (Halakha), a Jewish man must divorce his wife if she fails to bear him children after ten years of marriage.

4   Nira Yuval-Davis suggests that "the emotional needs of a people in a permanent war society, where husbands and sons might get killed at any moment, and cultural familial traditions probably play a more central role [in the decision to have children in Israel] than anything else" (1987: 85). She quotes Geula Cohen, a former right-wing Knesset member, who elaborates on this concept of a "permanent war society" and the role of Jewish mothers in it: "The Israeli woman is an organic part of the family of the Jewish people and the female constitutes a practical symbol for that. But she is a wife and a mother in Israel, and therefore it is of her nature to be a soldier, a wife of a

soldier, a sister of a soldier, a grandmother of a soldier. This is her reserve service. She is continually in military service" (ibid.: 86).

5   In her article Yuval-Davis is critical of Israeli demographic policies. She explains Israeli pronatalism and the encouragement of Jewish birthrates thus: "One of the basic concerns of the Zionist movement, especially the Labour Zionist movement, since the beginning of the Zionist settlement in Palestine, has been the creation of a Jewish majority in the country as a precondition for the establishment of the Jewish state there. . . . Gradually the objective and subjective conditions for aliyah (Jewish immigration to Israel) have dwindled and Israeli Jewish national reproduction has come to rely more and more on Israeli-born babies" (1987: 62).

6   Certainly, Palestinians living in the Occupied Territories may receive fertility treatment in Israeli hospitals, though the extent to which this treatment is subsidized varies according to the form of health insurance they carry. The National Health Insurance Law covers 98 percent of all resident Israelis, regardless of religion or ethnicity, but it only covers Jews living in the Occupied Territories, not Palestinians.

Interestingly, I often encountered Palestinians from the territories in Israeli fertility clinics. Indeed, after the complete closure of the Occupied Territories was imposed following the bus bombings in February–March 1996, I met a Palestinian couple who were undergoing fertility treatment at Hadassah Hospital in Jerusalem; the clinic had written them a medical letter that allowed them to bypass the military checkpoints on the way between Nablus and Jerusalem.

1 "The time arrived but the father didn't":
      A New Continuum of Israeli Conception

1   In 1993, 10 percent of the households in Israel were headed by a single parent; of these, 64 percent were headed by a single woman, either unmarried, widowed, divorced, or waiting for a divorce (Israel Women's Network 1995 Report on the Status of Women in Israel [hereafter cited as Women's Network 1995]). The Jewish divorce rate in Israel remains low compared to other developed countries; in the early 1990s it was 1.4 per 1000 (Avgar 1994).

2   Secular Israelis sometimes make the choice not to get married in an effort to avoid the involvement of the orthodox rabbinate, which has exclusive control over all marriages between Jews in Israel.

3   Of the immigrants who arrived in Israel from the former Soviet Union between 1990 and 1994, 13 percent were single-parent families, most of them headed by women. Statistics reveal that this

wave of immigration increased the number of single-parent families headed by women by over 14 percent (Women's Network 1995).

4   Some plans require women receiving donor sperm to pay 180NIS ($60) for each sample of sperm they receive, but there seems to be some variation in how various health plans subsidize artificial insemination. Some women I interviewed received sperm samples without paying anything, others paid up-front and were later reimbursed by their insurance, and still others paid for their sperm samples and were told they were not entitled to reimbursement.

5   The Center for Alternative Parenting in Tel Aviv, founded in the early 1990s, brings unmarried men and women together to form nonsexual, nonromantic contractual arrangements designed for the express purpose of having children in pseudonuclear families. Such arrangements operate not unlike custody arrangements after divorce. The first organization of its kind in the world, it was slowly becoming a more popular parenting option, particularly for gay men and unmarried heterosexual women in Tel Aviv.

6   "Just Me and My Sperm Donor," *Yediot Aharanot,* December 1994.

7   The California Cryobank provides extensive information about sperm donors, some of whom have agreed to be identified when the child(ren) conceived with their sperm turn eighteen years old. Though legally complicated and expensive, some Israeli women had succeeded in importing sperm from the California Cryobank and other sperm banks in America, but they must secure special permissions from the Israeli ministry of health.

8   Fear of AIDS among women seeking artificial insemination has been well documented (Weston 1991) and must be understood as part of the reason that artificial insemination is privileged over sexual intercourse. Contamination is feared from both sexual intercourse and tainted sperm.

9   The "inefficiency" of sexual intercourse as a means of getting pregnant is repeatedly invoked in medical and popular discourse about the advantages of the new reproductive technologies and has been persuasively criticized by Janice Raymond (1993) and others.

10   The psychiatric interview required of prospective unmarried inseminees was recently amended in the wake of the Supreme Court's decision in the Yarus-Hakak case (see chap. 2). As a result of the court's ruling in favor of the petition, unmarried women are now no longer required to undergo psychiatric evaluations.

11   According to a report in the newspaper *Haaretz* (23 December 1994), there is a thriving black market in "pirate insemination" services. The report indicates that "hundreds of illegal inseminations are done each

year" in Israeli fertility clinics, though most are performed for married women whose husbands are infertile. These inseminations are illegal because fresh sperm is bought from donors at prices above those set by the ministry of health and then sold to clients for a profit. This is a risky business, since fresh sperm is not screened for the HIV virus or for other diseases. Clients who are concerned about AIDS may pay black-market prices for the screening and freezing of sperm to be used in their inseminations. In addition to the health concerns involved in this practice, there are the obvious ethical issues involved in the buying and selling of biogenetic material, which, like the buying and selling of organs, is illegal in Israel. Those who donate sperm legally are compensated for their medical examinations and their time, they are not paid; an important, if somewhat blurry, legal distinction. "Pirate inseminations" are attractive to prospective inseminees because the recipients have more say about the particular characteristics of the sperm donor and more assurance that the donor is of "above average intelligence, like a medical student." They are also attractive because doctors who provide illegal inseminations do not require their clients to go through the regular insemination bureaucracy of psychiatric and social worker interviews. In addition, some doctors who provide illegal inseminations will perform genetic tests on the donated sperm to determine the existence of hereditary diseases and genetic compatibility with the recipient. This kind of testing can be expensive and, except for Tay-Sachs testing, is not provided in legal inseminations. The downside to "pirate inseminations" is that they are significantly more expensive than legal inseminations, which are almost entirely subsidized by National Health Insurance.

12 A woman I interviewed in Tel Aviv was an exception. She explained matter-of-factly: "With the public clinics, it's a problem. I don't want them in my business. I don't want to be bothered. I paid more money and had it done privately."

13 Exceptions to these regulations may be made in extreme, extenuating circumstances. If a child born via artificial insemination is diagnosed with an illness or disease to which there is a known genetic component, and if the child's prognosis is dependent on the medical history of the sperm donor, then a court order may be issued to identify the donor.

14 In a short newspaper article in the major daily *Yediot Aharanot* (28 March 1995) it is reported that at one Israeli fertility clinic, Assaf HaRofe, most unmarried women who seek artificial insemination prefer "blond, blue-eyed" sperm, even if they themselves are "dark." Light skin is believed to represent greater social privilege in Israel, as in many other countries.

15 See footnote 11 regarding the possibility of genetic screening of donor sperm in "pirate inseminations."

16 For a compelling analysis of "living IVF" see Franklin 1997.

17 Though there are rabbinic textual precedents for understanding conception without sex (see chap. 3), they are relatively obscure and were never invoked by the women I interviewed as historical antecedents or useful analogues to their pathways to pregnancy.

18 See Weston 1991; Lewin 1993; Agigian 1998.

19 Solomon 1991.

20 Yarus-Hakak successfully challenged the regulation that demanded psychiatric evaluations for unmarried women. See the discussion of her case in chapter 2.

21 Devorah Ross (1998) identifies the only other published rabbinic opinion on this issue, Rabbi Ben Zion Ferrer in *Noam*, book 6.

22 Responsa of the Va'ad Halakha of the Rabbinical Assembly of Israel, vol. 3. 5748–49. (Golinkin's responsa on single women and artificial insemination is summarized fully in appendix D.)

2 Not *Mamzers:* The Legislation of Reproduction and the "Issue" of Unmarried Women

1 Daniel Nahmani v. Ruti Nahmani, Assuta Ltd. Private Hospital, Attorney General (C.A. 5587/93:66–67), translated from Hebrew by Abra Siegel.

2 See Dolgin 1997; Shalev 1989.

3 Haim Zadok, Knesset Record 1994 32: 156, as quoted by Rabbi Dr. Mordechai Halperin in his dissenting opinion (hereafter cited as Halperin 1994) to the Aloni Commission Report.

4 See Rakover 1989.

5 Article 4a of the Law of Return: The right of a Jew under the Law of Return and the rights of a new immigrant under the Nationality Law are also vested in a child or grandchild of a Jew, the spouse of a Jew, and the spouse of a grandchild of a Jew, except for a person who has voluntarily changed his religion.

Article 4b of the Law of Return: For the purposes of this Law, "Jew" means a person who was born of a Jewish mother or has become converted to Judaism and who is not a member of another religion.

6 This rabbinic control is the subject of ongoing debates about the qualifications for citizenship in Israel, including "Who is a Jew" for purposes of immigration and marriage, and so forth. For more on the relationship between secular and religious law in Israel see Kretchmar 1993.

7   Knesset Record 1992 125: 3782–83, as quoted in Halperin 1994.

8   Part of the British colonial enterprise in Palestine was based on the adoption of certain ordinances from the preexisting Ottoman system, including tolerance of the rights of religious minorities to practice their religions and run independent religious courts.

9   Emanuel Rackman compares Jewish and Christian views on illegitimacy thus "that Jewish law is much more liberal than Christian law is due to the fact that the two legal systems parted ways centuries ago with regard to their conceptions of illegitimacy. According to Judaism, the child of an unwed mother is not illegitimate. A child is illegitimate only when it is conclusively established that it was born of an adulterous or incestuous relationship" (1956: 1,210).

10   For a full text of the ministry of health regulations regarding reproductive technology see my appendixes A, B.

11   The American Fertility Society's report titled "Ethical Considerations of the New Reproductive Technologies" differs from the aforementioned reports because it was not independent. It was not commissioned by the U.S. government but by the American Fertility Society as a way to provide support for the use of these technologies (Raymond 1993: 127).

12   For an in-depth discussion of the threat of mamzerut as historically specific see Falk 1991.

13   A sperm donor directory would still be a compromise for many rabbis who would prefer to outlaw sperm donations by Jews altogether. The Halakhic complications of anonymous Jewish sperm donation, including problems of sperm procurement and heightened risks of incestuous relationships among the children conceived with donor sperm, make the use of Jewish donor sperm Halakhically prohibitive. In the opinion of one ultraorthodox fertility counselor in Jerusalem, the current regulations, which allow for artificial insemination with Jewish donor sperm, create a situation in which "*mamzers* are being conceived in-vitro everyday" in clinics in which there is not Halakhic supervision (see chap. 1).

3 Jewish and Gentile Sperm:
Rabbinic Discourse on Sperm and Paternal Relatedness

1   David Schneider explains that "when I say that 'all human cultures have a theory of human reproduction,' I mean that we have an analytic category which corresponds to the cultural category which is called 'their folk theory of reproduction' (or biological relatedness).

If, in the native culture we are examining, there is nothing whatever that corresponds to our analytic category, then our analytic category is not applicable" (1984: 120).

2   See, for example, "At the Last Minute, the Mixing of Two Different Women's Eggs Is Found" (in Hebrew), *Yediot Aharanot*, 27 July 1995; "Orthodox Fertility Inspectors Found Three Mistakes in the Last Year in In-Vitro Fertilization Procedures" (in Hebrew), *Ha'aretz*, 31 March 1995; "Rabbi Bakshi Doron Says: Don't Have Fertility Treatment without Halakhic Inspection" (in Hebrew), *Davar*, 12 August 1994.

3   Moshe Drori puts it concisely: "Unlike secular legal systems, in which central legislative and judicial bodies create a more or less monolithic legal structure, and unlike religious legal systems in which there is one authority whose utterances reflect the binding religious law, Jewish Law, with no unified religious leadership, allows for Halakhic pluralism" (1984: 213). See also Elon 1994, 2: 477–545.

4   For a full discussion of the nature of rabbinic decision making see Berkovits 1983; Gordis 1979: 263–82; Roth 1986; Elon 1973.

5   See Rabbi J. Simcha Cohen:

> How does one *posken* (rule on) an Halakhic Question not overtly ruled in the *Shulkhan Arukh*? There are a variety of rules regarding the proper Halakhic methodology. An interesting and concise formulation was articulated by the 17thC Polish scholar R. Aaron b. Avraham of Solnik. He suggested Halakhic decision-making utilize the following procedures: 1) majority opinion, 2) Talmudic or rabbinic proof, 3) ruling of a great sage. Each process has its limitations:
>
> Problems with (1) are that many lesser rabbis can overrule a great rabbi.
>
> Problems with (2) are that great mental agility is required and a great contemporary sage is required to do a brilliant analysis.
>
> Problems with (3) are that it is difficult to determine who was the last great sage.
>
> It is necessary for Halakhic decisions to be circulated among scholars so that the proper policies may be formulated. This does not preclude any Rav or Rosh Yeshivah from making decisions on matters posed to them. It suggests merely that positions be made public so that general Halakhic policy may be organically generated. (1991: 76)

See also Drori 1976: 85–86.

6   "The Torah is all-inclusive. It comprehends the entire life of the Jewish people. Halakha, therefore, has to interpret the intention of the Torah for all the areas of Jewish existence, the spiritual, the ethical,

the economic, the socio-practical. It also has to define the functions and powers of the teaching and implementing authority envisaged by the Torah" (Berkovits 1983: 3).

7 Halperin 1988: 25.

8 For a full discussion of this issue see Y. Jakobovits 1993.

9 "1) It is improper to emit seed for naught and this sin is more serious than all the sins in the Torah. Therefore, a person should not thresh on the inside and sow on the outside and he should not marry a minor who is not capable of giving birth. 2) Those who commit adultery with their hands by emitting seed, not only is it a great prohibition, but a person who does so is considered excommunicated and of him it is said: 'Your hands are full of blood' (Isaiah 1:15) *and it is as if he had committed murder"* (*Shulkhan Arukh, "Even HaEzer"* 23: 1–2, translated by Rabbi David Golinkin).

10 Rav Feinstein, one of the leading rabbinic decisors of the twentieth century, uses the Talmudic text *Yevamot 76a,* in which the Gemara describes a semen test for a man (to see if his genital deformity prohibits him from getting married), as a basis for permitting the emission of semen if it is for purposes of procreation (in Cohen 1987: 49–50).

11 Indeed, to collect sperm for analysis (spermogram) as opposed to insemination, some rabbis have ruled that a woman should go to the doctor's office immediately after sex in order to have a sample of her husband's sperm removed from her vagina. This way, the husband does not have to masturbate in order to produce sperm; his sperm has been released in the "natural" way with the "natural" intention to fulfill the commandment to be fruitful and multiply.

To collect sperm for insemination, some rabbis permit masturbation because the intention of the act is to be fruitful and multiply. Other rabbis advocate the use of a perforated condom, so that sperm can be symbolically released in the "natural" way yet still be collected for lab preparation for artificial insemination.

Yoel Jakobovits, summarizing the guidelines suggested by Rabbi E. Waldenburg, outlines the preferred methods of sperm procurement thus:

—The preferred method of semen collection is from the vagina following normal coitus.

—Where that is not possible because of technical or emotional reasons, sperm may be procured after coitus interruptus.

—Where that is unsuitable, the collection should be made using a condom—preferably one with a perforation worn during intercourse.

—If that is impossible, a receptacle should be placed intravaginally.

— Finally, if that is impractical, sperm may be obtained by masturbation. Penile stimulation should preferably be achieved by a mechanical stimulator, though self-stimulation is also permitted. (1993: 245)

12 Priests (Kohanim) were biblically prohibited from marrying any woman other than a virgin (see Leviticus 21:14).

13 "A son born in this way would not have exactly the same standing as if born as a result of procreation in the usual way. He is legitimate, but if no other children are born of the marriage, a widow must receive *halitza,* that is, ceremonial permission from the nearest relative of the deceased husband, before re-marriage, just as if no children had been born at all" (Rosner and Bleich 1979: 111).

14 See Rav B. M. Uziel, Responsa, *Mishpete Uziel, Even HaEzer* (in Hebrew), sec. 19; Rav M. Feinstein, Responsa, *Iggerot Moshe, Even HaEzer* (in Hebrew), vol. 1, sec. 10; vol. 2, sec. 11, 71; vol. 3, sec. 11; Rav Y. Breisch, Responsa, *Chelkat Ya'akov* (in Hebrew), vol. 1, sec. 24; Rav Y. Weinberg, Responsa, *Sedrei Esh* (in Hebrew), vol. 3, sec. 5.

15 He explains further that marital fidelity for a woman is a restriction on her sexuality only, not a restriction on her reproductive capacity (*Iggorot Moshe, Even HaEzer* 71 (in Hebrew). This is not to suggest that Rav Feinstein advocated artificial insemination with donor sperm from a Jewish third party, it simply means that when considered after the fact, he did not consider such an act to constitute adultery. Indeed, we will see how Rav Feinstein, and indeed every twentieth-century orthodox rabbinic authority, explicitly forbade artificial insemination with donor sperm from a Jewish third party.

16 Avraham Steinberg explains: "All of the rabbis are of the unanimous opinion that there exists a prohibition against using unknown Jewish donor sperm for a married woman . . . most of the *poskim* [rabbinic decisors] say there is not a *d'oraita* [biblical] prohibition against implanting *zera psoul* [wasted seed] into the womb of a woman, but the main basis of the prohibition is the act of penetration and the pleasure of intercourse. Together, all the commentators forbade insemination from an unknown Jew to a married woman. The prohibition against this act arises both from a moral consideration and from a fear of various legal considerations (1975: 132–33) (my translation).

17 R. Y. Teitelbaum, Responsa, *Divrei-Yoel, Even HaEzer* 107: 5.

18 For many contemporary rabbis, the problem with relying on such texts as precedents in order to make current rulings about artificial insemination is that these texts only discuss accidental, indirect impregnation; artificial insemination as it is practiced today is premeditated and planned. The distinction is crucial, for Jewish law makes

clear divisions between acts that are done passively and acts that are done actively. See J. David Bleich and Fred Rosner, "Artificial Insemination in Jewish Law," in Bleich and Rosner 1979: 113; Responsa, *Helkat Ya'akov*.

19 See Rav Yonathan Eibeshutz, *Bene Ahuvah, Ishut,* sec. 15; Rav Y. L. Zirelson, *Ma'arche Lev,* sec. 73; Rav Y. Teitelbaum, "Responsa Concerning Artificial Insemination Using a Foreign Donor's Seed," in *HaMaor* 16: 9–10, Elul 5724 (Jewish month and year); Rav Y. Waldenburg, Responsa, *Tsits Eliezer* (1951), vol. 9, sec. 51, pt. 4, pt. 3, 27, and *Tsits Eliezer* (1978), pt. 13, sec. 97; Rav Ovadia Hadaya, Responsa, *Yaskil Avdi* (1958), pt. 5, 10 (all of the above in Hebrew).

20 For a discussion of the legal consequences for a wife who undergoes artificial insemination without her husband's consent see Rav Katzbourg, *Tel Talpiot* (in Hebrew), sec. 79; Rav Zirelson, *Ma'arkehei Lev* (in Hebrew), sec. 141; Rav Waldenburg, Responsa, *Tsits Eliezer* (in Hebrew), pt. 13, sec. 97; Schereschewsky 1974: 312.

21 There are conflicting versions of *Sefer Mitzvot Katan,* which are interpreted today to have different Halakhic implications for the use of artificial insemination.

22 Rav Peretz of Corbeil in *Hagahot Semak,* quoted by Rabbi Joel Sirkes in his commentary on Rabbi Jacob ben Asher's *Tur Shulkhan Arukh,* sec. *Yoreh Deah,* chap. 195.

23 "Midrash Alef-Bet of Ben Sira" (in Hebrew), in Eisenstein 1928: 43. The current critical edition of this story in *Toledot Ben Sira* is in Eli Yassif's "Sippurei Ben Sira Biyemei Habeinayim," Jerusalem, 1984: 198–99. It is first quoted by R. Moshe Hadarshan, France, eleventh century and the Arukh, Italy, eleventh century, and Yassif dates it to Bavel, ninth–tenth centuries, Yassif, 19–29. (I am grateful to Rabbi David Golinkin for this bibliographic source information.)

24 See Yoel Jakobovits 1993: n. 15.

25 For a full discussion of this issue see Yoel Jakobovits 1993.

26 The question regarding sperm donation and levirate marriage is: If a Jewish man who is married but childless donates sperm and then subsequently dies, is he considered to be childless even though his sperm has successfully conceived children, albeit not with his wife? And if so, is his brother still obligated to marry his wife in order to carry on his name, commensurate with the obligation of levirate marriage (yibbum)? Contemporary rabbis have expressed differing interpretations of this issue.

27 "Adoption" in a legal sense does not exist in Jewish law; unlike contemporary adoption practices in the West, traditional Jewish law does not recognize legal adoption. People who bring an orphan into

their home to raise are understood in legal terms to be acting as agents of the biological parents, not as replacements for them (Dorff 1998: 108).

28 Rav Waldenburg explains: "The very essence of this matter — namely, placing into the womb of a married woman the seed of another man — is a great abomination in the tents of Jacob and there is no greater desecration of the family in the dwelling places of Israel" (Waldenburg, *Tsits Eliezer,* vol. 5, sec. 1, cited in Zohar 1998: 80).

29 See Waldenburg 1982.

30 See, for example, Loike and Steinberg 1998: 31–47.

31 Avraham Steinberg explains: "It's clear to all that (a child born with non-Jewish sperm) is not a mamzer and is part of Israel like his mother. He does not have to convert and he is not disqualified from being a Kohen if his mother is a Kohen. The husband must separate from his wife three months before she inseminates with non-Jewish sperm and three months after she gives birth for reasons of distinction. In the event that the insemination was done with sperm from an unknown donor, a number of commentators have said you should presume that the sperm is that of a non-Jew, because most people in these countries are non-Jews, especially since the act of emitting sperm is a prohibited act and it should be assumed that Jews do not do this, thus the child is kosher. But as one of the authors has pointed out, these facts only apply abroad and that in our country the *poskim* should agree that we should not make such presumptions here" (1975: 135) (my translation).

32 See Babylonian Talmud, *Kiddushin* 66b, 68b; Maimonides, *Mishneh Torah, The Book of Holiness: The Laws of Forbidden Intercourse* 15: 4; *Shulkhan Arukh, Even HaEzer* 4: 5, 19, 8: 5; Dorff 1998: 70 n. 11. In addition, Steinberg points out that in rabbinic discussions about the use of non-Jewish sperm "there is no discussion whatsoever about the issue of maintenance (between a non-Jewish sperm donor and his child) because this obligation falls only on the father and the child is considered to have no father" (1975: 136).

33 One fertility specialist I interviewed told me of an orthodox couple for whom non-Jewish sperm was "a particular blessing." In this couple, the husband was a Kohen, a patrilineal status that designates membership in the "priestly class" believed to be linked directly back to the time the Temple stood in Jerusalem. He suffered from a severe form of infertility, and the treatment indicated was artificial insemination by donor. In consultation with their rabbi, the couple imported non-Jewish sperm from the United States in order to avoid adulterous or incestuous complications, and the wife became preg-

nant. What was unusual was how they dealt with the problem of the husband's status as a Kohen, which is traditionally passed through the patriline from father to son. The woman was given hormonal treatment to stimulate her ovaries so that they would produce an abundance of eggs. These eggs were then surgically removed, fertilized with the donated non-Jewish sperm, and the resulting embryos were implanted in her uterus. As so often happens in these cases, an overabundance of fertilized embryos began to grow in the uterus, and the woman had to undergo a procedure called "embryo-reduction" in order to prevent the spontaneous abortion of the embryos. In this case, the couple had access to advanced technology that allowed the doctor to determine the sex of the developing embryo. The couple had the embryos sexed and then asked to have the male embryos aborted so that only daughters would be born. Since Kohen status is passed through the patriline from father to son, sons born to a man who is a Kohen would be expected to perform the many public duties of a Kohen, including the recitation of the "priestly benediction" in synagogue and to observe the restrictions imposed on a Kohen, including not visiting cemeteries and not marrying divorced women. But since sons born from non-Jewish donor sperm do not inherit identity from their Jewish social fathers, a son conceived with non-Jewish donor sperm whose social father is a Kohen is not a Kohen himself, even though some rabbis have innovatively ruled that in such a case the son could inherit Kohen status from his mother. See Rav Shlomo Auerbach 1958 *Noam* (in Hebrew), 1: 165. This couple decided, then, that since daughters born to a Kohen do not have the public obligations of a Kohen, a daughter born from non-Jewish donor sperm would avoid the social expectations that would be demanded of her brother. Thus the couple succeeded in having children while avoiding Halakhic and social complications related to the patrilineal inheritance of Kohen status.

34 It is important to point out, however, that even among those rabbis who look more favorably on the use of non-Jewish sperm, none have issued a blanket ruling that states positively: It is permitted to use non-Jewish sperm. The ruling is not prescriptive legislation but is determined on a case-by-case basis.

35 *Hazra'ah Malakhutit, Noam,* 1958: 1: 165–66, as translated in Lasker 1988.

36 *Iggorot Moshe, Even HaEzer* 71 (in Hebrew).

37 See Zvi Hirsch Friedman. 1965. *Sefer Sedeh Hemed* (Brooklyn: Hemed), 34.

38 Mayer Amsel, "Od Peratim Nehuzim be-Issur ha-Hazra-ah Ma-

lakhutit" *HaMaor* 15, 1 (Oct.–Nov. 1964), as translated in Lasker 1988: 11–18. Daniel Lasker explains that this concept of pollution as a characteristic of non-Jews is derived from the rabbinic statement: "When the serpent had relations with Eve, it implanted her with pollution . . . the pollution of Israel, who stood on Mt. Sinai, has ceased: the pollution of the idolaters, who did not stand on Mt. Sinai, has not ceased" (*Shabbat 15a–b, Avodah Zarah 23b, Yevamot 103b*). Lasker goes on to explain: "While most Jewish thinkers do not believe in the concept of original sin, this concept was adopted by the Kabbalah. Thus, the pollution of the non-Jews in the case of artificial insemination from a non-Jewish donor is apparently an hereditary form of such original sin" (1988: 9).

39 Rav Waldenburg, *Tsits Eliezer* (in Hebrew), 12: 251–52.

40 In Cohen 1987: 58.

41 R. Halberstam, "Pamphlet for the Saving of Jewish Purity and Lineage," cited in Lasker 1988: 8.

42 This genealogy of ideas, reflective of a certain kind of Jewish racism, was outlined for me by Rabbi David Golinkin.

43 Mary Douglas's assessment of attitudes toward pollution among minority groups is illuminating here, particularly since she makes explicit mention of the so-called Israelites: "The Israelites were always in their history a hard-pressed minority. In their beliefs all the bodily issues were polluting, blood, pus, excreta, semen, etc. The threatened boundaries of their body politic would be well-mirrored in their care for the integrity, unity, and purity of the physical body" (1966: 125).

44 See Howards 1995.

45 Debates about the transmission of Judaism through the patriline are the subject of ongoing political discussion in Israel, where the fact that citizenship for Jews is determined by Orthodox definitions of relatedness is hotly contested. For a discussion of the patrilineal principle see J. David Bleich, "The Patrilineal Principle: The Crucial Concern," in Bleich 1989.

4 Eggs and Wombs: The Origins of Jewishness

1 I address these issues in another context: see Kahn 2000.

2 Some women recovered more slowly. Some said they felt significant cramping for a few days after the oocyte pick-up, in addition to nausea and exhaustion. Moreover, the operation and associated hormonal treatments are not without their considerable risks. In 1987 a woman named Rivi Ben Ari died in Tel Aviv following Pergonal

treatments, which are often a prelude to the oocyte retrieval (Solomon 1991: 102–4).

3　See *Talmud Bavli Niddah 17b* and *Shulkhan Arukh, Yoreh De'ah* 183: 1.

4　The principal Halakhic source that contemporary rabbis interpret in relation to this question is the thirteenth-century *P'sak Halakha* (ruling) of Rav Peretz of Corbeil, discussed in chapter 3.

5　For a fuller discussion of these issues in the context of fertility treatments see Grazi 1994. In his chapter "Diagnostic Evaluations," Grazi explains the differences between a niddah and a *zavah;* the former is defined as "a woman who experiences vaginal bleeding from the uterus during her expected menstrual period, and a *zavah* is a woman who experiences bleeding at times other than her expected period" (80). Both statuses render a woman ritually "unclean," though the period of uncleanliness differs. Grazi makes clear that bleeding produced "from a wound" incurred during diagnostic procedures in gynecological exams and fertility tests falls under a different Halakhic category: *makkah.* There is considerable rabbinic disagreement as to what constitutes a wound and how you can determine whether the source of bleeding is a wound or menstruation.

6　For a full discussion of the problems associated with artificial insemination and embryo transfer during the niddah period see Green 1984.

7　Rabbi J. David Bleich explains: "An organism that can be seen only by means of a magnifying glass or under a microscope is an organism of which Jewish law takes no notice. . . . (Hence) when the developing (human) organism is still sub-visual, the law takes no cognizance of its existence." See Bleich, "Ethical Concerns in Artificial Procreation: A Jewish Perspective," 1986: 144.

8　See Halperin 1988.

9　Rav Zalman Goldberg (1987) explains: "Rav Yosef Engel (Bet Otzar, 'Av') argues that there is a legal distinction between maternity and paternity. Paternity is determined at conception, as stated in the Talmud. Maternity, however, depends on birth and not on conception. He bases this distinction on a comment of Rashi (Meg. 13). The Gemara states that Queen Esther's father died when she was conceived and her mother died when she was born. Rashi explains that the statement is based on the verse '. . . and when her father and mother were dead' (Esther 2,7). It previously states that '. . . she had neither father nor mother.' The redundancy teaches us that: 'she did not have a father or mother even one day. When she was conceived her father died, hence she did not have a father from the time that he was eligible to be considered a father. When she was born, her mother died; hence (her mother) was not eligible to be considered a mother.' We see here that there is a difference between maternity and paternity. The reason is that the father is irrelevant to the birth; hence his relationship is necessarily dependent on his role in conception. Maternity, however, is determined by the birth, since the mother gives birth to the baby. . . . it follows that birth is the determinant of maternity . . . the possibility exists, however, that birth is not the sole determinant of maternity." See also discussions of Midrashic sources regarding the intrauterine transfer of Dinah from the womb of Rachel to Leah, and the transfer of Joseph from the womb of Leah to Rachel as a model for understanding parturition as the determinant of maternity (Bleich 1983: 92–93); Rav Ezra Bick's discussion of this issue (Bick 1987); Gemara, *Yevamot* 97b, for the Halakhic source that indicates parturition is the determinant of maternity; and Bleich 1994.

10 See Bleich 1991.

11 Rav Waldenburg, *Tzits Eliezer* (in Hebrew), 15: 45, as reprinted in *Sefer Assia,* 5, Jerusalem 5746; R. Gershuni, *Kol Zafayikh,* Jerusalem 5740, as reprinted in Bleich 1991.

12 For a fuller discussion of the various rabbinic opinions on the determination of maternal identity see Bleich 1979, 1983, 1991.
— 1981. Bleich, "Survey of Recent Halakhic Periodical Literature" in *Tradition,* 19 (4).
— 1984. *Tehumin* 5: 248–274. (In Hebrew)
— 1986. *Tehumin* 7: 266–270. (In Hebrew)

13 Interestingly, this agricultural model of conception, known anthropologically as the "monogenetic theory of procreation," has been well documented among other Middle Eastern peoples and could be understood as one of the most compelling kinship myths indigenous to the region (Delaney 1991; Inhorn 1994).

14 For example, Regulation (4) of the ministry of health regulations (1987) provides: "Eggs shall be taken from women only for whom the following conditions exist: 1) The patient is involved in medical treatment as the result of fertility problems. 2) A responsible doctor determines that the removal of eggs will advance this treatment." Regulation (12b) states: "An egg which was taken from a woman for donation will be implanted in another woman only if she gave her consent to the donation."

15 For a fuller discussion on the religious status of children born to Jewish women from non-Jewish eggs see Bleich 1991.

16 See Bleich 1991. Bleich also provides an interesting discussion of rabbinic attitudes toward conversion of a child in utero in response

to the question: could a Jewish woman carrying an embryo conceived with a non-Jewish egg immerse in a ritual bath and thereby convert the child in utero? (1991: 88–89).

17   For more information about Islamic rules concerning the new reproductive technologies see Inhorn 1994.

18   Many women I spoke to, all Jewish Israelis, have made it clear that though it is not an easy decision, they agreed to donate eggs because they wanted to help alleviate someone else's childlessness, a form of suffering they know all too well.

19   See Marcia Inhorn (1994) on Islamic law and the use of third-party donor material in infertility treatment.

20   See Klass 1996.

21   See also *Talmud Bavli Hullin* 79a, for a Talmudic discussion that favors determining species by descent.

5 Multiple Mothers:
Surrogacy and the Location of Maternity

1   The passage of the surrogacy law was greeted by Israeli mainstream women's organizations as a legitimate, albeit complicated solution to the suffering of childlessness. "We regard it as a humane, moving and important step that will allow women who can't have babies themselves to raise children from babyhood," said WIZO-Israel chair Helena Glaser. Na'amat, the women's division of the Histadrut, an organization that runs childcare centers and offers other services to women, issued a statement that the surrogacy law "will open new possibilities for thousands of couples who are not wealthy enough to have a family (through adoption)" (*Jerusalem Post,* 7 March 1996). The Israel Women's Network, the umbrella organization of the feminist movement in Israel, issued a lonely yet sharp condemnation of the surrogacy law, asserting that it opened up an avenue for the exploitation of women.

2   For a full discussion of the way consent for reproductive technology is manufactured in the media see Van Dyck 1995.

3   Translated from the Hebrew by Abra S. Siegel. For a complete text of the Embryo-Carrying Agreements Law see appendix E.

4   The approvals committee appointed by the ministry of health to oversee such agreements is to be composed of two obstetrician/gynecologists, an internal medicine specialist, a psychologist, a social worker, a lawyer, and a clergyman (*ish dat*) of the same religion as the parties involved.

5 The practice of surrogacy among Christians and Moslems in Israel, while fascinating, is beyond the scope of this chapter. Moreover, rabbinic understandings of relatedness, not Christian or Moslem understandings, influenced the construction of the new law. Thus I only examine Jewish understandings of surrogacy and the use of Jewish surrogates in Israel.

6 This last provision represents a highly controversial concession on the part of the orthodox religious representatives who were involved in the legal negotiations about the law. Secular legislators bargained for the inclusion of this provision in exchange for the religious demand that the sperm used in surrogacy agreements may only come from the contracting husband and not from an anonymous donor (Dr. Carmel Shalev, letter to author, 1997).

7 In chapter 2 we learned that the structure of the Israeli parliamentary system is such that orthodox rabbis can exert unusual pressure on secular lawmakers in various legal spheres, and the assisted reproduction of new Jewish citizens is one of them. Thus rabbinic beliefs about kinship are explicitly manifest in secular legislation regarding the appropriate uses of reproductive technology.

8 Rav Eliyahu, Former Chief Sephardic Rabbi, addressing a convention on Medicine, Ethics, and Jewish Law at Shaare Zedek Hospital in Jerusalem, 15 July 1996, my translation. Rav Eliyahu is not alone among prominent orthodox rabbis who condemn surrogacy: Rav Shalom Eliashev and Rav Shlomo Zalman Auerbach have also issued sharp condemnations of surrogacy (see *Nishmat Avraham* by Dr. Avraham Steinberg). In *Tsits Eliezer* Rav Waldenburg suggests that it is not even worthwhile to go into all the reasons why surrogacy should be prohibited, because to list the reasons would just be an invitation to try and reason around them.

9 See chapter 4 for a discussion of the Halakhic debates about the appropriate determinants of maternity. Rabbi Mordechai Halperin and others have suggested that maternity must be understood to have two components, genetic and gestational; therefore, a child conceived through a surrogacy agreement in effect has two mothers. See Halperin and Priner 1996.

10 Certainly, a child gestated by a non-Jewish surrogate mother could be converted to Judaism, but there have been ongoing Halakhic and political disputes about the conversion of non-Jewish children and the subsequent procedures for adoption in Israel, disputes that most secular lawmakers and contracting couples in Israel would prefer to avoid.

11 Legislators deliberately chose not to utilize a preexisting channel for

the transfer of guardianship known as an "order of adoption" (*tsav imutz*), in order to normalize these instances of reproduction.

12 See Chapter C, Embryo-Carrying Agreements Law in appendix E.

13 Halakhic concern over the status of the child, and concern that the child of a woman born within a surrogacy agreement could grow up and marry a child born to his Halakhic mother (i.e., the surrogate), is circumvented in the law by the provision that all children born to a surrogate mother must have the name of the birth mother, and the legal mother, listed on their birth certificates. This way, when a child born to a surrogate goes to get married, rabbis can check to make sure that the proposed union is not an incestuous one between two children born to the same Halakhic mother. One wonders whether two children, born to different surrogates but conceived with the same contracting mother's egg, would be considered siblings in the Halakhic imagination, for as we have seen, most rabbis discount genetic substance as the ultimate referent for maternity.

14 I understand the methodological problems involved in examining media narratives as "authentic" narratives, for no matter how diverse they appear, they are inevitably products of agenda-driven editorial processes. I suggest that media representations of surrogacy in Israel be understood as vehicles intended to manufacture public consent to these extraordinary procreative relationships. The notion that "consent" is "manufactured" is Herman and Chomsky's, who suggest that the function of the news media as an institution is to "inculcate individuals with the values, beliefs and codes of behavior that will integrate them into the institutional structures of the larger society" (1988: 1). Embedded in public consent for surrogacy are related issues of consent to reproductive technology in general, the pronatalist project of the state, and the centrality of the traditional family's "natural right" to have children. For a full discussion of how the media manufacture consent for reproductive technology see Van Dyck 1995.

15 In a discussion with Etty Dekel, the secretary of the surrogacy committee at the ministry of health, I learned that four months after the law had been passed, sixty couples had been in contact with the ministry of health and had requested application forms for surrogacy agreements, three agreements had been signed, and twenty contracts were being actively processed. Two private "surrogacy centers" have been established, one in Haifa and one in Tel Aviv, where for a monetary fee they will help a couple locate a surrogate and provide counseling throughout the procedure.

16 The question of whether unmarried women without children should be prevented from entering into surrogacy agreements was a subject

of contention in the Aloni Commission Report. The majority opinion states that there is no evidence to suggest that a woman without children is any less likely to honor the surrogacy contract than a woman with children, and in the absence of such evidence it suggests that women without children should not be prevented from becoming surrogates (7.12). In Rabbi Halperin's minority opinion, he states that the unmarried woman without children should be protected from unanticipated emotional suffering and physical harm, for if something went wrong with the contracted pregnancy and the surrogate was unable to give birth to her own children, a great injustice would be done (7.12–7.17).

17 The discussion of appropriate payment to the surrogate mother was the subject of ongoing discussion in the Aloni Commission's deliberations on the matter. In the report, it is stated: "precisely because women are economically vulnerable, it was contended, the financial temptation to enter a surrogacy agreement should be precluded. Indeed, the fear was expressed during the Commission's deliberations that some women might find in surrogacy an occupation or the only means to support their families. . . . A contrary view was that a woman is exploited precisely if she is NOT paid, and that she has the right to be paid for her work. A distinction should be made between purchasing the child and paying for the services of the woman. The surrogate should be paid in installments throughout the course of the pregnancy and not in a lump-sum payment following the birth" (7.20, 7.21). The commission ultimately concluded that payment to the surrogate mother should not be prohibited: "The Commission recommends that the Multi-Disciplinary Committee be authorized to approve an agreement that includes monthly payments to the surrogate mother in amounts that shall be specified in Regulations. Such payments would cover the actual expenses of conception, pregnancy and birth, and would *compensate* the surrogate mother for her time, suffering and loss of income or temporary loss of earning capacity, so that she not suffer financial loss. *No additional payment to the surrogate mother shall be allowed.* In order to prevent professionalism, the number of times that a woman may serve as a surrogate mother should be limited, just as it is recommended to limit the number of gamete donations from any one donor. The Commission recommends that a woman not be permitted to serve as a surrogate mother more than once, except in the case of a second pregnancy for the same commissioning couple" (7.23, emphasis mine). Chapter B (6) of the Embryo-Carrying Agreements Law reads: "The approvals committee is entitled to approve terms in the agreement re-

garding monthly payments to the carrying mother to cover actual expenses involved in the performance of the agreement, including expenses for legal counseling and insurance as well as compensation for time lost, suffering, loss of income or temporary loss of ability to work for a salary, or any other reasonable compensation."

18   Chapter D (19b) of the Embryo-Carrying Agreements Law reads: "A party to an embryo carrying agreement or his agent who offers, gives, asks or receives monetary or equivalent compensation in connection with the performance of an embryo carrying agreement, which has not been approved by the approvals committee, is subject to one year in prison."

19   The correlation between genetic heritage and parental relationship has been well documented by Emily Martin (1987, 1994) and others who analyze the meanings accorded to genetic inheritance in Euro-American culture.

20   Indeed, we saw in chapter 1 how economic well-being is one of the central criteria used by social workers to vet unmarried women for artificial insemination in Israel.

6 Consequences for Kinship

1   See Klein 1998.

Bibliography

Agigian, Amy. 1998. *Contradictory Conceptions: Lesbian Alternative Insemination*. Ph.D. diss. Brandeis University.

Amir, Delila, and Navon, D. 1989. *The Politics of Abortion in Israel* (in Hebrew). Research report, Pinchas Sapir Center for Development. Tel Aviv: Tel Aviv University.

Auerbach, Rav Shlomo. 1958. *Noam* 1 (Hebrew language journal).

Avgar, Amy. 1994. *Reproduction, Health, and Well-Being among Women in Israel*. Israel Women's Network. Jerusalem.

Berkovits, Eli. 1983. *Not in Heaven: The Nature and Function of Halakha*. New York: Ktav.

Bick, Ezra. 1987. "Maternity in Fetal Transplants." In *Crossroads: Halakha and the Modern World*. Alon Shvut-Gush Etzion: Zomet, 79–85.

———. 1993. "Ovum Donations: A Rabbinic Conceptual Model of Maternity." *Tradition* 28 (1): 28–46.

Bleich, J. David. 1979. *Contemporary Halakhic Problems*. Vol. 1. New York: Yeshiva University Press.

———. 1983. *Contemporary Halakhic Problems*. Vol. 2. New York: Yeshiva University Press.

———. 1986. "Ethical Concerns in Artificial Procreation: A Jewish Perspective," *Publications de l'Academie du Rovaume du Maroc, vol. X: Problemes d'ethiques Engendres par les Nouvelles Maitrises de la Procreation Humaine*: 144.

———. 1989. *Contemporary Halakhic Problems*. Vol. 3. New York: Yeshiva University Press.

———. 1991. "In-Vitro Fertilization: Questions of Maternal Identity and Conversion." *Tradition* 25 (4): 82–102.

———. 1994. "Maternal Identity Revisited." *Tradition* 28 (2): 52–57.

Bleich, J. David, and Fred Rosner, eds. 1979. *Jewish Bioethics*. New York: Hebrew Publishing Co.

Bloch, M., and H. Jean. 1980. "Women and the Dialectics of Nature in c18 French Thought." In *Nature, Culture, and Gender*, edited by C. MacCormack and M. Strathern. Cambridge: Cambridge University Press.

Borneman, John. 1996. "Until Death Do Us Part: Marriage and Death in Anthropological Discourse." *American Ethnologist* 23 (2): 215–34.

Boyarin, Daniel. 1993. *Carnal Israel: Reading Sex in Talmudic Culture.* Berkeley: University of California Press.

Boyarin, Jonathan. 1992. *Storm from Paradise: The Politics of Jewish Memory.* Minneapolis: University of Minnesota Press.

Broyde, Michael. 1999. Assisted Reproduction and Jewish Law. The Twenty-second Annual Rabbi Louis Feinberg Memorial Lecture in Judaic Studies. Department of Judaic Studies. Cincinnati: University of Cincinnati.

Butler, Judith. 1993. *Gender Trouble: Feminism and the Subversion of Identity.* New York: Routledge.

Cohen, Alfred S. 1987. "Artificial Insemination." *Journal of Halakha,* no. 13: 43–59.

Cohen, J. Simcha. 1991. *Timely Jewish Questions, Timely Rabbinic Answers.* London: Jacob Aronson Publishers.

Colen, Shellee. 1995. "Like a Mother to Them: Stratified Reproduction and West Indian Childcare Workers and Employers in New York." In *Conceiving the New World Order: The Global Politics of Reproduction,* edited by Faye Ginsburg and Rayna Rapp. Berkeley: University of California Press.

Corea, Gena, et al. 1987. *Man-Made Women.* Indianapolis: Indiana University Press.

Delaney, Carol. 1986. "The Meaning of Paternity and the Virgin Birth Debate." *Man* 21: 494–513.

———. 1991. *The Seed and the Soil: Gender and Cosmology in Turkish Village Society.* Berkeley: University of California Press.

Dickens, Bernard. 1994. "Legislative Approaches." *Journal of Assisted Reproduction and Genetics* 11 (17).

Dolgin, Janet. 1997. *Defining the Family: Law, Technology, and Reproduction in an Uneasy Age.* New York: New York University Press.

Donzelot, Jacques. 1980. *The Policing of Families: Welfare versus State.* London: Hutchison.

Dorff, Elliot N. 1998. *Matters of Life and Death: A Jewish Approach to Modern Medical Ethics.* Philadelphia: Jewish Publication Society.

Douglas, Mary. 1966. *Purity and Danger.* London: Routledge.

Drori, Moshe. 1976. "The Concept Shgaga in Jewish Law: Mistake of Law and Mistake of Fact" (in Hebrew). *Shenaton ha Mishpat LaIvri* vol. 1, no. 72: 85–86.

———. 1984. "Artificial Insemination: Is It Adultery?" In *Jewish Law and Current Legal Problems,* edited by Nahum Rakover. New York: Library of Jewish Law.

Eisenstein, L. D. *Otzer HaMidrashim.*

Elon, Menachem. 1994. *Jewish Law, History, Sources, and Principles.* Jerusalem: Jewish Publication Society.

———. 1973. "Principles of Jewish Law." In *Encyclopaedia Judaica.* New York: Macmillan.

Encyclopaedia Judaica. 1972. Cecil Roth, editor in chief. New York: Macmillan.

Falk, Zee'v. 1991. *Religious Law and Ethics.* Jerusalem: Meshavim.

Field, Martha A. 1988. *Surrogate Motherhood.* Cambridge: Harvard University Press.

Franklin, Sarah. 1995. "Postmodern Procreation: A Cultural Account of Assisted Reproduction." In *Conceiving the New World Order: The Global Politics of Reproduction,* edited by Faye Ginsburg and Rayna Rapp. Berkeley: University of California Press.

———. 1997. *Embodied Progress: A Cultural Account of Assisted Conception.* London: Routledge.

Franklin, Sarah, and Helena Ragone. 1998. *Reproducing Reproduction: Kinship, Power, and Technological Innovation.* Philadelphia: University of Pennsylvania Press.

Ginsburg, Faye D., and Rayna Rapp. 1991. "The Politics of Reproduction." *Annual Review of Anthropology* 20: 311–43.

Ginsburg, Faye D., and Rayna Rapp, eds. 1995. *Conceiving the New World Order.* Berkeley: University of California Press.

Goldberg, Rav Zalman N. 1987. "Maternity in Fetal Transplants." In *Crossroads: Halakha and the Modern World.* Zomet: Alon Shvut-Gush Etzion.

Gordis, Robert. 1979. "A Dynamic Halakha: Principles and Procedures of Jewish Law." *Judaism* 28 (3): 263–82.

Grazi, Richard. 1994. *Be Fruitful and Multiply: Fertility Therapy and the Jewish Tradition.* Jerusalem: Genesis Press.

Green, Joseph. 1984. "Artificial Insemination in Particular Cases of Infertility (in Hebrew). *Assia* 10 (32): 17–29.

Halperin, Mordechai. 1988. "In-Vitro Fertilization, Embryo Transfer, and Embryo Freezing." *Jewish Medical Ethics* 1 (1): 25–30.

Halperin, Mordechai, and Yeruchim Primer. 1996. *Medicine, Ethics, and Jewish Law: The Second International Colloquium.* Jerusalem: Schlesinger Institute.

Herman, Edward S., and Noam Chomsky. 1988. *Manufacturing Consent: The Political Economy of Mass Media.* New York: Pantheon Books.

Howards, Stuart S. 1995. "Treatment of Male Infertility." *New England Journal of Medicine,* 2 February (in Hebrew).

Inhorn, Marcia. 1994. *Quest for Conception: Gender, Infertility, and*

Egyptian Medical Traditions. Philadelphia: University of Pennsylvania Press.

Israel Women's Network. 1996. *Women in Israel: Information and Analysis.* Jerusalem: Israel Women's Network.

Jakobovits, Yoel. 1993. "Male Infertility: Halakhic Issues in Investigation and Management." *Tradition* 27 (2): n.p.

Jordanova, Ludmilla. 1980. "Natural Facts: A Historical Perspective on Science and Sexuality." In *Nature, Culture and Gender,* edited by C. MacCormack and M. Strathern. Cambridge: Cambridge University Press.

Kahn, Susan Martha. 2000. "Rabbis and Reproduction: The Social Uses of New Reproductive Technologies among Ultraorthodox Jews in Israel." In *Interpreting Fertility,* edited by Marcia Inhorn and Frank Van Balen. Berkeley: University of California Press.

Klass, Perry. 1996. "The Artificial Womb Is Born." *New York Times Magazine,* 29 September.

Klein, Michele. 1998. *A Time to Be Born: Customs and Folklore of Jewish Birth.* New York: Jewish Publication Society.

Kretchmar, David. 1993. *The Mini-Revolution in Israel's Constitutional Crisis.* Israel Law Review.

Lasker, Daniel J. 1988. "Kabbalah, Halakha, and Modern Medicine: The Case of Artificial Insemination." *Modern Judaism* 8 (1): 1–15.

Lewin, Ellen. 1993. *Lesbian Mothers: Accounts of Gender in American Culture.* Ithaca: Cornell University Press.

Livnon-Keshet, Naomi. "Surrogacy: Looking for a Womb in Good Condition" (in Hebrew). *L'Isha,* August 28, 1995.

Lloyd, Genevieve. 1984. *The Man of Reason: "Male" and "Female" in Western Philosophy.* Minneapolis: University of Minnesota Press.

Loike, John D., and Avram Steinberg. 1998. "Human Cloning and Halakhic Perspectives." *Tradition* 32: 31–47.

Marcus, George E. 1995. "Ethnography in/of the World System: The Emergence of Multisited Ethnography." *Annual Review of Anthropology* 24: 95–117.

Martin, Emily. 1987. *The Woman in the Body: A Cultural Analysis of Reproduction.* Boston: Beacon Press.

———. 1991. "The Egg and the Sperm: How Science Has Constructed a Romance Based on Stereotypical Male-Female Roles." *SIGNS* 16 (3): 485–501.

———. 1994. *Flexible Bodies.* Boston: Beacon Press.

Mednek, HaRav Haim. 1953. "A Short Answer in the Matter of Artificial Insemination" (in Hebrew). *HaPardes* 27 (11): 2–4.

Noam. 1958. Jerusalem: Shlomo Torah Institute.

Rackman, Emanuel. 1956. "Morality in Medico-Legal Problems: A Jewish View." *New York University Law Review* 31: 1205–14.

Ragone, Helena. 1994. *Surrogate Motherhood: Conception in the Heart.* Boulder, Colo.: Westview Press.

Rakover, N. 1989. *Lines for Integrating Jewish Law and Israeli Law.* Israel Ministry of Justice. Jerusalem.

Raymond, Janice. 1993. *Women as Wombs.* San Francisco: Harper.

Rapp, Rayna. 1999. *Testing Women, Testing the Fetus: The Social Impact of Amniocentesis in America.* New York: Routledge.

"Report of the Public-Professional Commission in the Matter of In-Vitro Fertilization." The Aloni Commission Report. 1994. State of Israel. Jerusalem: Ministry of Justice.

Rosner, Fred. 1972. *Modern Medicine and Jewish Law.* New York: Yeshiva University Press.

Ross, Devorah. 1998. "Artificial Insemination in Single Women." In *Jewish Legal Writings by Women* (in Hebrew), edited by Micah D. Halpern and Chana Safrai. Urim. Jerusalem.

Roth, Joel. 1986. *The Halakhic Process: A Systematic Analysis.* New York: Jewish Theological Seminary.

Schereschewsky, B. 1967. *Dine Ha'Mishpahah.* Jerusalem: Reuven, Mass.

Schneider, David M. 1984. *A Critique of the Study of Kinship.* Ann Arbor: University of Michigan Press.

Sered, Susan Starr. 1992. *Women as Ritual Experts: The Religious Lives of Elderly Jewish Women in Jerusalem.* New York: Oxford University Press.

Shalev, Carmel. 1989. *Birth Power: The Case for Surrogacy.* New Haven, Conn.: Yale University Press.

———. 1998. "Halakha and Patriarchal Motherhood — An Anatomy of the New Israeli Surrogacy Law." *Israel Law Review* 32, no. 1: 51–81.

Sofer-Avraham, Avraham. 1994. "In-Vitro Fertilization on Shabbat and Holidays" (in Hebrew). *Assia* 14 3: 42.

Solomon, Alison. 1991. "Anything for a Baby: Reproductive Technology in Israel." In *Calling the Equality Bluff,* edited by Barbara Svirsky and Marilyn Safir. New York: Pergamon.

Spallone, Patricia. 1989. *Beyond Conception: The New Politics of Reproduction.* Granby, Mass.: Bergin and Garvey.

Stanworth, Michelle, ed. 1987. *Reproductive Technologies: Gender, Motherhood, and Medicine.* Cambridge: Cambridge University Press.

Steinberg, Avraham. 1975. "Artificial Insemination in Light of the Halakha" (in Hebrew). *Assia,* no. 12.

Strathern, Marilyn. 1980. "No Nature, No Culture." In *Nature, Culture,*

and Gender, edited by C. P. MacCormack and M. Strathern.
Cambridge: Cambridge University Press.

———. 1992a. *After Nature: English Kinship in the Late Twentieth
Century.* Cambridge: Cambridge University Press.

———. 1992b. *Reproducing the Future: Anthropology, Kinship, and the
New Reproductive Technologies.* New York: Routledge.

———. 1993. *Technologies of Procreation.* Manchester: Manchester
University Press.

———. 1995. "Displacing Knowledge: Technology and the Consequences
for Kinship." In *Conceiving the New World Order: The Global
Politics of Reproduction,* edited by Faye Ginsburg and Rayna Rapp.
Berkeley: University of California Press.

Van Dyck, Jose. 1995. *Manufacturing Babies and Public Consent.* New
York: New York University Press.

Waldenburg, Rav E. "In-Vitro Fertilization: A Medical Halakhic
Discussion" (in Hebrew). *Assia* 33.

Weston, Kath. 1991. *Families We Choose: Lesbians, Gays, Kinship.* New
York: Columbia University Press.

Yuval-Davis, Nira. 1987. "The Jewish Collectivity." In *Women in the
Middle East,* edited by Magida Salman. London: Zed Books.

Zohar, Noam. 1991. "Artificial Insemination and Surrogate
Motherhood: A Halakhic Perspective." *S'vara* 2 (1): 13–19.

———. 1998. *Alternatives in Jewish Bioethics.* Albany: State University
Press of New York.

Index

Susan Martha Kahn is Senior Research Director of the
Hadassah International Research Institute on Jewish Women
at Brandeis University.

Library of Congress Cataloging-in-Publication Data

Kahn, Susan Martha, 1963–
Reproducing Jews : a cultural account of assisted conception in
Israel / by Susan Martha Kahn.
p.   cm. — (Body, commodity, text)
Includes bibliographical references and index.
ISBN 0-8223-2601-9 (cloth : alk. paper) —
ISBN 0-8223-2598-5 (pbk. : alk. paper)
1. Human reproductive technology — Law and legislation —
Israel.   2. Human reproductive technology — Social aspects —
Israel.   3. Human reproduction technology — Religious
aspects — Judaism.   4. Human reproduction (Jewish law)
5. Law — Israel — Jewish influences.   I. Title.   II. Series.
KMK1527 .K34 2000
306.83 — dc21   00-030856